SOCIAL AND ECONOMIC
FOUNDATIONS OF THE
ITALIAN RENAISSANCE

MAJOR ISSUES IN HISTORY

Editor

C. WARREN HOLLISTER,

University of California, Santa Barbara

C. Warren Hollister: *The Twelfth-Century Renaissance*
William F. Church: *The Impact of Absolutism in France: National Experience under Richelieu, Mazarin, and Louis XIV*
C. Warren Hollister: *The Impact of the Norman Conquest*
Roger L. Williams: *The Commune of Paris, 1871*
L. Pearce Williams: *Relativity Theory: Its Origins and Impact on Modern Thought*
Loy Bilderback: *Conciliarism*
Robert O. Collins: *The Partition of Africa: Illusion or Necessity*
J. B. Conacher: *The Emergence of Parliamentary Democracy in Britain in the 19th Century*
Frank J. Frost: *Democracy and the Athenians*
Paul Hauben: *The Spanish Inquisition*
Bennett D. Hill: *Church and State in the Middle Ages*
Boyd H. Hill: *The Rise of the First Reich: Germany in the Tenth Century*
Thomas M. Jones: *The Becket Controversy*
Tom B. Jones: *The Sumerian Problem*
Anthony Molho: *Social and Economic Foundations of the Italian Renaissance*
E. W. Monter: *European Witchcraft*
Donald Queller: *The Latin Conquest of Constantinople*
Jeffrey Russell: *Medieval Religions Dissent*
Arthur J. Slavin: *Humanism, Reform, and Reformation*
W. Warren Wagar: *The Idea of Progress Since the Renaissance*

SOCIAL AND ECONOMIC FOUNDATIONS OF THE ITALIAN RENAISSANCE

EDITED BY

ANTHONY MOLHO

JOHN WILEY & SONS, INC.
New York   London   Sydney   Toronto

Copyright © 1969, by John Wiley & Sons, Inc.

10 9 8 7 6 5 4 3 2 1

Library of Congress Catalogue Card Number: 78-88317

Cloth: SBN 471 61310 X   Paper: SBN 471 61311 8

Printed in the United States of America

SERIES PREFACE

The reading program in a history survey course traditionally has consisted of a large two-volume textbook and, perhaps, a book of readings. This simple reading program requires few decisions and little imagination on the instructor's part, and tends to encourage in the student the virtue of careful memorization. Such programs are by no means things of the past, but they certainly do not represent the wave of the future.

The reading program in survey courses at many colleges and universities today is far more complex. At the risk of over-simplification, and allowing for many exceptions and overlaps, it can be divided into four categories: (1) textbook, (2) original source readings, (3) specialized historical essays and interpretive studies, and (4) historical problems.

After obtaining an overview of the course subject matter (textbook), sampling the original sources, and being exposed to selective examples of excellent modern historical writing (historical essays), the student can turn to the crucial task of weighing various possible interpretations of major historical issues. It is at this point that memory gives way to creative critical thought. The "problems approach," in other words, is the intellectual climax of a thoughtfully conceived reading program and is, indeed, the most characteristic of all approaches to historical pedagogy among the newer generation of college and university teachers.

The historical problems books currently available are many and varied. Why add to this information explosion? Because the Wiley Major Issues Series constitutes an endeavor to produce something new that will respond to pedagogical needs thus far unmet. First, it is a series of individual volumes—one per problem. Many good teachers would much prefer to select their own historical issues rather than be tied to an inflexible sequence of issues imposed by a publisher and bound together between two covers. Second, the Wiley Major Issues Series is based on the idea of approaching the significant problems of history through a deft interweaving of primary sources and secondary analysis, fused together by the skill of a scholar-editor. It is felt that the essence of a historical issue cannot be satisfactorily probed either by placing a body of undigested source materials into the hands of inexperienced students or by limiting these students to the controversial literature of modern scholars who debate the meaning of sources the student never sees. This series approaches historical problems by exposing students to both the finest historical thinking on the issue and some of the evidence on which this thinking is based. This synthetic approach should prove far more fruitful than either the raw-source approach or the exclusively second-hand approach, for it combines the advantages—and avoids the serious disadvantages—of both.

Finally, the editors of the individual volumes in the Major Issues Series have been chosen from among the ablest scholars in their fields. Rather than faceless referees, they are historians who know their issues from the inside and, in most instances, have themselves contributed significantly to the relevant scholarly literature. It has been the editorial policy of this series to permit the editor-scholars of the individual volumes the widest possible latitude both in formulating their topics and in organizing their materials. Their scholarly competence has been unquestioningly respected; they have been encouraged to approach the problems as they see fit. The titles and themes of the series volumes have been suggested in nearly every case by the scholar-editors themselves. The criteria have been (1) that the issue be of relevance to undergraduate lecture courses in history, and (2) that it be an issue which the scholar-editor knows thoroughly and in which he has done creative work. And, in general, the second criterion has been given precedence over the first. In short, the question "What are the significant historical issues today?" has been answered not by general editors or sales departments but by the scholar-teachers who are responsible for these volumes.

University of California,   *C. Warren Hollister*
Santa Barbara

PREFACE

The editor of an historical anthology is invariably tempted to organize his material in a manner meant to confront the undergraduate student with a clear and challenging problem. "The Renaissance—Mediaeval or Modern?", "Machiavelli—Patriot or Cynic?" are currently available titles dealing with the Renaissance that reflect this tendency. Clearly, the subjection of historical data to such an interrogation is a useful pedagogic device. One may ask, however, if all historical material, when presented to the modern student, should be organized in this manner. After all, a practicing historian, when investigating a problem, is forced to confront a body of evidence and impose upon it a structure that is the product of the interaction between his mind and the evidence. This contrapuntal relationship, involving as it does a constant dialogue between the student and his evidence, is the principal ingredient of what one might call "historical thinking." Thus, I suspect that little harm can be done by compelling the neophyte student of history to initiate such a dialogue about a past historical era. Moreover, this anthology does not purport to investigate one problem. Rather, it examines a number of salient features of an epoch; within this epoch, one can identify and investigate any number of interesting and challenging problems. For these reasons, I have conceived my purpose in preparing this anthology as one of providing the student with certain types of information that recent manuals and textbooks of the period have tended to overlook in favour of the intellectual currents of that age. Aided by the readings of this anthology and by information culled from other assignments, the student will undoubtedly raise a number of questions about the historic trends that shaped and moulded the Italian *Trecento*, *Quattrocento*, and early *Cinquecento*.

It has been my experience when offering courses on the Renaissance that I tend to concentrate very heavily on the Italian developments of the 14th and 15th centuries and that I draw many of the examples and illustrations for the generalizations that I formulate in my lectures from the history of Florence. I trust that such an emphasis on Italian and Florentine affairs is not simply an outcome of my own prejudiced view of that period but that, rather, the very history of the period justifies this focus. Professor Roberto Lopez has rightly suggested that Italy's place in the early modern era was comparable to England's during the Industrial Revolution. When dealing with the processes of industrialization and modernization in the 18th and 19th centuries, one obviously focuses one's attention on English history, particularly on the history of certain counties and provinces in which these processes were first developed. Similarly, when dealing with the history of urban, financial and, to an extent, political institutions from the 13th through the 15th centuries, one is forced to concentrate on Italy and, particularly, its principal urban centers, the most important and famous of which was Florence. This reason and the fact that I happen to have studied the history of that city in much greater detail than that of any other Italian commune of the Renaissance explain, in the following pages, the prominence that the history of Florence enjoys.

Finally, I thank Professors Paul Grendler of Toronto and William Church and Bryce Lyon of Providence for their useful suggestions.

Florence, 1969   ANTHONY MOLHO

CONTENTS

Introduction   1

The City   12

  1. Padua in the Age of Dante, *by J. K. Hyde*   12
  2. The Greatness of Florence, *by Giovanni Villani* 18

Sources of Wealth and Techniques of Business   23

  3. The Commercial Revolution of the 13th Century,
     by Raymond de Roover   23
  4. Economic Conditions in the Communes during the
     13th and 14th Centuries, *by Gino Luzzatto*   26
  5. Florentine Families and Florentine Diaries,
     by P. J. Jones   33
  6. Investment and Usury, *by F. C. Lane*   41
  7. How To Succeed in Business While Trying, *by
     an Anonymous Merchant of the 14th Century*   53
  8. The Troubles of a Moneylender,
     by a 14th Century Moneylender   58
  9. Song on Worthy Conduct, *by Dino Compagni*   64
 10. The Physiognomy of the Florentine Merchant,
     by Armando Sapori   65

The Crisis of the 14th Century   77

 11. Population, Plague and Social Change,
     by David Herlihy   77

ix

12. The Impact of the Black Death, *by William Bowsky*   91

The Economy, 1350–1500   95

13. Hard Times and Investment in Culture,
        by R. S. Lopez   95
14. Renaissance Economic Historiography,
        by W. K. Ferguson   116
15. Economic Change and the Emerging Florentine
        Territorial State, *by M. B. Becker*   123

The Commune   132

16. The Pattern of Social Change, *by Gene A. Brucker*   132
17. The Government of the Petty Bourgeois,
        by Giovanni Villani   140
18. A Story About a New Knight, *by Franco Sacchetti*   142
19. The Equalization of Classes, *by Jacob Burckhardt*   145
20. The Family: The Significance of a Tradition,
        by Lauro Martines   152

A New Aristocracy   159

Alfieri Foundation   159
21. Ludovico Sforza—New Ruler of Milan, from the
        History of Milan of the Treccani degli
22. The Two Aristocracies—The Case of Genoa,
        by J. Heers   164
23. The Triumph of the Aristocracy in the Veneto,
        by A. Ventura   169

The Merchant and His World   173

24. A New Attitude Toward Wealth, *by Hans Baron*   173
25. Florentine Painting and its Social Background,
        by Frederick Antal   182

26. A Quattrocento Father Advises his Son,
    by Giovanni Rucellai 194

27. The Happiest Man in the World,
    by Giovanni Rucellai 200

27. A Mother's Advice,
    by Alessandra Maccinghi negli Strozzi 201

28. Civic Humanism at Pistoia, *by David Herlihy* 205

The Court and the Courtier 214

29. The Making of a Courtier, *by Lodovico Alamanni* 214

30. The Manners of a Courtier, *by Baldassare Castiglione* 220

31. The Justice of the New Court,
    by Anton Francesco Donni 230

Suggestions for Further Reading 234

SOCIAL AND ECONOMIC FOUNDATIONS OF THE ITALIAN RENAISSANCE

SAVOY
Turin
Milan
MILAN
MANTUA
Venice
VENICE
Genoa
GENOA
MODENA
FERRARA
Bologna
Pisa Florence
FLORENCE
Siena
PAPAL
THE MARCHES
DALMATIA
Corsica
(to Genoa)
SIENA
UMBRIA
STATES
Rome
Adriatic
Sea

Sardinia
(to Aragon)
Naples
KINGDOM
OF
NAPLES
(to Spain 1504)

RENAISSANCE
ITALY

Holy Roman
Empire

Republic

Duchy

KINGDOM OF
SICILY
(to Aragon)

Map by J. Donovan

INTRODUCTION

In the last generation or so a new school of Renaissance historians has focused an increasing amount of attention on the economic and social foundations that gave rise to the culture of the Italian Renaissance. Surely, economic historians interested in the Italian experiences of the 13th through the 16th centuries had written on the subject since the turn of the last century. But the primary thrust of past Renaissance scholarship, the areas which it had investigated methodically and painstakingly, were the realms of ideas and the arts. The great work of Burckhardt, Voigt, and Burdach belongs in the category of such older scholarship which, in recent years, has been continued by Cassirer, Kristeller, and Panovsky. The new brand of Renaissance scholarship, without being necessarily revisionist in its interpretation, has shifted the focus of its attention and sought to discern the relationship between the intellectual and artistic developments, on the one hand, and the broad contemporary social, economic, and political currents, on the other. Thus, increasingly, recent Renaissance scholarship had been primarily cultural in its approach, attempting to analyze the Italian history of the 14th and 15th centuries by using the historical categories devised and refined by the great French historian Marc Bloch.

One of the problems in dealing with the economic and social foundations of the "Italian Renaissance" lies in the definition that past and current scholarship has given this historical term. When does the Renaissance begin? Does the art of Niccola Pisano (second half of the 13th century), with its classical tendencies and its renewed emphasis on the magnificence of the human form, belong to the new age? Does Dante? Or Petrarch and Boccaccio who vacillated between the composition of amorous poems and the crises of conscience that plagued "mediaeval" men? Possibly their great contemporary, the painter

Giotto? Or should one start with the intellectual revolution that was being completed in the last quarter of the 14th century? Clearly, the definition of the historical term will depend, to a great extent, on the chronological boundaries that one chooses to assign to the period. However, as long as the "Renaissance" is defined primarily in terms of its intellectual components, one's point of departure will be some time in the second quarter of the 14th century. But any date chosen by intellectual or artistic criteria compels the economic and social historian to discuss currents and trends that had been initiated well in advance, reaching their maturity in the 14th and 15th centuries. Two facts are clear:

1. Italian civilization beginning in 1200, possibly one or two centuries earlier, is an urban phenomenon; it evolves in cities; it is characterized by attributes that are foreign to most other European regions. That is why one cannot formulate generalizations about the Renaissance based on comparisons between the patriotic, secular, and rational Italian of the 15th century and his counterpart shackled to feudal institutions and plagued by ignorance in North Europe. In addition to oversimplifying the Transalpine situation, these comparisons overlook the fact that this description of the 15th century Italian might fit his ancestors of 300 years past. It may be that many of his qualities were rechanneled in the course of the *Trecento* and *Quattrocento* and that they were articulated in new styles and forms. But the Sienese banker, the Venetian trader, the Pisan poet of the 12th and 13th centuries could also be characterized as patriotic, rational, and secular in their outlook—or, at least, no less so than their descendants of the 1300's and 1400's. Therefore, Italian economic and social history from (about) 1200 to 1500 must be considered as a unity—as suggested several years ago by Armando Sapori, the dean of Italian economic historians.

2. The great period of economic expansion, demographic growth, town and road building, agricultural innovation, land reclamation, construction of new town walls and great cathedrals occurred in the mid- and late 13th century. Certainly, no other period of Italian history until the late 1950's and early 1960's with their much publicized *boom economico* witnessed such a

phenomenal rate of economic growth. The section of this anthology entitled "Sources of Wealth" will offer an idea of the broad movement and dimensions that the Italian economy assumed in this era of great expansion.

Questions, of course, have arisen about the economic fluctuations following the visitation of the devastating plague of 1348. In recent years, the research of several scholars has demonstrated that the 1340's were in fact a sad and desperate decade. The plague was but the *coup-de-grâce* in a series of disasters that had caused havoc and undermined the social, economic, and moral foundations laid in previous decades of patient work. Surely, if the plague had never arrived, the bankruptcy of the giant Florentine banking houses in the previous decade was bound to leave indelible marks. To compound the problem, floods, crop failure, and famine were to follow, so that the plague was but the culmination in this succession of tragic and devastating blows. One cannot doubt its vastness and severity in terms of deaths and material damage to every facet of Italian life.

But does it necessarily follow that after 1348 the Italian economy entered upon an unchecked downward spiral for several centuries to come? Opinion is divided on this issue. Some, among whom are Professors Lopez and Miskimin in the United States and Professor Fiumi in Italy, insist that the peak reached at the turn of the 13th century was not to be reached again and that the era of great cultural efflorescence of the 15th century coincided with an economic depression. Others, primarily Professors Ferguson and Cipolla, insist that 1348 was but a temporary setback and that the losses in industrial and agricultural production of the late 14th and 15th centuries were compensated by the sharp diminution of the Italian population, thus creating a new and dynamic economic equilibrium. One is very aware today that economists are sharply divided about their prognostications and diagnoses of the contemporary economy. How much more difficult it is, then, to diagnose properly and accurately the workings of the Italian economy of the 14th and 15th centuries! The mountains of data available to answer similar questions about the modern scene simply do not exist for the premodern era, and economic historians are forced to generalize on the basis of fragmentary and inconclusive evidence.

One should be cautious in suggesting that the outcome of the mid-14th century crisis resulted in the mass exodus from the cities to the country and that men, having lost confidence in the safety of business and industrial investments, channeled their funds to agricultural enterprises. P. J. Jones makes it clear that there was no mass exodus from the cities to the land. The Florentines of whom he talks, as well as other Italians of the late 14th and early 15th centuries, never abandoned the land when they settled in the cities. Strong ties between city and country surely mark one of the most important and unique aspects of Italian culture from the year 1000 until the 16th and early 17th centuries. It is also clear that by the late 15th century this picture was beginning to change and that a division between a commercial and landed aristocracy was gradually being forged. But, as Professor J. Heers states, this was a phenomenon of the "late Renaissance" and not of he 14th and early 15th centuries.

Max Weber in the late 19th century based his far-reaching thesis on the growth of capitalism and of the "bourgeois spirit" on his study of the industrial and commercial activities of Calvinist Swiss and Scottish merchants. Yet, generalizations about the commitment to a supposedly "bourgeois spirit" solely on the basis of investments in trade and industry overlook the important fact that land always remained one of the vital sources of revenue for all Italians, whether urban or rural dwellers, and that it was considered a proper source of "capitalistic" exploitation. Anyone who has seen the richly cultivated Tuscan and Umbrian slopes will realize the enormous amount of effort and investment poured into the proper operation of agricultural enterprises.

The point is that, once we ascertain that land always remained an important source of investment and that the second half of the *Trecento* was not marked by a drastic reorientation from the city to the country, we must undertake a discussion of agricultural production in our consideration of a possible overall economic decline or stability in the century or two after the onslaught of the Black Death. And to do that is to ask of the economic historian an enormously complex and taxing question for which the sources are fragmented, widely dispersed and, more often than not, do not exist. A pioneering job has been undertaken by an Italian scholar, Elio Conti. and the results promise to clarify some of the confusion and add much to our knowledge.

A proper evaluation of the growth or stagnation of the Italian economy in the 14th and 15th centuries must also take into consideration the new financial and fiscal institutions which emerged in that period. Some decades ago, Professor Gino Luzzatto pointed out the phenomenal growth of the Venetian public debt and suggested the importance of this institution in asserting the direction in which the Venetian economy was moving. In a series of recent articles, Marvin Becker has examined the same phenomenon in the development of Florentine history. For reasons that he discusses in detail from around the middle of the *Trecento*, the Florentine public debt *(Monte)* soared to astronomical figures. In an earlier era, the great fortunes of the city were in private hands but, after 1350, the main repository of Florentine patrimonies was the state itself. The consequences, as Professor Becker makes clear, were enormous. ⟨What needs to be emphasized at this point, however, is that in measuring the growth or stagnation of the Italian economy one must not rely solely on the criteria that were applicable to the pre-plague days, but should also make use of the developments, such as the public indebtedness and the consequent fiscal displacement, which came to the fore and became crystallized in the late *Trecento* and *Quattrocento*.⟩

One may say that the old view which discerned the concurrent, almost synchronized progress of cultural and economic activity must be set aside. In absolute terms, the late 13th century remained the peak. But it seems unjustifiable to suggest that the Italian economy of the late 14th and 15th centuries lacked vitality and energy. Time and again, reacting after a natural calamity, it rebounded and acquired new vigour. A graph depicting economic developments during this period would be a serpentine line with a succession of ascents and descents reflecting the ups and downs of the economy.

* * *

While it is clear that urban nuclei had survived in Italy even during the blackest of the "dark ages," the Italian cities of the 12th through the 15th centuries were the products of the far-reaching economic and social revolution of the 11th through 13th centuries. The ultimate and most significant outcome of this revolution was the phenomenal increase of urban populations. Professor Hyde suggests that the population of Padua increased in a 150-year period from about 15,000 to nearly 35,000. Professor Herlihy's studies have led him to the conclusion that the Pisan population jumped from 11,000 in 1164 to about 38,000 in 1293. Similar patterns of growth were evident everywhere in Italy. The city attracted thousands of immigrants from the surrounding countryside and assumed an economic, cultural, and political preponderance in the life of the peninsula. It is not difficult to imagine the reasons that persuaded the myriads of immigrants to leave their rustic lives for the excitement of the urban environment. Cities have always exercised this kind of fascination on the minds of rural dwellers and, in this respect, the high Middle Ages did not differ from ours.

It seems clear that the wave of emigration from the *contado* (the rural district surrounding an urban center) to the city can be divided into two main periods. The first wave, lasting from the beginning of the demographic expansion until the mid-13th century, saw not only affluent rural dwellers acquiring palaces and towers in the bustling new cities but also thousands of workers seeking their fortune in the new environment. The prize sought by all was the citizenship of the city that they inhabited—a status conferring numerous economic, social, and political advantages on the recipient.

In the first era of emigration, the chances of an enterprising but indigent immigrant of attaining such a goal were reasonably fair. But the gradual institutionalization of the new urban forms and the emergence of a new and self-conscious elite made it increasingly difficult for the aspiring newcomers to obtain citizenship. The qualifications for acquiring this status were stiffened considerably, so that the aspiring new citizen was expected to be relatively wealthy, possessing a substantial residence in the city. (In Florence, for example, he had to own a home valued at 150 florins or more—a very considerable sum considering that the salary of a professional civil servant was in the vicinity of 75 to 100 florins a year, at most.) More often than not, he was expected to be a member of one of the professional guilds, each of which represented the interests of one or more occupations or crafts. Thus, with the mid- or late 13th century, the great amount of social fluidity and the numerous opportunities for social advancement came to an end, and Italian society began assuming an increasingly stratified appearance. After that time, the status of new citizen *(novus civis)* became a handicap from which it was fairly difficult to escape. Dante and many of his contemporaries spoke contemptuously of these new men whose presence in the city, they believed, diluted and undermined the existing standards of social and ethical behaviour, but who, nevertheless, hoped that their money was sufficient to secure for them a position of eminence in the city.

One of the crucial aspects of social development in Italy from the 13th through the 15th centuries is the fact, already mentioned above, that the division between the urban and rural patriciates was not nearly as marked as it was in Transalpine Europe. Feudal lords with castles in the *contado* and inherited baronial titles also possessed *palazzi* in the city and were not reluctant to invest money and time in the pursuit of profits in industrial and commercial enterprises. Nor did the new rich, having made their fortune in the city, forsake their rural origins. More often than not, they maintained a villa in the country and invested a share of their capital in the agricultural exploitation of the land. Thus, in many respects, a community of interests was created between these two ruling groups—a community not only of financial interests but also a common mode of life and a similar outlook toward the crucial problems confronting the new class. Reinforcing this amalgamation was the fact that, from a very early stage, intermarriages between members of the two patriciates became quite common, so that by the late 13th century it was fairly difficult to trace the ancestry of a family either to "lordly" or *nouveaux riches* roots. The ruling class of the 14th and 15th centuries, to whose patronage one must partly attribute the striking cultural efflorescence of the epoch, as well as the elaborate stratification of society that persisted through the 14th and 15th centuries, was the product of the late 13th century.

Jacob Burckhardt, undoubtedly the most influential historian to have written on the Renaissance for over a century, when formulating his famous thesis on "renaissance individualism" had in mind precisely the phenomenon described above. For the creation of a new ruling class out of the fusion of two distinct elites was an indication to him that the 14th and 15th centuries had witnessed the survival and triumph of the fittest elements from each of the two classes. Birth no longer guaranteed one an eminent position in society. It was rather merit, one's intellectual and spiritual endowment, that determined the measure of his success. Man now stood alone and waged his battles as an individual, no longer supported by the prestige and authority of the institutions to which he had belonged in the Middle Ages. While mediaeval man had derived his existential identity from his sense of belonging to a group, the Renaissance man proudly asserted his individuality fully aware that success would be proportionate to his personal merits.

We must recognize, however, that "individualism" is a relative concept. In measuring the "individualism" of an age, we must compare it to that of a previous or future epoch. When, for example, we compare the 15th century with the 9th or 17th, we discover that there was more social fluidity, more room for individual initiative and less oppression from a predetermined social order in the 15th century than either before or after. But, at the same time, we cannot apply to Italian society from 1200 to 1500 characteristics of individualism derived from the 19th or 20th centuries. To us, "individualism" conjures up such images as the breakup of the patriarchal family; the assertion of an individual's will over social or natural forces; the shaping of one's life, that is, according to one's own will, desire, or inclination. It is clear that none of these images is applicable to Italian society of the period that interests us.

Italian society from the 13th through the 15th centuries, even at its most flexible and dynamic stages, nurtured institutions which by contemporary standards circumscribed an individual's freedom of movement and his latitude of action. The most important and influential of these institutions was the family. Some debate has arisen recently about whether the traditional familial bonds, first forged in Italy during the Lombard invasions (6th to 7th centuries) and reinforced in subsequent centuries were in fact weakened or destroyed in the course of the 14th and 15th centuries. Yet, a reading of the sources leaves little doubt about the continuing viability and strength of the Italian family. Professors Brucker and Martines make it abundantly clear that an individual derived his political identity primarily from his membership in a family. One was known as a Malatesta, an Acciaioli or Medici, a Mocenigo or Foscari, or a Panciatichi. Being identified with a family meant that, in addition to carrying a name, an individual was identified with a tradition that he was obligated to uphold. Contemporaries were invariably amazed when, occasionally, members of the same family found themselves on opposite political sides. The family remained at the center of an individual's life and interests. Giovanni Rucellai, that interesting 15th-century Florentine who (among other things) commissioned Leon Battista Alberti to design the magnificent facade of the great Dominican cathedral in Florence, Santa Maria Novella, captured vividly in the pages of his diary the spirit of strong family solidarity that pervaded all facets of Italian life in the course of the *Quattrocento*. One's first and foremost concern must be the well-being of his family, for all the public honours amassed by an individual would not feed the family, and it is to one's children and relatives that one owes one's first and foremost allegiance. In addition to the family, there were numerous other institutions that bound an individual's commitments and identified him as a member of a group, for example laymen's religious confraternities, professional associations, and guilds. The strongly corporate bonds that had fashioned Italian society in the 13th and 14th centuries did not disappear in the 15th, although, as becomes apparent from the analysis of Ludovico Sforza's policies, these bonds were considerably weakened by the rising power of the state.

By the mid- and late 15th centuries, the social elasticity and flexibility that characterized Italian society since the beginning of the great economic revolution in the 12th and 13th centuries started giving way to a more stratified social structure. Political developments were not unrelated to this phenomenon. The ascendancy of numerous tyrants and the creation of courts tended to foster a clear-cut division between the rulers and the ruled, and between those favored by the new political masters and those not favored. F. Braudel, who has probably contributed, more than any other scholar, to our understanding of the economic and social processes of the "high Renaissance," has described the gradual but unmistakable fossilization of the social order. Even where political tyrannies did not triumph, in the oligarchic cities of Venice and Lucca, a more artistocratic and patrician atmosphere prevailed. With the establishment of this new order which, according to all indications, had become well-entrenched by the first quarter of the 16th century, we observe the arrival of a new type of man: the courtier. Intent upon gaining the approval and sympathy of his lord, interested in refining his manners and learning, concerned, above all, to impress his superiors and peers (for his well-being now rested almost entirely in their hands), the courtier dominated Italian society for the next three centuries. Thus, one era of Italian history had come to an end. One cycle had been completed, and the peninsula, embittered by a series of political and diplomatic failures and disappointments, lost its vitality and momentum because of the rigidity injected in its social structure and now embarked upon a new stage of its history.

One of the habitual characterizations of Italian history from 1200 to 1500 is that it was an "era of transition." In that era, it is alleged, Italy traversed the chronological frontier that separates the Middle Ages from modern society. Yet, it seems to me that this characterization misses too many of the essential and peculiar elements of that epoch. Every age is an age of transition. But as long as we view historical epochs—in this case, Italian history from 1200 to 1500—in teleological terms alone, content to trace through them characteristics that seem to triumph in the modern and contemporary eras, we shall remain blind to the contradictory, the tenuous, and the intensely peculiar aspects of each past epoch. It should be well, when studying the period with which this anthology deals, to remember Frederick Antal's advice: "We are not concerned with general classifications; our problem is rather to bring out the specific, definite features of each period, each decade even." One hopes that some of these specific and definite fatures of Italian history from 1200 to 1500 will become unravelled in the following pages.

THE CITY

1

J. K. Hyde

Padua in the Age of Dante

One of the most interesting and important Italian communes of the 13th and 14th centuries was Padua, the seat of the great university and the neighbour of Venice. Professor J. K. Hyde of the University of Manchester offers a brief description of the city and then discusses the problem of demographic growth in the 13th and early 14th centuries. It is interesting to observe the techniques and methods on which Mr. Hyde, as well as most demographers of premodern Europe, have to rely to obtain an estimate of general population trends.

The description of Paduan society must begin from its physical setting, from the topographical and economic structure of the city and its territory which exercised a persistent and sometimes a determinant influence over its whole development. Nothing is more characteristic of the modern historical outlook than its way of regarding the relationship between economy and society, and in the following pages some attempt will be made to answer the kind of questions which occur to the modern mind, even though this means that in many cases the sources have to be worked against the grain and made to yield up evidence on matters which they were not designed to record. For it goes without saying that the outlook of the thirteenth and fourteenth

SOURCE. J. K. Hyde, *Padua in the Age of Dante* (Manchester: Manchester University Press, 1966), pp. 29–35 and 37. Copyright 1966 by J. K. Hyde. Reprinted by permission of Manchester University Press and the author.

centuries was not ours, yet it would be a serious omission to ignore their ideas, for the contemporary understanding of the city and its environment is an integral part of the world we are seeking to recreate. And, in the case of Padua, the sources do permit a glimpse of the city as it appeared to contemporary eyes.

Padua is one of the few cities for which there exists a literary description from the mediaeval period. This is the *Visio Egidii Regis Patavie* of Giovanni da Nono, whose title refers to the opening passage, in which the author imagines Egidius, a mythical king of Patavium, a refugee at Rimini after the destruction of his city by Atilla the Hun. The king falls asleep and is comforted by a vision in which an angel prophesies the rebuilding of the city and its future greatness. This device enables Da Nono to put into the mouth of the angel a description of Padua as he knew it in the early fourteenth century; internal evidence makes it possible to date the work with reasonable certainty between the years 1314 and 1318. In undertaking a formal description of his native town, Da Nono was placing himself in a long-standing but diffuse tradition of town-descriptions leading back to antiquity, most of which was unknown to him, for although he was a judge, it is evident that his literary culture was small. From this tradition, which probably reached him through the popular *Mirabilia Urbis Rome*, Da Nono drew the overall plan of the *Visio* which concentrates first on the gates and walls of the city and then on the chief 'palaces' or public buildings, but within this outline the writer was free to follow his own interests and inclinations, and to this extent the *Visio* is both a description of the city and a window into the author's mind.

The first part of the *Visio Egidii* is devoted to the major and minor gates of the city and the principal buildings and other features associated with them. Da Nono begins with the Porta Pontemolino, which took its name from the numerous mill wheels in the river below, which in his day numbered thirty-four. Standing at the head of the Via Maggiore which had been the principal north–south street of Roman Patavium, the gate gave access over a fine bridge to the suburbs of S. Giacomo and Codalunga. For Da Nono, each principal gate was associated with the territory beyond, which in the case of the Pontemolino meant the region beyond the Brenta, a fast-flowing river which, leaving the Alpine foothills at Bassano, ran south to within a few miles of Padua before turning east to the lagoon almost opposite Venice. The chief centre of the Paduan Oltrebrenta was the walled town of Cittadella, built by the commune in 1220 to guard the route to the north and the open north-eastern frontier with Treviso. But the Pontemolino was also the gate for Padua's north-western neighbour Vicenza, which was reached by turning left at the head of the bridge and following the road which ran roughly parallel to the other major river of the Paduan territory, the slow-flowing Bacchiglione. It was by this route, Da Nono remarks, that a Paduan expedition left to take control of the neighbouring city in 1266.

The old western and southern gates of Padua were known as the Porta S. Giovanni and the Porta Torricelli, the latter taking its name from the many towers which stood in that quarter until the time of Ezzelino. These gates gave access to two of the most important parts of the Paduan contado: the region of the Colli Euganei, known in mediaeval times as the Pedevenda, and the plain beyond, between the hills and the Adige, to which the old name of the Scodosia was attached. The Colli form a striking contrast with the plain which makes up the rest of the Paduan contado, from which they stand out like islands. In Da Nono's mind, they were connected with the earliest history of Padua, for he believed that the first city, called Euganea, had been founded by the fugitive Antenor of Troy on the Monterosso; down to his own day, the Pedevenda was associated in a special way with the oldest Paduan nobility and it was there that they were reputed to have their castles and country houses. The importance of the Scodosia rested on the fact that in or near it were situated Monselice, Este and Montagnana, three of the four largest dependent towns in the Paduan contado which looked out towards the river Adige marking the natural frontier of Paduan territory.

The last of the four main gates was the Porta Altinate, through which the main roads passed for Venice and Treviso. Just outside the walls, the Via Altinate served the port of Ognissanti which was connected by canal to the lower part of the Brenta and Venice, while near by was the salt port from

which it was possible to navigate to the salt pans near Chioggia
by way of the lower Bacchiglione. Almost as important as the
Porta Altinate was the Porta S. Stefano, a short distance to the
south, from which the Via S. Margherita ran in a south-easterly
direction to the Pontecorvo to form the backbone of that part
of the town known as Rudena. Near the Pontecorvo were two
of Padua's greatest religious houses, the Benedictine monastery
of S. Giustina and the Franciscan church of S. Antonio which
Da Nono describes in detail. The road continued from the
Pontecorvo for some ten miles to Piove di Sacco, the chief town
of the south-eastern part of the Paduan contado which was
occasionally referred to as the Plebatus.

Despite its apparent comprehensiveness, the first part of the
Visio Egidii presents a very incomplete picture of fourteenth-
century Padua. The walls which it describes are the ancient
ones, constructed about the end of the twelfth century, which
enclosed the western island formed by the Bacchiglione, on
which the cathedral and the centres of business and the administration were situated. But by the fourteenth century, this was
less than half the built-up area of the city which extended for a
considerable distance on all sides of the old walls, especially to
the east on the island bounded by the Arena, S. Sofia and the
Pontecorvo. In fact, there was probably never a time when the
city was confined to the western island, for ancient Patavium
had stood on both islands astride the Bacchiglione, which was
spanned by Roman bridges. traces of which are visible to this
day. Legend derived the name Rudena from the ruins of
Patavium which Attila had destroyed. Thus Da Nono's description was realistic only in its details; as a whole it was highly
stylised, the exact verbal equivalent of the city represented on
the seal of the commune—walled, moated and four-square,
while the surrounding inscription names the mountains, the
sea and the rivers Adige and Musone as the ideal boundaries of
the Paduan state. The city was thought of as a fortified square
within the larger square of her territories.

For indications of the probable course of Padua's urban
development, it is necessary to turn to records of a very different
kind. For the twelfth century, there is an inscription copied
into the *Liber Regiminum* which records that in 1174 a fire de-

stroyed 2,614 houses in the city, which are said to have been three-quarters of the whole. If these figures can be relied on, they would suggest a total population of the order of 15,000 at that date. Eighty years later the next milestone is reached with the oath which Ezzelino da Romano ordered to be taken by all the citizens, promising to uphold his treaty with Oberto Pelavicino of Cremona. Altogether 665 members of the Consiglio Maggiore and 1,941 other inhabitants are named as having taken the oath. While these figures cannot be used to estimate the total population, they do give some indication of its distribution, as the names of the ordinary inhabitants, though not of the councillors, are listed under the various *centenarii* into which the city was divided. The administrative divisions are in themselves a sign of the development of the city; the four quarters of Pontemolino, Duomo, Torricelli and Ponte Altinate obviously derive from the gates of the old walls, but of the twenty *centenarii*, nine were mainly outside of the confines of the western island. In 1254 the oath-takers in these extramural *centenarii* amounted to 1,135 as against 806 from within the gates, those showing the highest numbers being Rudena (234) and S. Sofia (207) on the eastern island, followed by the outlying suburb of S. Croce (137), separated from the city by the great open space of Prato della Valle. Even allowing for the fact that the great majority of the 665 councillors probably came from within the walls, while the lists reflect Ezzelino's reliance upon the lower classes of the city in the last years of his *signoria* when he had quarrelled with almost all the nobility and many of the substantial members of the *popolo*, it is probable that at least half the population lived outside the walls which had been reconstructed only fifty years before. 146 persons who took the oath, including 15 members of the council, were described as immigrants from the contado or from other cities. Taken as a whole, it is likely that the first half of the thirteenth century was a period of considerable urban growth in Padua.

From 1254 to 1320 the evidence for the growth of Padua is almost entirely indirect; the political successes and the public works of the commune in this period suggest a prosperous and growing community. The eastern suburbs of the city were already fortified in 1256, when the Guelph army had to force an

entrance near the Pontecorvo; the western arc of the new circuit known as the *murus spaldi*, was begun by the victorious army in the same year and completed in 1270. Among the public buildings, the Palazzo del Podestà was erected in 1281, the hall of the Consiglio Maggiore in 1284; the Palazzo degli Anziani followed in 1285 and a communal archive was provided in 1297. The record with regard to bridges, markets, river-ports and the paving of streets in this period is equally impressive. The early fourteenth century which saw the completion of the basilica of S. Antonio and the reconstruction of the Palazzo Comunale, which was decorated with frescoes ascribed to Giotto, was the golden age of mediaeval Paduan architecture. Private documents provide some evidence for continuing immigration into the city. Most of the individuals found in these records were men of some property, who when they reached the city, particularly favoured certain occupations such as notary, taverner and university professor. Behind them must be imagined an unknown mass of poor labourers who have left no mark on the records.

The most important evidence for the demography of mediaeval Padua belongs to the year 1320. It consists of a detailed survey undertaken by the communal authorities while the city was besieged by Cangrande which has survived through two independent transcripts made in the sixteenth and seventeenth centuries. These give the number of men and/or families living in each street or *centenario*, together with the names of the leading inhabitants. Fortunately, unlike some other records of this kind, neither the names nor the figures seem to have been deliberately tampered with. Although there are some discrepancies and omissions in each manuscript, the survey appears to be substantially complete since the sum of the details tallies fairly well with the total, and the census leaves no obvious gaps when plotted on the map.

The real difficulties in the interpretation of the census of 1320 arise not so much from the nature of the record itself as from the circumstances in which it was compiled. At the time, Padua was closely besieged by the Veronese, and sonsequently the outlying parts of the city which were outside the defended area were omitted, while the population within the defences was undoubtedly swollen by an uncertain number of refugees from the contado. Thus an element of uncertainty is introduced into the use of the census to answer the question both of urban growth and of the total population in 1320. With regard to the former, the survey mentions three localities known as Borgo Nuovo in different parts of the city, and opposite these and several other streets in the outskirts is noted *omnes artifices*, probably indicating industrial suburbs of recent origin. But the outer suburbs beyond the *murus spaldi* are omitted; in particular, the Borgo Ognissanti with its two ports, which had supported a considerable population in 1254, was not recorded. The most important evidence bearing upon the population of the city is the figure of 11,131 men given by the census; if, as is most likely in the context, men of military age are understood, this would represent a total population of over 40,000. The problem is to decide how far this represents the normal population of the city and its suburbs. Some allowance must be made for the presence of refugees from the contado—162 families in this category are expressly recorded in the *centenario* of S. Nicolò— but against these must be offset a number of political exiles, as well as the inhabitants of the outer suburbs who should certainly be included in the normal population of the city. Bearing in mind that in a census compiled for military purposes under difficult conditions there are likely to have been some omissions, it seems reasonable to say that in 1320 Padua was a city of at least 35,000 inhabitants. This means that by population, Padua belonged to the middle rank among Italian cities, being about a third of the size of the great centres like Venice, Milan and Florence, and about half the size of contemporary Bologna. On the other hand, she was as large as almost any city north of the Alps, and about the equal of London in 1377.

2
Giovanni Villani
The Greatness of Florence

Giovanni Villani, himself a Florentine businessman, wrote a chron-icle of his city, which has earned him the reputation of an acute and

*judicious observer of his times. In the following passages, a veritable
panegyric of his city's magnificence, Villani captures the enormous
amount of dynamism and excitement that characterized the bustling
urban areas of Italy at the height of the economic expansion before
the onset of the "14th century crisis." Villani died in 1348.*

Since we have spoken about the income and expenditure of the
Commune of Florence in this period, I think it is fitting to mention this and other great features of our city, so that our descendants in days to come may be aware of any rise, stability,
and decline in condition and power that our city may undergo,
and also so that, through the wise and able citizens who at the
time shall be in charge of its government, [our descendants]
may endeavor to advance it in condition and power, seeing our
record and example in this chronicle. We find after careful
investigation that in this period there were in Florence about
25,000 men from the ages of fifteen to seventy fit to bear arms,
all citizens. And among them were 1,500 noble and powerful
citizens who as magnates gave security to the Commune. There
were in Florence also some seventy-five full-dress knights. To be
sure, we find that before the second popular government now
in power was formed there were more than 250 knights; but
from the time that the people began to rule, the magnates no
longer had the status and authority enjoyed earlier, and hence
few persons were knighted. From the amount of bread constantly needed for the city, it was estimated that in Florence
there were some 90,000 mouths divided among men, women,
and children, as can readily be grasped [from what we shall say]
later; and it was reckoned that in the city there were always
about 1,500 foreigners, transients, and soldiers, not including in
the total the citizens who were clerics and cloistered monks and
nuns, of whom we shall speak later. It was reckoned that in this
period there were some 80,000 men in the territory and district

SOURCE. Giovanni Villani, *The Chronicle of Giovanni Villani*, Book XI,
Chapter 94; from R. S. Lopez and I. W. Raymond, *Medieval Trade in the
Mediterranean World* (New York: Columbia University Press, 1966), pp.
71–74. Reprinted by permission of Columbia University Press and the editor.

of Florence. From the rector who baptized the infants—since he deposited a black bean for every male baptized in San Giovanni and a white bean for every female in order to ascertain their number—we find that at this period there were from 5,500 to 6,000 baptisms every year, the males usually outnumbering the females by 300 to 500. We find that the boys and girls learning to read [numbered] from 8,000 to 10,000, the children learning the abacus and algorism from 1,000 to 1,200, and those learning grammar and logic in four large schools from 550 to 600.

We find that the churches then in Florence and in the suburbs, including the abbeys and the churches of friars, were 110, among which were 57 parishes with congregations, 5 abbeys with two priors and some 80 monks each, 24 nunneries with some 500 women, 10 orders of friars, 30 hospitals with more than 1,000 beds to receive the poor and the sick, and from 250 to 300 chaplain priests.

The workshops of the *Arte della Lana*[1] were 200 or more, and they made from 70,000 to 80,000 pieces of cloth, which were worth more than 1,200,000 gold florins. And a good third [of this sum] remained in the land as [the reward] of labor, without counting the profit of the entrepreneurs. And more than 30,000 persons lived by it. [To be sure,] we find that some thirty years earlier there were 300 workshops or thereabouts, and they made more than 100,000 pieces of cloth yearly; but these cloths were coarser and one half less valuable, because at that time English wool was not imported and they did not know, as they did later, how to work it.

The *fondachi* of the *Arte di Calimala*,[2] dealing in French and Transalpine cloth, were some twenty, and they imported yearly more than 10,000 pieces of cloth, worth 300,000 gold florins. And all these were sold in Florence, without counting those which were reexported from Florence.

The banks of money-changers were about eighty. The gold coins which were struck amounted to some 350,000 gold florins

[1] The guild of wool merchants and entrepreneurs in the woolen industry.
[2] The guild of importers, refinishers, and sellers of Transalpine cloth. Their name is derived from Calle Mala, the 'bad street,' where their shops were located.

and at times 400,000 [yearly]. And as for deniers of four petty each, about 20,000 pounds of them were struck yearly.

The association of judges was composed of some eighty members; the notaries were some six hundred; physicians and surgical doctors, some sixty; shops of dealers in spices, some hundred.

Merchants and mercers were a large number; the shops of shoemakers, slipper makers, and wooden-shoe makers were so numerous they could not be counted. There were some three hundred persons and more who went to do business out of Florence, and [so did] many other masters in many crafts, and stone and carpentry masters.

There were then in Florence 146 bakeries. And from the [amount of the] tax on grinding and through [information furnished by] the bakers we find that the city within the walls needed 140 *moggia*[3] of grain every day. By this one can estimate how much was needed yearly, not to mention the fact that the larger part of the rich, noble, and well-to-do citizens with their families spent four months a year in the country, and some of them a still longer period.

We also find that in the year 1280, when the city was in a good and happy condition, it needed some 800 *moggia* of grain a week.

Through [the amount of] the tax at the gates we find that some 55,000 *cogna* of wine entered Florence yearly, and in times of plenty about 10,000 *cogna* more.

Every year the city consumed about 4,000 oxen and calves, 60,000 mutton and sheep, 20,000 she-goats and he-goats, 30,000 pigs.

During the month of July 4,000 *some* of melons came through Porta San Friano. and they were all distributed in the city. . . .

[Florence] within the walls was well built, with many beautiful houses, and at that period people kept building with improved techniques to obtain comfort and richness by importing designs of every kind of improvement. [They built] parish churches and churches of friars of every order, and splendid

---

[3] The *moggio* was a dry measure equal to 16.59 + bushels.

monasteries. And besides this, there was no citizen, whether commoner or magnate, who had not built or was not building in the country a large and rich estate with a very costly mansion and with fine buildings, much better than those in the city— and in this they all were committing sin, and they were called crazy on account of their wild expenses. And yet, this was such a wonderful sight that when foreigners, not accustomed to [cities like] Florence, came from abroad, they usually believed that all of the costly buildings and beautiful palaces which surrounded the city for three miles were part of the city in the manner of Rome—not to mention the costly palaces with towers, courts, and walled gardens farther distant, which would have been called castles in any other country. To sum up, it was estimated that within a six-mile radius around the city there were more than twice as many rich and noble mansions as in Florence.

SOURCES OF WEALTH AND TECHNIQUES OF BUSINESS

3   *Raymond de Roover*
The Commercial Revolution of the 13th Century

In the following passage Professor de Roover of Brooklyn College, New York City, examines some of the business practices developed by the enterprising Italian merchants in the late 13th and 14th centuries.

Professor Gras makes a distinction between petty capitalism and commercial capitalism and between the traveling and the sedentary merchant. The transition from the first of these systems to the second gave rise to a "commercial revolution," which occurred about the end of the thirteenth century and which cuts the Middle Ages into two periods: an earlier period up to about 1300 and a later period which includes the fourteenth and fifteenth centuries.

By a commercial revolution I understand a complete or drastic change in the methods of doing business or in the organization of business enterprise just as an industrial revolution means a complete change in the methods of production, for example, the introduction of power-driven machinery. The commercial revolution marks the beginning of mercantile or commercial capitalism, while the industrial revolution marks the end of it.

SOURCE. Raymond de Roover, "The Commercial Revolution of the 13th Century," in F. Lane and S. Riemersa, *Enterprise and Secular Change* (London: George Allen & Unwin Ltd., 1953), pp. 80–82. Copyright 1953 by George Allen & Unwin Ltd. Reprinted by permission of George Allen & Unwin Ltd., Richard D. Irwin, Inc. and the author.

In the twelfth and thirteenth centuries the fairs of Champagne were the great gathering place which attracted traveling merchants from Flanders and Germany on the one hand and from Provence and Italy on the other. At these fairs Flemish cloth was exchanged for spices, silk, and other luxury articles from the Levant. Historians have attributed the decline of the fairs to certain ill-advised fiscal measures of the French kings, to the beginning of regular voyages of galleys between Italy and Bruges, and to the social troubles in Flanders and the war between that country and France. None of these explanations is quite satisfactory, for reasons which we cannot stop to consider here.

The real cause for the decline of the fairs of Champagne lies in the fact that the Italian merchants became sedentary, established permanent agencies in Bruges, and began to buy Flemish cloth in the centers of production. This new form of business organization came into being because new techniques for control and management had been gradually developed:

(1) Instead of forming partnerships for the duration of a single venture, a new type of partnership agreement was evolved: the terminal or permanent partnership, which was to last for a number of years unless it was prematurely dissolved by the death of one of the partners.

(2) The traveling merchant knew the "letter obligatory" either given under seal ("letter close") or given under the form of a deed ("letter patent," notarial act). This instrument was inadequate when merchants ceased to attend the fairs and began to work with agents and correspondents abroad. The "letter of payment," or bill of exchange, was developed to meet the need for a more practical instrument. It made possible the transfer of money from place to place without the shipping of actual coins.

(3) The greater security along the roads made it henceforth unnecessary for the merchants to convey their goods themselves and to travel in armed caravans. Goods could safely be entrusted to specialized common carriers on land as well as on sea.

(4) The development of maritime insurance made it possible

to shift the sea risk to the underwriters, and consequently it was no longer necessary to divide that risk by shipping goods on different ships and by entering into partnership with several traveling merchants.

(5) The bookkeeping of the traveling merchant had been crude, though adequate for his purpose. Accounting records were merely memorandum entries of credit transactions; no record was kept of cash or barter transactions. Accounts between partners were settled very simply by deducting the expenses from the proceeds of each venture and by dividing the rest among the partners according to the rules agreed upon. This could be done on a scrap of paper.

In the late thirteenth and early fourteenth centuries, accounting advanced with great strides. One innovation of major importance was the current account kept in bilateral form, that is, the personal account divided vertically into two columns, one for the debit and one for the credit. Later, double-entry bookkeeping was introduced by adding impersonal accounts to the existing personal accounts. Good methods of bookkeeping were essential in order to keep accounts straight when two persons, residing in different cities, had numerous business dealings with each other. Merchants had to know where they stood, and accounting served as a guide by revealing profits and losses.

All these techniques were merely tools for control and management. They did not replace intelligence and common sense in the conduct of business enterprise.

The consequences of the commercial revolution may be summarized as follows:

(1) The Italians were the first to master the new techniques just mentioned. As a result, foreign trade in Western Europe became virtually an Italian monopoly. Italian supremacy did not break down until well into the sixteenth century, long after Italy itself had declined as a consequence of the geographical discoveries.

(2) The traveling merchants of Flanders, who used to visit the fairs of Champagne, were entirely eliminated. Foreign trade was taken out of the hands of the Flemings, who ceased to play an active rôle and confined themselves to acting as intermedi-

aries. The native upper class in Bruges, during the fourteenth and fifteenth centuries, was not made up of merchants but of brokers, innkeepers, *drapiers*, and commission agents.

(3) Any investigation into the origins of capitalism should concentrate on Italian practices. There is in America a tendency to overrate the importance of England. Until the reign of Elizabeth, England was commercially backward. (It was mainly an agricultural country with wool as its principal product for export.) One example will suffice to bring this out: the bill of exchange remained unknown to English merchants until the fifteenth century.

(4) The Italians controlled foreign trade in the Levant, in Southern Europe, in France, in Flanders, and in England. For various reasons they did not penetrate into Germany. The Baltic trade, in particular, remained the monopoly of the Hanseatic League.

4   *Gino Luzzatto*
              Economic Conditions in the Communes
                 during the 13th and 14th Centuries

Until his death in 1964 Gino Luzzatto enjoyed the reputation of one of Europe's most distinguished economic historians. The booklet from which the following selection was borrowed was written as a general introduction to Italian economic history from the fall of the Rome Empire to the 16th century.

In strictly formal terms the urban commune can be considered a creation of feudal society; it came into existence with the

SOURCE. *Gino Luzzatto, An Economic History of Italy from the Fall of the Roman Republic to the Beginning of the Sixteenth Century.* Translated from the Italian by P. J. Jones (Routledge & Kegan Paul Ltd., 1962), pp. 91–98. Copyright 1962 by Routledge & Kegan Paul Ltd. Reprinted by permission of Routledge & Kegan Paul Ltd. and Barnes and Noble, Inc.

transfer of certain public rights, by sovereign concession, from a feudal lord to a group of vassals associated for the purpose. But in practice this transfer of power was encouraged and often caused by the revival of the towns as centres of exchange and the consequent formation of a bourgeois class.

One effect of the immigration was a sharp and general increase in urban population, an increase described by several of the chroniclers, and illustrated, we have seen, by the steady enlargement, often on a massive scale, of the walled urban perimeter. Many towns must have trebled their population in little more than a century. Inside the walls new public buildings and churches, often of enduring beauty, shared the crowded space with the towered palaces of the immigrant nobility and the wood and stone hovels of the common people.

Side by side with this renovation and expansion of the city, changes of equal magnitude developed in society and economic life. In particular the subjugation by the commune of the lords of the *contado* destroyed once for all the vestiges of economic unity on manors and fiefs, and widened increasingly the range of urban markets. As the last manorial workshops began to disappear, even rustics had to turn to urban industry for what they could not make themselves. And so in Italy the political division to town and country was cancelled and replaced by an almost complete economic division of labour, whereby the country supplied food and raw materials and the towns practiced trade and industry. Inside the city, however, divisions of a different kind appeared, in the growth of class distinctions. On the one hand an aristocracy arose composed of great landowners, jealous for their ancient immunities, their share in public revenues, and all their traditional rights over dependent *homines*; on the other hand were the dependants themselves, who had entered some urban trade or profession and would tolerate no claims to ancient rent and services. But more important for urban history was the fact that, in between the old landed aristocracy and the manual workers who had turned from agriculture to industry, stood another class, the merchants; and the merchants were not mere shopkeepers selling goods from stalls in the *piazza*, but—in those communes at least where they formed an organized class—consisted of men of wealth and substance, engaged in foreign trade and travel and in the import of merchandise which the local town and territory were unable to produce. Merchants of this type were the natural leaders of the new middle classes, and in some communes we already find them sharing power with the nobles in the period of consular rule. As industry and trade intensified, they were quickly joined by other groups, not indeed by the mass of manual workers, but by the master craftsmen of the richer and more powerful guilds, which had been established in most cities of north and central Italy in the later twelfth century. In combination with the lesser merchants, who had not yet entered the nobility, the wealthier guildsmen came to form what was known in every town as "the people" *(popolo)*, a middle-class alliance, which during the thirteenth century began to gain control of the commune.

As the government passed increasingly under middle-class influence, economic policy conformed increasingly to middle-class interests, interests, however, which were often common to the urban population at large. But what served the city did not serve the country. On the contrary the rural population was now subjected to a policy of systematic exploitation for the benefit of consumers and producers in the town. It is perfectly true that, by suppressing many feudal rights and freeing the class of serfs, the towns had contributed, directly or indirectly, to improving social conditions in the countryside. But when the feudal lords had been deprived of power, the towns simply took their place and proceeded to treat the country like colonial territory, as a source of food and a market for manufactures. In accord with this policy attempts were made to prevent households in the country from making goods produced in the towns More revealing still, laws were introduced forbidding peasants to "fly" the land, the effect of which was to revive in favour of urban landlords a condition little different from the old praedial servitude.

Another matter which closely affected the economic relations of town and country was the food policy pursued by the urban communes. One supreme concern of all municipal governments was to avoid any shortage of food or rise in the cost of living, which would lead to a demand for higher wages. In years of abundant harvest the problem hardly arose, for even the towns with the densest industrial population and the least adequate supply of home-grown food could easily import corn and other basic produce from less populous regions nearby. But in years of scanty harvest the barriers were raised relentlessly between each commune and the next. And so, to avert the misfortune of too frequent famine, special officials were appointed (called officials of the *annona, grascia,* or *abbondanza*), whose task it was to study the periodic census of all persons above the age of infancy, check the local stocks of grain, estimate the need of the following year, and determine the measures to meet it. Then, on the bases of their calculations, the commune or prince proceeded to purchase large quantities of corn, if possible from neighbouring states which were not threatened with shortage, but more often from one of the maritime cities, which imported it mainly, as we have seen, from the Maremma, Apulia, Sicily, and the Byzantine East.

This dependence on food supplies from outside was one reason why the urban economy, in the larger towns at least, ceased to be a closed system in which town and territory could combine as a self-sufficient community. But other reasons were no less important. Thus the massive development of particular industries in different towns led to a local specialization and reciprocal trade. At the same time a number of inland towns, where the merchants had managed to accumulate substantial capital, began to play a part in international commerce. As early as the twelfth century numerous merchants of Asti, Chieri, Piacenza, Lucca, and Siena, were in the habit of visiting markets in southern France, Paris, and Champagne. Not long after, we find them also in London and Bruges. In all these places the Italians took up banking as well as trade, partly encouraged by the popes, who often made them agents for the transmission of papal taxes. Many were simply pawnbrokers, known collectively in northern towns as "Lombards," who did a thriving business in petty loans on small security. But some became financiers to princes and monarchs, great feudal lords and prelates. The bankers of Lucca, Siena, and particularly Florence, were the principal creditors of kings. The risks involved were certainly great, but so were the advantages obtained in the export of merchandise and the farm of customs and other revenues.

Among the towns most actively engaged in this mercantile enterprise of the twelfth and thirteenth centuries were certain communes of northern Italy, in particular Asti and Piacenza, Cremona and Milan. From the twelfth century on, we find merchants and bankers of Asti at work in France, Burgundy, and England; they formed a primary group among the so-called "Lombards," who gave their name to the street still occupied by many of London's principal banks. Piacenza, which remained a centre of banking business down to the early seventeenth century, became commercially important because of its position at the junction of the Po with several busy high-ways: the Via Francigena (which led from England and France to Lucca, Siena, and Rome), the Via Emilia, and one of the main roads from Genoa to Milan. Cremona was another notable trading city on the Po, distinguished especially in the Middle Ages for its unrivalled fustian industry. The greatest town of all, however, was Milan, which after the decline of Pavia became the leading centre of trade and industry throughout the whole of Lombardy and the valley of the Po. Milan was already strong enough to rouse the jealousy of its neighbours in the early twelfth century. At the time of the struggle with the Emperor Barbarossa the merchants of Milan already possessed an organization with consuls of their own. And after the defeat of Barbarossa (1176) the Milanese gave further proof of their resource and wealth by starting to build the canals, drainage and irrigation works, to which lower Lombardy has ever since owed most of its prosperity. About the same period a woollen industry developed in the city, with help from the Umiliati brotherhood, and very soon it was producing abundant cloth for export. The most famous Milanese industry, however, was metallurgy, and especially the manufacture of arms.

Industry flourished also in the larger communes of Venetia, particularly Verona and Padua. The main commodity produced for export was woollen cloth. But not only trade was lucrative; in Dante's day we also hear of wealthy capitalists who engaged in moneylending on a very large scale. From time to time both Padua and Verona managed to extend control over great part of the Veneto, especially after the late thirteenth century, when the two towns were ruled by despotic families, the Scaligeri and Carraresi; but local rivalries and the jealousy of two great neighbouring powers, Venice and Milan, prevented them from ever establishing a durable dominion.

In Emilia, by contrast, none of the various urban communes scattered at regular intervals along the Emilian Way seriously disturbed the local balance of power during this period. Bologna, it is true, had particular advantages. It surpassed the other towns in industrial development. It also occupied a favoured position at the junction of the Via Emilia and the road from Venice to Florence and Lucca. In those days, moreover, it commanded access by water to the Po and the sea, which it later lost because of changes in the river system of the region. And finally the University, which was famous throughout Europe, drew people and trade to the town. But for all that, Bologna never developed so large a population or so great a surplus of production as to be impelled to undertake territorial conquest.

The first town in Tuscany to attain more than local economic importance was Lucca. Lucca was also the first town in upper Italy to engage in the manufacture of silk. For more than a century the Lucchese silk industry maintained an unchallenged supremacy; and when political unrest drove many of the merchants and craftsmen into exile, Lucca became inadvertently responsible for the growth of similar industries in Florence, Bologna, Venice, and Genoa. But the business men of Lucca had always been merchants rather than manufacturers, and as merchants they occupied a leading position in the trade of western Europe, and especially France. right down to the beginning of modern times.

Roughly contemporary with the rise of Lucca, though rather different in form, was the economic development of Siena. One source of Sienese wealth was mining, which was practised on a very large scale (for those days) in various parts of the wide Sienese dominion. But the main source was commerce. Siena was the meeting-place of two main roads to Rome: the Via Francesca from Piacenza and Lucca, and the road from Bologna and Florence. Such a situation not only favoured trade; it also encouraged frequent intercourse with the capital of Christendom, and this no doubt explains why pope Gregory IX chose Sienese merchant-bankers to collect the crusading tenth in the countries north of the Alps. The commission served the Sienese well; for it enabled them to increase their trade with the northern countries, and also probably their banking activity. Banking in fact was the main concern of the great Sienese families, who made their fortune during the thirteenth century—the Bonsignori and the Piccolomini, the Salimbeni and the Tolomei. Too often, however, these fortunes built on banking proved precarious. Loans to the popes and to foreign nobles, prelates, and princes, tied up so much capital that in the second half of the thirteenth century many Sienese houses, including the most powerful and famous of them all, the Tavola dei Bonsignori, went irredeemably bankrupt. The result was that the Sienese finally lost their dominant position in the Tuscan banking world to the great business companies of Florence, which had secured and distributed their capital better, by investing in larger and richer rural estates and exploiting a rapidly expanding industry.

The rise of Florence to supremacy in Tuscany occupied the best part of two hundred years, and as late as the mid thirteenth century the city was still closely encircled by independent urban communes and powerful feudal lords. Florentine wealth was derived from commerce, combined from an early stage with industry. Chief among the trade corporations *(Arti)* of the town was the guild of the Calimala merchants, so called from the street where they had their shops. The principal business of these merchants was the importation of French, Flemish, and English cloth; but since their trade involved them in close relations with countries abroad, they often engaged in banking as well, though at first on a limited scale. More important in the thirteenth century was the industry they developed for processing northern textiles to suit the taste of markets at home and in the Levant, to which they re-exported the dyed and finished cloth by way of Pisa, Venice, and later also Fano.

Quite independent of the Calimala guild was the purely industrial clothmakers' guild, or *arte della lana*, which by the early fourteenth century administered the greatest industry in Florence and possibly in the whole of Italy. At that time, according to the chronicler Giovanni Villani, the looms of Florence were producing more than 100,000 pieces yearly, though only of moderate quality; thirty years later, the same authority tells us, production had dropped by about one-third, but had so improved in quality that the finer cloth, intended mainly for export, was fetching a price equal to or above that of the most highly prized fabrics of Flanders or France.

Long before this, however, the position which Florentine merchants had reached in the markets of western Europe was vividly revealed and powerfully strengthened by the gold coinage issued by Florence, concurrently with Genoa, in the year 1252. This coin was introduced in order to replace the Byzantine *hyperperon*, which had served as international currency for all Christian countries down to the twelfth century, but had then been rapidly and seriously debased. In the event the florin was far more successful than the Genoese coin or *genoino*, and it soon placed Florence in the front rank of the financial powers of Europe. But its triumph was not so much the cause as the measure of Florentine influence, and this was due to the great expansion of Florentine business in the markets of France, England, and the Low Countries, Rome and southern Italy, and even, to some extent, the Orient as well.

5   *P. J. Jones*
        Florentine Families and Florentine Diaries

P. J. Jones is a lecturer of mediaeval history at Brasenose College, Oxford University. Drawing heavily from the account books and personal diaries (ricordanze) *of 14th and 15th century Florentines, he formulates a carefully drawn image of the complex world in which these men lived and establishes the fact that a clear division between a landed aristocracy and a commercial class did not exist in Florence during the 14th and 15th centuries.*

It is difficult to decide what distribution of capital should infallibly mark the family active in trade, still more a society dedicated mainly to business. The tax-returns of Nofri di Palla Strozzi and his son reveal only a small proportion of their declared capital invested in trade, but they were business men and came of a business family; even the Medici in 1427–1430 appear from their tax statement to have had less money placed in commerce than in land or government stock. The distribution of investments can be determined only statistically, but comprehensive statistics are lacking in Florentine records before the *catasti* of 1427 and even then are unreliable. It was traditional to declare as few commercial investments as possible and represent business as bad, and there is no doubt that returns of business capital were falsified to an extent which made all attempts to tax it ineffective. It must also be noted that many firms and business families operated extensively with deposit capital. According to his tax-return of 1378, Francesco Rinuccini possessed land to the value of 30,000 florins, government securities totalling 14,500 florins, and only 2,500 florins nett. "tra mercatanzia e danari,"[1] yet Francesco had wide-flung business enterprises, was possibly the richest man in Florence, and when he died in 1382 was said to have left 180,000 florins, "contanti d'oro"[2] apart from land.

It is doubtful therefore whether any reliable means exists of measuring the general tendency of investments in fourteenth century Florence; certainly no movement away from business, no "new direction" in the placing of capital, can be convincingly proved from the random evidence of *ricordanze*. Instances are still not difficult to find in late medieval Florence of men whose wealth lay least in land, beside them no less certainly was a class of individuals or families, old and new, the *scioperati*, who lived by land alone and the interest of government stock. Paolo

---

[1] In cash and business investments.
[2] 180,000 gold florins in cash.

SOURCE. P. J. Jones, "Florentine Families and Florentine Diaries in the Fourteenth Century," *Papers of the British School at Rome*, XXIV (n.s., Vol. XI) (Rome: British School at Rome, 1956), pp. 197–205. Reproduced with permission from the Papers of the British School at Rome and the author.

da Certaldo treated as normal the case of those who drew their income only from land, though he also said: "The country produces good animals but bad men, therefore use it little: stay in the city, practise some craft or trade, and you'll get on." Over a century later Guicciardini described the class of "pernicious citizens who live by their fat revenues from land" and government investments. Such families, the later aristocracy of Medici Tuscany, were probably increasing; but it is notable how many Florentine houses continued to produce business men and business capital uninterruptedly from the thirteenth to the sixteenth century. During the sixteenth century it is generally agreed that a new spirit of disdain for trade and industry, even agricultural industry, spread universally in Italy; but it seems no less agreed that if the Italians were losing their monopoly of international trade and banking, their primacy was slow in passing and there was no sudden decay. Florence specifically was still in the early sixteenth century considered a mercantile and industrial city, as before in the fifteenth and the later fourteenth century. The "new direction" was followed only gradually, and the "return" of Italians "to the land" was the process of generations.

One proof offered in tracing this movement in Florence to the fourteenth century is the substantial return that might be had from landed investments. It has been argued that later medieval business profits, which were anyway subject to violent fluctuation, did not if properly estimated normally rise above 15 per cent. Much capital was also deposited "sopra corpo" at a fixed interest rate of 6 to 10 per cent. It is therefore possible to show that the return from land in the fourteenth century might sometimes be as high as the payment on deposits, or as much as 8 per cent. But, as Rodolico rightly emphasises, there were other motives than profit for acquiring land, and land and business were never considered merely alternative forms of investment.

There was first the simple desire to possess a country house and estate in land. This no doubt was "not in the course of nature," but it was an ambition none could resist. The possession of castles or *ville* to which great families could periodically retire for pleasure or to organise political resistance is a commonplace of Italian municipal history. Of the Florentines, the Venetian ambassador observed in 1527 that "they have this weakness, that they go about the world to make a fortune of 20,000 ducats and then spend 10,000 on a palace outside the city." This was not new in the sixteenth century nor even in Dante's day; Dante himself deplores the practice, and after him a long line of writers describe the villa landscape of the Florentine *contado* and the custom, particularly among magnate families, of spending summer months in the country. It was also during Dante's lifetime that the first essays in agronomic literature appeared which with works in praise of country life became generally popular in the sixteenth century. All over Tuscany the *curtis* of the feudal past was emerging transformed in the country "casa da signore" or the more pretentious towered villa and *palatium* of the urban landlord, set beside the dwellings of his tenants (the "case da lavoratore"). Few *ricordanze* fail to mention them, and all the families "new" and "old" whose diaries have been noticed here possessed what Francesco Datini called a "nest." Already before 1260 the ownership of town and country palaces is plainly characteristic of the upper classes generally and not simply the feudal families of Florence. The fortified country-house—*domus murata, casa turris,* or *palatium*—was taking its place beside the older "palaces" or "towers" established inside walled *castella*. These in turn were changing as their feudal lords ecclesiastical and lay bought up the lots within *castella* to plant new palaces and castles. Merchant families soon joined or displaced the old, acquiring or building castles of their own, which in the course of generations were converted into villas. The fourteenth century villa was still partly fortified, like the French *manoir*, and with good reason; but it was no less a mark of social elevation. The Peruzzi had a villa built at Baroncelli; they also bought and crenellated a country palace of the Mozzi; but they were proud as well to own the ruined *castellare* of Baroncelli for the honour ("orevolezza") it conferred.

Whether agriculture was as much affected as the aspect of the countryside by these villa-building families is not clear. It cannot be assumed that they were more methodical or harsh than landlords in the past, but the evidence, not least of *ricordanze,* does imply an active interest in exploiting and improving the land, if no changes may be proved in agricultural technique. On large estates *castaldi* or factors were employed, but it does not seem that management was left irresponsibly to them. The estate-accounts of Nofri di Palla Strozzi, who employed a factor, indicate careful and energetic supervision by the landlord. Smaller men dealt only with their tenants, who Paolo da Certaldo advised should be called to town for settling accounts, since in the country the landlord's bargaining position would be weaker.

An interest in farming is suggested by the practice of working some lands, especially vineyards, directly and by the preference shown for *mezzadria*. *Mezzadria* obliged the landlord to play an active part in agriculture; it was in fact less a lease than a form of hiring labour, and was precisely suited to urban families so many of whom were immigrant landowners. The agricultural expenses of *mezzadria* were increased by others, very prominent in *ricordanze*, on building and improvement, with particular care once again for vineyards. The object was to produce for both consumption and the market. There may have been no Florentines so rich in land that they might like certain of the Sienese nobility starve their city of corn, but they could hoard and force up grain prices, and the evidence abounds that sale of produce by landowners great and small was usual. Nofri di Palla Strozzi sold systematically oil, wine, and above all, grain to bakers, millers and corn-dealers of all kinds, and his son Palla was reported to draw from his estates 600 *moggia* (*c.* 14,400 bushels) of grain, which would have fed the whole of Florence for several days. A man was commonly said to consume one bushel (*staio*) of grain a month, but in the greater families the rate was certainly higher. During the year 1314-1315 the families of Giotto and Tommaso Peruzzi consumed about 2,000 bushels of grain, with wine, oil and meat in proportion; much of this was certainly bought, yet Giotto Peruzzi was assiduous in planting vineyards and marketing produce and expressly bought property in Florence for storage and sale of wine. The Frescobaldi even built a villa from the profits of their vineyards. The commercial spirit detected here was present also in other forms of speculation, particularly stock-raising "a soccida." In Emilia this was a regular type of capital investment for citizens of all classes; so in certain parts of Tuscany, and the same is suggested of Florence by *ricordanze*.

The Florentine "business class" then, like that of other towns, turned the land and its resources to profitable account. But a further and final motive for acquiring land, as is often pointed out, was its security. The unlimited liability of medieval business firms encouraged investment in land to guarantee their credit and meet the "subite perdite"[3] that frequently followed the "subiti guadagni"[4] of trade. The great security of land was already emphasised by medieval writers. Ser Lapo Mazzei in a letter to Francesco Datini reminds him how unstable business profits are, "here to-day, gone to-morrow," while L.B. Alberti, M. Palmieri and in general all who touched the subject urged the widsom of investing in land: "they were unconscious physiocrats." It was on land that creditors distrained when, as happened frequently in fourteenth century Florence, firms fell bankrupt. Bankruptcy however brought few families to total ruin; most managed to save a part of their possessions, sometimes like the Antellesi concluding fictitious sales in frustration of their creditors. Bankruptcy proceedings always lasted years, and one problem was to trace the bankrupts' lands; to make this possible a description of properties was several times attempted between 1346 and 1358 but had to be abandoned as impracticable. So land was secure enough. All the same, great estates were dismembered by bankruptcy proceedings and much property transferred in this way from one business family to another. As a result, economic and political supremacy changed hands from period to period, until the most enduring families, new and old alike, became united in the landed aristocracy of ducal Tuscany.

In this process the fourteenth century cannot be said to represent a decisive stage. A landowning merchant class was either new in 1300 nor peculiar to Florence or to Italian cities generally. The urge of business families to invest increasingly in land belongs to all times and places and at Florence may be

---

[3] Sudden losses.
[4] Sudden gains.

traced in every age. In this sense the "return to land" was continual and prompts the further question how far the land had ever been abandoned? Disregarding local variation it might be urged that in north and central Italy generally the typical figure remained at all times the landowner; not the Bardi or Medici, Pepoli or Bentivoglio, but the Scaligeri, Visconti, Estensi or Malatesta were most representative of their society. Yet even these great families did not always disdain to trade, for the link of land and trade was traditional and close in Italy, where the landowning *negotiator* was far older than the commune, where commercial and landed investments were combined—most obviously at Genoa and Venice—from the earliest time, and where the frequent origin of merchant capital and merchant enterprise in landowning families, great and small, old-established or newly immigrant, is plainly indicated.

At Florence, merchant origins are more difficult to trace than in certain towns. The twelfth century consular aristocracy was already composite, as in other communes, admitting merchants as well as *milites*[5] to office. After 1200 in the struggle of nobility and *popolo* the merchant families of many towns—those pursuing "noble" trade in Lapo's sense—were doubtful in their sympathies and consequently classed as magnates. Nearly half the town-dwelling *grandi* of Florence were merchants, but not all of these were *gente nuova:* of the 51 ancient families named by Villani, 15, and of the 114 or so ancient families named by Malespini, 52 at least can be shown to have shared directly in trade or banking. The other merchant *grandi* (Cerchi, Bardi, Frescobaldi, etc.), were "new" and probably belonged to the great class of migrants form the country who, whether lords like the Alberti or Franzesi or tenants like the Niccolini, had land already but sought enrichment in the town. Their final aim it has been said was simply to increase the family property; if so, many were successful, which often makes it hard to distinguish the ancient lands of a family from the new.

Most families preserved some tradition of their origins: the Pitti and Velluti claimed to come from Semifonte, the Niccolini from Passignano, the Morelli from Mugello and so on. As these

---

[5] Knights.

examples show, such traditions were already formed by the fourteenth century and certainly combined much fact with fable. Giovanni Morelli, starting to write in 1393 the history of his family, explains that 300 years before they were settled at S. Cresci in Valcava. All that can be proved is that in the fourteenth century some of them bought land and held *livelli* of the bishop there, and that Giovanni himself had a deep affection for Mugello. He tenderly describes its castles and villas, its great fertility, its dancing feasting country folk, its "boschetti acconci per diletto" where one may safely walk barefoot; idyllic detail is not spared. The Morelli had risen through the *arte della lana*, which they combined with banking, trade in cloth, and money-lending in the country to "peasants and poor men." They continued members of the wool guild to the sixteenth century, but this is no proof of active trade; Giovanni's own brother, though belonging to the guild, preferred to live 'iscio-perato' and never earned a farthing by trade.

Giovanni himself was a merchant and in the words of advice to his family expresses unambiguously the spirit of his age. He was a good Guelf, favoured the "buoni mercanti," and preached political conformity. In trade he urged honesty and caution and above all personal attention to management; riches would follow, but riches should never be displayed, still less declared for taxation. A wise man would always challenge his tax-assessment and complain that trade was bad. He would also say his farms were not producing, for every man, Giovanni assumed, would have estates in the country, spending part of each year in *villeggiatura*. All crops would be sold above the minimum needed in the home and the citizen would attend as carefully to his lands as to his business, dealing circumspectly with his tenants *(mezzadri.)* If his sons should show no inclination to trade, then he must buy them land near Florence to support them in their idleness.

This is the advice and this the outlook of the fourteenth century Florentine. Engaged in trade, engaged in agriculture, engaged in politics and office, he is a man of business in them all, though ready enough to praise the consolations of philosophy, recommend pious reading, and uphold the example of "nostri padri signori Romani che come da loro siamo discesi, per essenzia, cosi dismostrassimo in virtù, e in sustanzia."[6]

6   *F. C. Lane*
                Investment and Usury

Past president of the American Historical Association, Frederick Chapin Lane is Professor Emeritus of History at the Johns Hopkins University. In the following selection, he examines some of the questions that traditionally have drawn the curiosity and interest of students of the Middle Ages and the Renaissance. For example, what was the relationship between the ecclesiastical teachings on usury and the commercial growth of the 12th through the 14th centuries? How were fortunes accumulated and men induced to violate ecclesiastical laws in pursuit of monetary profits? Did the doctrinal strictures on the collection of interest effectively hinder the economic development of Europe? By studying these questions in the Venetian context, Professor Lane arrives at some interesting hypotheses, which merit our careful consideration.

The recent economic pre-eminence of the West was obviously connected with the high position that businessmen held in western civilization in the nineteenth century, and the priority of the West in economic development was linked to their earlier role. This role depended in very large measure on their com-

[6] "Our fathers the Romans from whom, as we are their spiritual descendants, we should demonstrate our descent by virtuous and practical actions as well."

SOURCE. *Venice and History–The Collected Papers of Frederic C. Lane*, edited by a Committee of colleagues and former students, "Investment and Usury," (Baltimore: Johns Hopkins University Press, 1966), pp. 56–68.

mand of credit, that is, it depended on the ability of businessmen to invest in trade and industry *more* than their own personal funds. Like many other fundamental features of western civilization, the practice of doing business with borrowed money took root in the Middle Ages. In the period when the Christian church was at the peak of its power as an institution, when canon lawyers, theologians, and popes were condemning interest as usury, organizations for conducting business with other people's money became a basic part of western economic life.

This apparent paradox is partly removed, but only partly, by an explanation of the rather ambiguous terms "borrowing" and "usury." A man who is out to produce some goods or services with an eye to his own profit and who lacks for his purpose sufficient money of his own can use a variety of legal forms in inducing others to give him the use of their funds. Waiving legal technicalities, I have referred to his "borrowing." But the managers of a modern corporation who want more money for their schemes and who obtain it by selling stock are not in a legal sense borrowers. Similarly, a thirteenth-century businessman seeking the use of other people's funds could do so by various means. Whether the relationship created by a particular contract was a loan or a partnership could be a difficult legal and moral question. If it was what they would call a loan, a *mutuum*, and if he paid interest on it, in our sense of the word "interest," it was in principle sinful in the eyes of the church, being usury even if the rate of interest was extremely moderate. But there were contracts that were morally approved, perhaps because they were called partnerships, which permitted a businessman to mobilize under his command other people's resources. I will use the word "investment" to avoid the legal problem raised by either "loan" or "partnership."

Among all the cities of medieval Europe, Venice was the first to become capitalistic in the sense that its ruling class made their livelihood by employing wealth in the form of commercial capital—cash, ships, and commodities—and used their control of government to increase their profits. How did commercial investment develop at Venice? How was it affected by the condemnation of usury? I shall consider first the kinds of contracts used in commercial investment and how they changed, and then the reasons for these changes.

The early commercial documents show the use at Venice on the one hand of the kind of ordinary loans on security which the church fathers censored as usurious and on the other hand of real partnerships, a form of contract which was never condemned. Approval of partnerships was a matter of course and was so assumed by Pope Innocent III about 1200 when he recommended that a dowry be committed to some merchant in order that from the honest gain so won the husband might better support the burdens of matrimony. Full partnership had the disadvantage, however, that it involved the investor in liabilities that were theoretically unlimited and of which the practical range was difficult to foresee. Neither the ordinary loan nor the ordinary partnership was as popular in twelfth-century Venice as was a third form provided for in Roman law, namely the sea loan. This was distinguished from the ordinary loan by the fact that the lender took the risks of shipwreck or piracy and was allowed therefore a higher rate of return.

Another form of credit unknown to Roman lawyers but in use since the tenth century was what the Venetians called a *colleganza*. It was a kind of profit-sharing sea loan or agency having some of the features of a partnership. Of the two parties to the contract, one, the *tractans* or *procertans*, undertook to travel and trade with the fund which was the subject of the contract. He may be called the active or traveling merchant. The other, who is often referred to as the *stans* or stay-at-home, I think it generally best to call the investor, for whether he moved about or stayed put was not essential to the contract. The essential was that he put up funds on which he took the risk of loss by shipwreck or piracy and on which he received a return that depended on profitable trading conducted by someone else. If there was profit, he received three fourths of it, the other fourth going to the traveling merchant.

These were the essential features of what at Venice and Ragusa was called a *colleganza* and was elsewhere, as at Genoa, called a *commenda*. It appears in most general discussions under the name *commenda*, but in speaking exclusively of Venice it seems best to use the Venetian name, *colleganza*. The *colleganza* may be thought of as developing out of the sea loan when investors agreed to accept a percentage of the profit instead of requiring a fixed sum or a stated percentage on this loan. Other features distinguishing the *colleganza* then followed logically, for once the investor's gain depended on the amount of profit, he was interested in requiring an accounting of all pertinent expenses and receipts. Venetian laws required an accounting within thirty days after return to Venice and stipulated how much of his personal as well as traveling expenses the traveling merchant could charge as costs against the return on that investment.

In the earliest *colleganza* contracts the traveling merchant supplied one third of the trading fund, the investor supplied two thirds. The profits were then divided equally. This is called the two-sided *collegantia*, or *societas maris*. In such an arrangement the investor was receiving exactly the same amount he would have received if the contract had provided that he get three fourths of the profit on his two thirds (since $3/4$ times $2/3$ is $6/12$). The two-sided *colleganza* thus gave exactly the same claim on profits as a one-sided. In the two-sided form, the traveling merchant contracted to administer as a unit a fund to which he contributed one third and to account for it as a unit. He had to commit some of his own funds to the same purchases or ventures and to charge expenses to the combined account.

Surviving contracts indicate that the one-sided *colleganza* almost completely displaced both the sea loan and the two-sided *colleganza* early in the thirteenth century. Venetian legislation clearly indicates that the unilateral *colleganza* became the form which merchants seeking funds to take overseas were expected to use. Conversely, it was the form most used by those who had money available for investment. Indeed, since opportunities to invest in land were restricted in Venice, *colleganze* and government loans were almost the only means by which widows or pious foundations or wealthy merchants on their retirement could obtain an income on their funds; and the Venetian equivalent of government bonds—namely forced loans which the lenders could sell—did not become available in much quantity until very late in the century.

The amount of commercial credit embodied in *colleganze* became so large that it disquieted the governing councils of Venice. In 1324 they forbade anyone to send or carry overseas in *colleganza* a sum greater than the amount for which he was assessed in the government's levying of forced loans. After being periodically thus restricted, *colleganze* gradually ceased to be important in financing the Levantine trade. Commission agents were used instead. Merchants no longer made a practice of traveling out and back with the same fleet; the commission merchant resided in an overseas port for several years. He accepted goods or cash on consignment, sold and bought as ordered, and charged for his services a small percentage of the total value of the turnover. Larger and more permanent associations of capital were arranged through full partnerships.

Having been ousted from its great role in international trade, the *colleganza* continued in three forms. For trading voyages into little known territory, such as that of Alberto Loredano to Delhi, India in 1338, it was used in its old form. At Chioggia it was slightly modified to allow for the ownership by the active merchant of the vessels used for trade, probably in nearby markets. But most contracts of *colleganze* in the fourteenth century were loans to shopkeepers and craftsmen or to banks for use "in Rialto," as the expression went. This form, called the local *colleganza*, involved no sea risk. The loaner often took the risks of thievery and fire, and did not specify the return exactly. In practice the loans were generally renewed at some standard rate, 8 per cent in 1330 and 5 per cent after 1340.

What relation does all this have to the teachings about usury, this development from sea loan to two-sided *colleganza*, then to one-sided *colleganza* so extensively used that it crowded out even the sea loan, and then to the use of commission agents in overseas trade, and within Venice to a kind of *colleganza* that provided capital for local trade and banking? Not as much as is commonly supposed. The changes can just as well be interpreted as adjustments of commercial customs to changing economic needs. There has been a tendency to attribute to the usury laws every departure from what seems natural to us in the light of modern practice, even when the forms used can be satisfactorily explained by their suitability to the economic conditions of the times.

A reasonable explanation of the changes in the forms of investment can be found primarily in the larger supply of funds seeking commercial investment. Evidence that the flow of capital into the Levant trade was excessive in the eyes of contemporaries is strongest in the early fourteenth century, but when one considers the general increase of wealth in the cities of Italy and particularly in Venice, it seems reasonable to suppose that the same factor—the funds accumulating in the hands of pious foundations and of old families—was operating throughout the centuries between 1000 and 1300. References to a standard interest rate of 20 per cent in the twelfth century and 5 per cent in the thirteenth is some indication of such a change.

Consider first the change from sea loan to *colleganza*. It substituted for a fixed obligation an obligation to share profits. To that extent it was like issuing common stock to finance an expansion of business, instead of selling bonds. It placed more of the risks on the investors.

The fact that early *colleganze* were two-sided may be considered a concession to investors that was necessary when the supply of capital was still relatively small. In order to persuade investors to take some of the commercial risk, the managing merchants had for a time to commit part of their own capital to the same ventures. In the thirteenth century, investors became so eager that this was no longer necessary.

When commercial practices were then made the subject of legislation in Venice, the sea loan and the two-sided *collegantia* were passed over as obsolete. The one-sided *collegantia* was being used by men and women of widely diverse occupations and conditions to participate in maritime trade. A very wide popular participation in overseas commerce occurred and can be even more thoroughly demonstrated at Genoa at the beginning of the thirteenth century; the prevalence there of one-sided *commenda* contracts rose from 22 per cent of all contracts in the mid-twelfth century to 91 per cent in the early thirteenth. With a large number of relatively uninformed investors eager to place funds, a managing merchant could take advantage of the situation, pad his expense accounts, charge more expenses to one investor than to another, consign to other agents funds or goods he had contracted to handle himself, and delay making his report, even after coming back to Venice. Venetian lawmakers were concerned to prevent such practices, in short, to protect investors who were no longer in a sufficiently good bargaining position to protect themselves.

The ever-expanding volume of funds seeking investment played a role also in the next step, the use of commission agents instead of *colleganze* in overseas trade. Many changes in commercial technique contributed to this change—quicker, more regular voyages, bills of lading, better bookkeeping, etc.—but for Venice, at least, Professors Luzzatto and Cessi, who have studied in detail the disuse of the maritime *collegança* ascribe much importance to alarm at the volume of capital being invested in the Levant.

Although the shift from one form of contract to another is not, in my judgment, to be attributed to the ecclesiastical prohibition of usury, the church doctrine may perhaps explain why a rate of return was not specified in the local *colleganze*. By leaving the amount of interest dependent on what certain banks would pay, these contracts intoduced an element of risk or at least uncertainty. Possibly a canonist favorable to the Venetians would have argued that these deposits at interest were legal because the return was uncertain. Such a crack in the doctrine, if widely accepted, would have burst the dam and swept away the whole usury doctrine or made it an anachronism. In fact, the rate of return on local *colleganze* seems often to have been well understood in advance, and courts enforced on recalcitrant debtors rates varying from 5 to 12 per cent.

One reason for not attibuting to the usury doctrine such a change as that by which the *colleganze* displaced the sea loans is the use even at the time when this change was going on of many contracts that were clearly usurious according to the teachings of the church. Loans at 20 per cent with land pledged as security were made by Pietro Ziani, who was doge from 1205 to 1229, and by his father Sebastian Ziani, who was doge from 1172 to 1178 and in the latter year entertained most magnificently Emperor Frederick I and Pope Alexander III. Another contract which would seem also to have been clearly usurious according to the teachings of the churchman was that by which a son in 1213 promised his widowed mother, Agnese Gradenigo, 10 per cent a year on her money and he took all the risks.

The reasons for using one form of contract instead of another can hardly ever be determined in an individual case. A few years after 1213, Domenico Gradenigo promised his mother three fourths of the profits on her money and she took the sea risk. Had Agnese Gradenigo felt guilty of exacting usury from her son? Or was the mother at the later date less concerned with an assured income? Or hoping for a higher return? If the only concern had been the illegality of usury, an agreement between mother and son for a fixed interest could easily have been hidden under a contract for a free loan. There are many examples of such loans *pro amore*. Some of these free loans probably hide the payment of usury; some were probably really accommodation loans such as businessmen have used during the centuries. When there is no evidence of the circumstances, there is little reason to jump to either conclusion about the individual case.

In regard to the general change, there is evidence on at least one point. The disappearance of the sea loan used to be ascribed to the decretal *Naviganti* of Pope Gregory IX of 1234. But at Venice the sea loan had gone out of use before 1234 so that its disappearance cannot be attributed to that specific decree.

Although the usury doctrine has been appealed to more often than necessary to explain features of medieval business practice, its general, long-run influence on economic life is not of course to be ignored. Its greatest importance was its moral influence. One could argue that the Venetians were at first quite unconcerned about the sin of usury and gradually became so as churchmen became more vehement and specific on the subject. The Ziani were following old Venetian customs in collecting 20 per cent, as they did even on well-secured loans, and they probably felt no sense of sin. Church doctrine was given more teeth during their lifetime, however, by the Third Lateran Councils of 1179, and was then energetically disseminated by the preaching friars. During the thirteenth century, Venetians certainly expressed a destestation of usury. In 1254 they began passing laws against it, and Da Canale's thirteenth-century chronicle lumps together heretics, usurers, murderers, and thieves—boasting that none of these dared live in Venice.

When the Venetians did become concerned about usury, they developed a standard different from that of the ecclesiastical authorities—what might be called a businessman's standard. Indeed, in the fourteenth century the Venetians applied a conception of usury much like that current today. It approved as nonusurious the payment on investment of a rate of return determined at least in theory by market conditions. Accordingly it approved as perfectly legal, in spite of the law against usury, the contracts described above as "local *colleganze*." Such a contract was considered usurious only if the borrower was charged an unusually high rate or taken advantage of in some way, such as being made to give unusual security.

A legal basis for these interest-paying deposits was laid in 1301 when a commission drew up regulations to prevent four kinds of illicit deals in money: in selling exchange, in buying or selling goods on credit, in dealing in futures, and in placing money at interest *(ad presam)*. In all four cases the exceptions were important, but the last is our concern here. Money could be placed at interest only with a bank, or other establishment which was well known as generally accepting money at interest. The establishment was not to pay a particular investor other than the same rate it was paying to other depositors. If it had no other money on deposit, it could not pay the depositor (or lender) more than one half of the profit that the establishment itself had made with the money placed with it. This last is in accord with the provision in the earliest example of *colleganza* for trade on the Rialto, which provided that each party receive one half of the profits.

No doubt these rules only sanctioned and perhaps restricted practices already current in the thirteenth century. Many contracts and court records show that these practices continued in the next century. Particularly significant is a petition asking for a pardon in 1339. Its significance does not lie in the fact that the pardon was granted to a certain Vitale Dente convicted of usury, nor even in the particular act for which he felt he had been unfairly condemned. Its significance lies in what he assumes to be a perfectly innocent practice; namely, that he had loaned 2,500 ducats with the provision that he would be repaid the capital and such profit or loss as was paid by stipulated banks, but not more than 14 per cent. What caused his condemnation by the magistrates for usury was a clause inserted in the contract saying that his word was to be taken concerning the profit or loss ("credi debeat suo verbo tam de prode quam de danno"). He maintained that he had regarded these words as meaningless notarial jargon. The magistrates said they had inquired of the bankers as to whether Vitale had ever asked them how much they were paying and the bankers said no. Hence, following the law, the magistrates said they condemned Vitale, but they made no protest against his pardon. Whether they or the nobles voting for pardon were moved by Vitale's arguments, or general good reputation, or by entirely different motives does not much matter. The standard of fair practice is evident in the general assumption that he would never even have been accused if his contract had called simply for collecting the going rate of interest actually being paid by bankers.

It has been asserted that the prohibitions of usury prevented the development of the concept of interest. Although it is true that Venetian businessmen did not distinguish clearly between interest and profit, certainly not in their language, they did conceive of interest rates as prices paid for the use of funds. They applied this concept also in setting prices on wares sold for delayed payment. For example, Andrea Barbarigo wrote to the agent who was selling his cloth in 1440, "I think they [some cloths he had shipped] will bring 30 ducats if sold for payment in six months and 28 ducats if sold for cash. If you cannot sell them for cash at 2 ducats less than the term price, I even prefer that you sell for cash at 3 ducats less, because one knows how to gain more than 12 per cent a year on one's money." And they were accustomed to figuring how sums grew at various rates of compound interest.

Venetian businessmen and the Venetian courts regarded usury as an abuse of practices which were normally used legitimately to collect a going rate of return. This conception may be regarded as a joint product of the church's teaching and of other

factors bearing on economic life. The importance in this connection of the church's teachings does not lie chiefly in their
effect on legal forms, since the changes in the forms of
commercial credit are best explained by other economic conditions. But among these other economic conditions one of the
most influential was the increasing volume of funds seeking
investment in commerce, and this demand for commercial
investment is itself to be explained in part by the condemnation
of usury. The usury doctrine's chief influence was thus indirect.

As soon as any appreciable amount of liquid capital was
accumulated in the hands of retired merchants, widows, or
institutions, they sought ways of making their wealth yield
income. In such cities as Venice, where investment in land had
limited possibilities, they put their money with someone who
could promise a return. Practical necessities of commerce and the
traditions rooted in Roman law shaped the forms of contracts.
When the moralists and the canon lawyers examined their contracts they denounced as usurious all loans bearing a fixed
interest even if the interest charge was very moderate and even
if contracted between businessmen as commercial investments.
But if there was risk and uncertainty about the return, the
transaction would probably be approved as a partnership. In
practice, loans to consumers were at a fixed rate and secured by
collateral. Businessmen were better able to obtain funds without
pledging specific security and without specifying the yearly
return. Therefore loans to businessmen more generally escaped
being obviously usurious. A distinction between productive
loans and those that were merely exploiting consumers was
recognized in the fourteenth century by the merchant nobles
of Venice and by some Roman lawyers. It is hinted at by
some moralists in the fifteenth century, openly championed in
the sixteenth, and practically recognized in the church's teaching generally in the seventeenth century.

In so far then as rich persons paid any attention to the teachings of the church and at the same time sought some returns
on their wealth they were under pressure to seek land or commercial investments. The Venetians assumed that a man had as
much right to income from commercial property as from
landed property. As long as he invested in commerce through

some contract by which he took a measure of the risk and the return was uncertain, he regarded his return as legitimate. If he was concerned about usury the effect would be to turn him from mere moneylending to commercial investment.

So far as this was true generally the practical effect of the usury doctrine was to increase the funds placed at the disposal of the businessman and thus to encourage economic growth. Consider from the point of view of growth the alternatives open to a person of wealth. If he spent it improving land that he owned, that of course contributed to economic growth, but merely buying land by itself did not. His purchase merely transferred his liquid wealth to other persons. If they consumed it, the wealth never became capital from a social point of view; it contributed nothing to economic growth. Similarly, the manifest usurer making consumption loans from his pawnshop added to his personal fortune but did not add to the aggregate wealth of the society.

In contrast, commercial investments—whether through sea loans, or *colleganze* of various kinds, or full partnerships—did on the whole contribute to economic growth. They built up a network of trade and transportation, a system of regional specialization, and a diffusion of technical skills.

When we inquire concerning the effect of the usury doctrine on economic growth, the most important question is whether it discouraged the kind of loans to consumers which were unproductive socially. To the extent that it did so, the doctrine created pressure on men possessed of liquid wealth to find some other way in which to make their wealth yield income. It thus encouraged the flow of capital into commerce. It is logical to conclude then that the usury doctrine is so far as it was effective stimulated economic growth. But whether or not it really did have that general effect is difficult to prove.

7   *An Anonymous Merchant of the 14th Century*
        How To Succeed in Business while Trying

Throughout the 13th, 14th, and 15th centuries Italian merchants and bankers dominated the European financial and industrial world. In the two following selections some of the remarkable spirit of acumen, realism, and enterprise that enabled the Italians to obtain and safeguard that position of predominance become abundantly clear.

In the first selection, written by an anonymous merchant in the mid-14th century, one gets a clear image of the enormous amount of reflection and calculation given to the conduct of business affairs. The author, in a long series of often repetitive pieces of advice, suggests those ways which, if followed, will bring success to an aspiring businessman. In selection 8, actually a business letter written by an Italian moneylender in France to his partner in Pistoia, the moneylender reflects on the continuous vicissitudes and uncertainties that Italian merchants encountered when dealing abroad. In this case, a decree of confiscation issued by the French monarch against the "Lombards," that is, the Italian moneylenders, forced the writer into all kinds of adventures, which are graphically described in the letter.

Whoever wishes to be a merchant must be endowed with three qualities: good sense, experience, and money.

GOOD SENSE

In order to know how to behave and act in every circumstance, that is, to know how to recognize and chose whatever

SOURCE. "Consiglio sulla mercatura di un anomino fiorentino," edited by Gino Corti in the *Archivio Storico Italiano*, CX (Florence: Olschki, 1952), pp. 117–119. Translated for this volume by Anthony Molho. Reprinted by permission of Casa Edetrice Leo S. Olschki.

must be done, and avoid whatever must be left alone. This means that one should not over extend oneself, nor undertake more than his purse allows him, and not to have patience with those whom one cannot trust, for these people are lords [*signiori*], or men with similar inclinations, poor and of ill repute.

One must take good account of the types of people one deals with, or to whom one entrusts one's goods, for no man is trustworthy with money.

It is convenient to be shrewd in words and actions which one undertakes, for many tricks are used to distract the merchant from his goal, everyone trying to improve himself at his expense. And everyone feels that all of the merchant's transactions are successful, and that in his hands bird droppings turn into gold, and that he earns from each transaction as much as he wishes.

It is not advisable to have everyone's friendship, particularly of those who are of low station and who do not enjoy a good reputation, that is sharpsters and slanderers and people who, in general, take pleasure by defaming others.

One must learn to protect oneself from jealousy, which is always disloyal, and a very bad enemy; thus, one should always act secretly, without advertising one's affairs, nor boasting of one's gains or riches, for then, whatever your gains, they would not be profitable to you, but would bring you great damage. For, some men, observing you speak in such fashion, would try to appropriate some of your goods, and a great loss would result to you only because of their jealousy and not because they had some good reason.

And keep in mind that this jealousy is found in the heart of everyone. I do not believe that there is any sin which is so great and ubiquitous as is this.

One should not be ambitious or aspire to fame only in order to show off, but only because he leads a judicious life. A good name is always derived when one leads a moderate life, for it is a precious and praiseworthy thing. This kind of life often aids and defends a man in circumstances in which ordinarily he would not be appreciated. Man does not have a clearer or dearer friend than his good name. For, whoever enjoys a good reputation cannot help but be good, just, and upright. All the things on this earth under the sky are here for whoever enjoys this condition of life.

Always guard yourself from bad habits, for in the end they always damage you.

If ever visitors come to your house who are not well-disposed toward you, you should not invariably throw them out or snub them. It is rather advisable to deal with them nicely and to feign good intentions toward them. For there are many who can harm a merchant, particularly when he is a foreigner. This last word means nothing more than a man who enjoys no favours at all.

Sometimes your actions should depend on the status of the men with whom you deal. For you may have to deal with someone who is more powerful than you are, or with a man of bad reputation, or with some one who always procrastinates, and in these cases it is better that they be in a position to ask favours of you, than you depending on them. The essence is that you recognize your own and your comrades's status. You should act accordingly.

It is not always a bad thing to pay more for something than it is worth, particularly to messengers, to one's employer, to a broker, or to such men in general. For, if ever they take offense they can cause a good deal of damage, particularly brokers and middlemen who are in a position to do much harm, and who should always be kept on good terms.

It is always good to have friends from every condition of life; but not useless men. Whoever can have good, wise, and wealthy friends would have the very best kind; if that is not possible, let them be good and wise.

One can never be too careful, particularly when collecting money, for the condition of the merchant is such that it is always subjected to infinite dangers. And one cannot collect money on short notice as some people seem to believe.

You should not postpone tending to your correspondence. Paper is cheap, and often it brings in good profit.

Expenses should always be curtailed, for they always bring damage, and money never returns to one's purse. Thus, if you save a little bit at a time, you will have a respectable sum at the end of the year. Let us say that you save 10 lire; in 10 years, if they are accumulated, they constitute a great sum; so great, in fact, that he who does not calculate it carefully would never believe it.

Careless and immoderate expenditures for clothes result in bad and dishonest earnings.

There is nothing that inflames one's ego more than a desire to lead an ostentatious life. There are some people who, before reducing their standard of living, would be willing to give their soul to the devil. There are many dangers inherent in leading a luxurious life which requires large expenditures.

Moreover, if ever you have an excess of money, it should always be saved. For, whoever spends moderately and with foresight is called wise and discreet. Whereas he who spends lavishly is called a bad provider and scatterbrained. The reason is that all temporal possessions are subjected to many dangers, and incessant expenses are like a continuous fever which kills men.

If you live in a foreign land keep in mind that your aid, defense, honour, profit and support come from your money; if you lose it one could say that you lived as if you were damned.

There are only a few reasons for which a citizen of a state would seek the friendship of a foreigner: either to improve his position by associating with the foreigner, or to have some of his money, or because he knows him to have a fine and subtle mind, or even because the foreigner is a good conversationalist or an imaginative historian, or is endowed with some such qualities. If you do not possess any of these qualities and, while living in a strange land a citizen seeks your friendship, beware, for he is probably trying to trick you.

If, while a foreigner, you have to sign an agreement with the citizen of a state do your utmost to behave as a mature and intelligent man. Keep in mind that your generosity toward him, rather than justice or reason, will dispose him favorably toward you. Remember that authority which says: "Gifts blind the eye of the wise, and alter the words of the just." [Deuteronomy, XVI, 19]

Even if I were to prolong this statement I would not be able to include anything on the question of accidents, which are infinite in number. Everything could not be specified here. Nevertheless, one must not have a frail mind, but one must have discretion which is the best of judges and most sensible. Discretion instructs you that you must not judge a document by its contents, but by its intentions. You must not say: Such and such authority, or that precedent instruct this course. But ask yourself: What was the intention of whoever wrote the document? Only then will you be able to understand and act according to the exigencies of a situation. And this is the most beautiful discretion.

EXPERIENCE

So that you may judge the quality of the merchandise, if it is good, average, or poor, and how long it may last without spoiling. It is also important to know the season in which each must be sold, and when it is the best time of the year to send it by boat or by an overland route. Moreover, one should know how to repair these goods if they are damaged on the way, for they can be damaged easily. Similarly, there are many remedies which may be used to conserve or repair them so that they may be better in appearance. In this question of adorning merchandise, there are any number of ways which may be used, and one must be an expert in such things so that he may not be tricked.

It is a very grave error to base one's commercial activities on mere opinion, and not on reason. That is why one must have experience, or at least be accompanied by an experienced person in mercantile affairs.

One must know how to keep books and records; to write and answer letters, which is not a small thing, particularly that of knowing how to dictate letters. For, of all the great friends that we have, language is one of the best, particularly to the man who knows how to use it well.

It is a most useful thing to know how to keep records properly; and this is among the principal lessons a merchant can learn.

MONEY

It is needed so that one may act with his own resources and not with those of others. For, whoever depends on the money of someone else has to pay a high price for it, even if he can borrow it at low interest rates, for it is always certain that the money has to be repaid, while profits are never certain.

Paying interest in order to be a merchant means nothing more than tiring oneself for someone else's benefit, and in the end with damage to oneself:

8   *A 14th Century Moneylender*
          The Many Troubles of a Moneylender

Beaulieu and Bourges, January 26, 1330

Greetings from Beaulieu. As I have written you by other letters, I am surprised that after you left us here we received no letter except the one which you sent from Nice. And were it not that I definitely think the fault is not yours—it is [the fault], I believe, of those to whom you entrusted the delivery—I should say that you have entirely forgotten us. I am not writing anything more about this, except that you should be careful to whom you entrust [letters], so that they be delivered to us.

I was in Paris the day before yesterday, I wrote you the reason and I shall write it once more here from beginning to end. And then I gave Bonagiunta Dondori two letters to send to you. I believe you should have received them, because he gave me his word that he would entrust them to someone who would certainly deliver them to you.

SOURCE. The Many Troubles of a Moneylender, from R. S. Lopez and I. W. Raymond, editors and translators, *Medieval Trade in the Mediterranean World* (New York: Columbia University Press, 1955), pp. 394–399. Reprinted by permission of Columbia University Press and the editor.

These are the new developments that have occurred here and are still [in progress]. First [of all], on the Thursday after All Saints' Day [November 8], all the Lombards in the kingdom who are in the profession[1] were arrested, with the exception of those in Touraine. And the latter remained [free] because the *bailli* was in his own country [place], so that, thank God, we had the time to put our business in good order. Later the *bailli* returned and had them arrested—[that is], those whom he could catch—with the exception of the sons of Messer Vinci-guerra and their factors, because Vanni procured his own liber-ation and that of his brothers, [together] with Cancellieri. Us he forgot. Yet Giovanni had been in Tours earlier and had asked Vanni to include him in the bond when paying the fine—and we would have paid whatever was our share. Giovanni and I decided that it would be the best course to let one of us be arrested, and that I should be the one, because he knew the ways of Paris better than I did. I was arrested—courteously—and inventory was made of all our goods; and then I was taken to Tours to the *bailli*. When I was in Tours, the *bailli* wanted 600 florins from me as a pledge that I would present myself in Paris 'by a certain day.' Gianni Cibotto and Gramma d'Oro, who had come to Tours with me to attend to business of their own, put up the pledges. I presented myself in Paris in the presence of the officials—"by the day." The officials at once had me put in Saint-Martindes-Champs, and they did the same to all those who presented themselves.

A few days after this, the king [Philip VI] had all of them released under pledges, the one [putting up pledges] for the other; and he issued certain ordinances by which commissioners were to go through every *bailliage* and *sénéchaussée*[2] of the kingdom in order to listen to all who wanted to place com-plaints against us, and to cause the return of all profits anyone had received from [loans to] the said persons who would place the complaints. And whoever had extended credit at [a rate of]

---

[1] That is, moneylenders. In time the word became a synonym of "usurer," but originally it was used for any merchant of Italian origin who made interest-bearing loans.

[2] That is, every province—*bailliages*, under *baillis*, in the north, and *séné-chaussées*, under *seneschals*, in the south.

more than one denier[3] should be subject to forfeit of body and goods at the will of the king. And it should be proclaimed that no one was to pay us, under penalty of body and goods; and that those who owed [money] to us and knew the terms were to disclose them, under the penalty mentioned above. And there are many other articles about which I do not write you fully because that course of action seems to have been abandoned, according to what Vanni has written. And they are following another, about which I am writing to you—and it is this, that one . . .[4] agreed that he must have 80,000 pounds; and we have to give a rebate to all our debtors of one fifth of what they owe us; and we must not extend credits at [a rate of] more than one denier per pound.

Vanni had sent [news] that the king wanted all the Lombards in the kingdom to go to live in Champagne. Now, in the last letter he sent us, he writes us nothing about this. I believe the king was saying this to bend us more to his intention. I pray God that He give us counsel, for we have been and still are in great trouble and conflict, and we have not yet gotten out of it. May God in His compassion free us from this; for the agreement is not yet clear in all details, although Vanni writes that they believe that it has been definitely made.

You ought to know that I have returned to Bartolomeo Dondori the 200 *reali* which were borrowed when you left. Vanni told me that he wants me to pay interest *(merito)* on them throughout the month of August because he kept them [ready] for us from St. Christopher's Day up to the day you took them. We, however, have not yet figured it out; hence, when we figure it out, I shall talk to him about deducting those 4 *reali* from the total of 200;[5] and if I can I shall pay [interest] only

---

[3] One denier per pound a month, or one shilling per pound (5 percent) a year—a much lower rate than those prevailing at the time.

[4] A blot caused dampness makes the original unreadable at this point.

[5] Apparently the interest—2 percent a month, or 24 percent a year—was concealed in the figure of the loan. The *reali* were French gold coins. Some French coins also were usually called florins, but the florins mentioned in this letter probably were a money of account pegged to the Florentine florin.

from the Kelends of September. Should I see that he does not feel satisfied, I shall do what he wants, so that he may not feel ill-paid by us. At any rate I want you to know what he has in mind.

We have no money here, nor is there anyone who pays us anything, both because the population is poor on account of the total loss of the vintage and because of the prohibition issued [by the king]. [The situation of] our debtors has not been carefully studied because Giovanni went to Paris on Saturday directly after you had left. And he stayed there up to vigil of All Saints' Day, and later, as I have written you above, we were arrested on the following Thursday.

As I have written you by other letters, your wine was sold to Jehan de Samson for £ 37. He has not yet fully paid us for it, and [the interest] for the remainder must be figured out with him. If I can help it, none of it will be rebated because he has delayed payment more than he should have.

The two horses were sold for 17 florins. The she-mule was sold in Bourges for fl.10 s.10. Pierrot de Châtillon gave me no more than fl.1 s.15; he told me that through[?] Lancia dell'Oro he would give me as much as he could. I do not want to antagonize him because it is not the [right] moment until contribution is levied upon us and our goods. Then, if I can make him pay by nice words, I shall do it; if not, I certainly shall use the arm of the Church. Should that be of no avail, I shall use the other.[6]

For the present I am sending you no money for the reasons mentioned above; and in regard to this I beg you for God's sake to be willing to consider me excused, since you see that the excuse is good. I am certain that when the contribution is levied upon us, we shall have to pay a great sum of money. Notwithstanding this, as soon as the agreement is made I shall

[6] Pierrot de Châtillon must have been an ecclesiastic against whom the bankers could invoke the assistance of the Roman Church. It was not uncommon for the pope to excommunicate insolvent or reluctant debtors of Italian moneylenders. The other power that could be used was that of the royal officials—once the agreement between the king and the Lombards had been concluded.

borrow from Bartolomeo Dondori 200 florins and send them to you; and if I can get more I shall send you more. And if in this interval you still need money and if Corrado is willing to be kind enough to lend you some, I would return it to them from here and would pay for it at the rate *(pregio)* at which one borrows here. And he could very well be kind enough to do so, if he wishes, because Vanni sent him a large amount of money after All Saints' Day.

Lapino, son of Cecco del Signore, is here with us and has been [ever] since you left. I told Giovanni that we did not need a factor and that we could easily handle what there was to do, and more if it were necessary. He answered me that it was his intention that Lapino be with us, so that if he wished to leave [at any time] between now and two or three years hence, he would want to have someone remain here in his place; and that I had Ranieri. At last, seeing that I could not do any better, I came to the agreement that so far as I was concerned he would bear nothing else but the expenses. And before coming to this agreement I had spoken about it with Bonagiunta and Bartolomeo, when we were in Paris, and to them it seemed that what I said was the best [solution]. Nevertheless he wanted [Lapino] to remain, and so he remains. So far as I can see up to the present, he is a good and loyal person. Then, when I spoke to Bonagiunta and to Bartolomeo, I told them that they should indicate politely to Giovanni, in any way that would seem proper to them, that he should not be so hard toward me. They told him this; he at once said that he wanted to leave the partnership, and told Giannotto, son of Messer Vinciguerra, to tell me this.

As I saw the great trouble in which we were, and I saw the great damage that might come to us and to him from this, I spoke to his uncle and to his cousin and showed them that this was his ruin and ours. They had a talk with him, so that matters remained just as they had been before.

His motive for leaving, according to what Vanni told me, was this: that I had complained to his uncle and to his cousin about him. And he made up reasons [such as these]: that I did not trust him and that I had said, "You are taking the money and leaving me the records." As a matter of fact, when he went to Paris he had 170 florins, and only 30 florins remained with me; and he came and asked for them, and I gave them to him. Only I told him, "You are leaving me here without money; neither the records nor the accounts will pay my expenses." That was all. I do not know whether you knew it. I am telling you that there is no one in the world who can do anything that pleases him. He wants to boss the entire world, and there is no valet nor maid who can put up with him for long. Nevertheless this does not disturb me, and I am looking to the profit which may come to us with the help of God, so that I am indifferent to his bossiness and with the help of God I have hope that my patience will get the better of his shouting and of his bad disposition, so that his conduct will not cause our business to run down. And be confident about it, because I know what benefit and grace have been granted me by God and by you; so that, if it pleases our Lord God, neither the folly of another nor my own folly will make me lose them. I believe that it is in our interest that you act as if you knew nothing at all about it. He told me and Giannotto many times that you have taken away all the furniture from this place, and Giannotto told me the same. I answered both of them that you have taken away what was yours—what you had bought with your own money—and that you had touched nothing that belonged to the business. I am writing you all this with the purpose that you may be informed. And he reproached me about the 20 florins you took away from the business, which we had lent you. I told him that he should take just as much and keep it as long as you had.

In Bourges there is no money, according to what they wrote me, because of these bad conditions. I have not yet gotten around to go there to see; I believe I shall go there now.

[*Postscript*]

After I had written this letter, I decided to go there so that I could better write you the truth, and I am here in Bourges. I have found bad debts. However, so long as one cannot make official prosecutions, one can hardly write the full truth about it. But so far as I can see, I believe we are quite close to the sum I have written to you another time. The horse which was bought in Bourges we have not yet been able to sell except in a way that would bring too great a loss.

The bishop of Noyon has been made archbishop of Bourges; the archbishop of Bourges has been made archbishop of Sens; the archbishop of Sens has been made archbishop of Rouen. So that, thanks be to God, we shall be near to Gaio, and we shall get from him good support and good advice, for we need it. When things have quieted down, we shall then see clearly our position here and in Beaulieu; and then I shall write you from beginning to end how things are and how they are developing.

Give my regards to Monna Lapa, and my greetings to all our friends over there. Giovanni Naldino and all our friends here send you greetings. Basiglia and Cibotto are writing to you. Jeoffroy Raers and his wife, the daughter of the late Giovanni Ribaldo, have died. The prior of Chartreuse and the others have been very kind to us, and they have done great services for us in going and in coming and in guarding our property.

We have done for them what we believed was proper. He told me the day before yesterday that he was surprised that you had not written him after you left. I said that you had written but that [the letters] had not been delivered either to him or to me. I believe it would be well for you to write to him and to the convent to show that you remember them. We are all well. Ranieri is a fine boy.

Done in Bourges, January 26, 1330.

The bearer of these letters is Ranieri, son of Ser Migliore, who has been in Laon with the sons of Messer Vinciguerra.

9   *Dino Compagni*
                  Song on Worthy Conduct

Dino Compagni, a Florentine merchant of the first half of the Trecento, wrote a chronicle of his city's affairs in which he inserted a poem entitled "Song on Excellence." The following stanza of this

poem reflects many of the popular ideas of Compagni's day on the
proper conduct of merchants.

A merchant wishing that his worth be great
Must always according as is right;
And let him be a man of long foresight,
And never fail his promises to keep.
Let him be pleasant, if he can, of looks,
As fits the honor'd calling that he chose;
Open when selling, but when buying close;
Genial in greeting and without complaints.
He will be worthier if he goes to church,
Gives for the love of God, clinches his deals
Without a haggle, and wholly repeals
Usury taking. Further, he must write
Accounts well kept and free from oversight.

10   *Armando Sapori*
          The Physiognomy of the Florentine Merchant

Like many of the Florentine humanists of the Quattrocento, Ar-
mando Sapori was born in the Florentine contado, but spent many of
his years in the great Tuscan city studying and elucidating its history,
particularly the activities of the great enterpreneurs of the 13th
through 15th centuries. The following selection was first delivered as
a lecture to a Florentine literary circle shortly after World War II.
In it Professor Sapori, with the sensitivity and sympathy that only few
scholars have been able to acquire in their studies, deals with the
Florentine merchants of the Trecento *and* Quattrocento, *whom Boni-*

SOURCE. Dino Compagni, "Song on Worthy Conduct," in R. S. Lopez
and I. W. Raymond, *Medieval Trade in the Mediterranean World* (New
York: Columbia University Press, 1955), pp. 425–426. Reprinted by permission of Columbia University Press and the editor.

face VIII had characterized as the fifth element of the late mediaeval universe.

There once was a city which was the mistress of the world. It was Florence, whose businessmen reached and even surpassed the levels attained by the magnates of modern international finance in the following realms: the volume of business, particularly if one considers the difference in population between then and now and the different purchasing power of money; political prestige; and the intensity of speculation. Let us remember that London had a few thousand inhabitants, and that all of England numbered some one million souls. Consider for a moment the expenses incurred by the priors[1] and compare this figure of a few florins to the one million which represented the yearly volume of business of the Bardi company. Consider also that the Florentine merchants controlled the collection of papal taxes all the way to Scandinavia, not to mention the finances of kings and counts. They were in fact the arbiters of Edward III's fate while he was engaged in the first campaigns of the One Hundred Years' war. Also remember that their familiarity with the various Courts was such that in their account books we find entries under the heading "Messer the Pope," and "Messer Edward," or "Phillip" with the comment when these were outstanding credits: "We shall have difficulty collecting even a portion." If we consider all this, then a comparison with a Ford or a Rockefeller will not seem exaggerated. Moreover, if we but remember the gold florin, which remained stable and dominated all markets for such a long period of time, surely we shall conclude that the success of the sterling pound, and later of the dollar, has a precedent which, without doubt, is striking.

[1] The nine officials, serving for two month periods, who constituted the highest executive office of the city.

SOURCE. Armando Sapori "I secoli d'oro del mercante fiorentino," in *Il Trecento* (Florence: Libera Cattedra di Storia della Civilta Fiorentina, 1953), pp. 179–189. Translated for this volume by Anthony Molho. Reprinted by permission of Casa Editrice G. C. Sansoni.

Shall we try to become more intimitely acquainted with the Florentine merchant? He was a complex man, much more so than men of any other time, and he enacted within his soul a drama of such intensity and nobility, which no other beings have ever had to suffer.

*   *   *

To begin with, he was profoundly religious, as one could not escape being in the religious ambience of Dante and Saint Francis. After all, he was responsible for the construction of the beautiful churches which exalt God's glory. But he was also living in the tumult of daily life which suggested—one might say imposed—on him attitudes different from those dictated by the Church. These were the two poles which attracted the soul of the merchant: between these two poles he was searching for some sort of equilibrium, a tomistic "just average," if in fact faith is open to such compromises. Obviously, the Church prohibited the practice of usury which it understood not in our terms of charging usurious interest rates, but as any interest at all. The merchant, however, needed increasing capitals for his work, and he could not find them without paying for them. As a result, when loaning money, he exacted a certain percentage. Nevertheless, he limited himself to a modest rate, accepted as normal by the public and which, the benevolent monks of the Inquisition, wisely overlooked. These latter were quite ready to suggest legal quibbles to justify such practices, always referring to the Thomistic explanation of *damnum emergens*[2] on the part of the creditor. The legal quibbles were these: The word "interest" was to be struck from the legal documents and substituted by that of "present" which was to signify a spontaneous payment given, so to speak, in good spirit, and not because—using a contemporary expression—of the coercion of a "fixed agreement." The justification for such a theory could be traced to St. Thomas who, deeply influenced by the thought prevalent in his days, had reasoned thusly: given the equality of all beings it should be intolerable to approve any action

---

[2] "Interest due because of 'loss arising' and 'gain ceasing.'" Florence Edler, *Glossary of Medieval Terms of Business—Italian Series* (Cambridge. Mass., 1934), 98.

which would benefit one person by harming another. Nevertheless, if he who issues a loan can prove that he is incurring a
real risk, then he would be justified in requesting some compensation. Clearly, such a reasoning, without rejecting the
canonical law on usury, opened the door to the collection of
interest on loaned money. Ecclesiastical thinkers, however, insisted on rejecting the further expansion of this reasoning which,
advanced by lay jurists, suggested that the very fact that the
creditor was being deprived of a sum was a risk in itself for
which he should be compensated. What nuances! In reality the
merchant could work in peace, at least as long as he did not
exaggerate. And under ordinary conditions he did not exaggerate, limiting himself to charging between 5 and 15% interest as
long as the transaction was relatively safe, that is, as long as he
was working at home, with well known persons and under the
protection of the city's courts. When, however, he speculated in
foreign lands things took a different form. On the whole, he was
poorly acquainted with his clients. The general environment
was inimical to him and more favourable to the local merchants; the courts did not offer any guarantee of impartiality;
the political authorities, above all the king, were ever ready to
sequester foreign goods and to impose difficulties on foreigners.

It is evident that if only two or three out of ten such transactions could be counted upon to bring in a profit, interest rates
would be as high as possible in order to cover all possible risks.
This is why outside of Italy we encounter incidents where the
interest charged amounted to 100 or 120%, without incurring
Rome's excommunication. The Church understood. The ecclesiastical controllers north of the Alps did not close only one
eye as they did in Italy; they closed both. And if ever, there
was a reckoning after death, in case a merchant left a truly
considerable legacy. If it could be proven that this fortune had
been created by usurious practices the Church had the right to
intervene and confiscate it, for a usurer's money was forever
damned if it passed on to his legitimate heirs. But it reacquired
its purity if taken over by the "Inquisitor of the heretical
depravity," the bishop or the Pope for, as they claimed, they
would have spent it on pious works. In fact, this was such a
profitable operation that when a really affluent businessman died

witnesses were invariably found willing to testify of his heretical practices. Thus the Church's aim was reached. One of numerous such examples is offered by the Florentine Scaglia Tifi who from his youth had few scruples about stealing substantial sums from the lords of Montbeliard whose treasurer he was. His father confessor, however, testified that Tifi had continued to frequent the Church and to receive the sacraments. In his old age, disillusioned by his adventurous life, and even maybe sincerely repentant for his younger years, he had closed himself in a monastery where he died in the presence of the Franciscan monks of Besançon whose prayers assisted him in his last agony. As I have already said, his patrimony was great, even after restitution was made for some ill-gotten gains. Thus, it proved easy to oppose the reverend confessor's testimony with that of others willing to attest Scaglia Tifi's depravity: according to his detractors he had led a truly diabolical life; he was quoted as saying that the earth is governed by the constellations; that matrimony is not a sacrament, and incest not a sin; that consecrated ground and a tuft of nettles are equally valid for interment. Brother Mino of Fiesole, the inquisitor of the Church of S. Marco, did not let go of the prize until he was confronted by the Pope himself who had the records of the trial sent to Rome and appropriated as much of Tifi's patrimony as was possible, with the exception of what little had been pinched by Mino himself.

I was saying that as long as the merchant was willing to content himself with a modest interest he lived in peace. I repeat that the international merchant in Florence was rather modest and did not risk his soul in order to consolidate his financial position. The practice of usury was left to the small merchant who, endowed with a more modest ingenuity and less audacity, still aspired to reach the levels of his superiors. Even more it was the Jews who were allowed to engage in usurious practices, for the Church could hardly threaten them with penalties. Certainly they could not be any more damned than they already were, and once damned it was just as well that they be allowed to exercise a function necessary to the growth of the economy. Usury was also left to the notaries who were thoroughly acquainted with all kinds of legal tricks and quite willing to put them into practice. Finally, and please do not recoil in amazement, it was the university professors who encouraged the students living as lodgers in their houses to cultivate their several vices, particularly gambling, and later settled the accounts with the student's parents.

Nevertheless, these shrewd merchants were well aware that despite their moderation and their good intentions they did in fact carry a slightly sinful burden, and feared that the true judge was more interested in one's intentions than in practices. Thus, they put into effect yet another game in order to escape the infernal flames. In their testament they would leave alms to the poor, or more often to the Church; or they might leave instructions to their heirs to restitute all usurious and ill-gotten gains. The heirs, observing the wishes of the departed, submitted his account books for examination to the monks who, at the very outset, assigned to themselves a salary for their labours. Then, remembering that they owed this salary to the people who had invited them, they asserted that it should be correct to respect the wife's dowry, and assure her of a revenue for her old days—all in recompense for the love and affection she had shown toward the dear departed; then they removed another portion of the patrimony for the children who were under age; finally, they cut another slice for the relatives who were in high political position. Whatever remained was restituted—one understands, not entirely—to the victims of usury. In any case, more often than not, the heirs did not take so much trouble: they accepted the heredity, enjoyed it, and in turn took on the responsibility to discharge their obligations to their descendants. In sum, all this was reduced to a formality, which, however, if one penetrates the soul and morality of the age one understands that it was not a mockery.

Would you like to have references of names and documents to prove all these curiosities? (Surely, they are more than curiosities for they bring to life such fundamental aspects of the merchant's existence.) In the course of my studies I have gathered a great quantity of such references which I cannot cite in this brief survey. In any case, as I remembered Scaglia Tifi earlier, one of the most complex figures of the 13th century, and one pregnant with humanity, now I refer to Bartolomeo

Cocchi Compagni of the second half of the 14th century whose testament can be taken as a model of the methods of the age as I have described them. Finally, in order to give an idea of the excesses of true usury, of which the Florentine merchant was immune, I shall mention the notary Neri Orlandi whose infamy was immortalized in the petition of the year 1308 filed by one of his victims, Lady Orevole. For a sum of sixty florins loaned to the son of one of his colleagues ser Neri succeeded in appropriating all the goods of the family, a house and hundreds of gold florins, while also obtaining from her promissory notes for very substantial sums. As a result, at the time of the death of the young man's father the family found itself completely destitute. The widow, followed by a household of young children, was constrained to go from door to door asking for alms. This spectacle gave rise to much grumbling against the usurer who, in turn, denounced the poor woman as a propagandist of revolutionary ideas—in those days they called her a ghibelline, yesterday they would have called her an anti-Fascist, and who knows what the term will be tomorrow—and had her exiled. A group of citizens took the matter to heart, presented an expose to the Councils, and finally justice was rendered.

* * *

Another aspect of the Florentine businessman's life and of his drama was his patriotism. No one could claim that people love their land when they damage it by splitting themselves into factions. Even more so, as was the case then, when each faction upon taking the upper hand, attacked the houses of its adversaries not to rob them, but to put the furnishings to the torch. Nevertheless, whoever studies that period, not with modern eyes and pre-suppositions, but views it from a mediaeval perspective, knows and feels that even those hatreds, in their own way, were an expression of deep patriotism. For, each wanted the city for himself not only for the obvious benefits accruing to those who govern, but even more because of the conviction that he was the only one who could benefit his small country. I should not want to draw parallels with our days when the first of these stated goals has such a preponderance over the second. And yet, even today there exists a trace of that remote past in those who believe that they have a monopoly of patriotism. What, however, has been entirely lost today from the great patrimony of the past centuries is the great love of country which in moments of need loosens the purse strings, and causes men to put their lives on the path of those who threaten the liberty of their country. In those days all—I say all—great merchants did not hesitate to invest (and I use this term consciously) enormous sums for the decoration of the city. Many grand and beautiful things are done today. But none so grand and beautiful as the mediaeval temples. In any case, today the technology is vastly different from those days, and the past required different kinds of sacrifices of men.

*   *   *

The third aspect of the personality and drama of the great Florentine merchant was his sensitivity toward the miseries of the poor, and at the same time his intransigence toward his workers. Here is an example: That little heretic, Scaglia Tifi, if indeed one is to accept the judgement passed on him in his post-mortem trial, bequeathed a substantial legacy to religious institutions: he requested that on the day of his funeral a piece of white cloth be distributed to each poor of the city; he ordered the prior of the convent of the Holy Spirit at Besançon that every year, before the rigours of the winter set in, he was to buy a sufficient amount of cloth to make tunics for the poorest monks, requesting (and this is significant) that the cloth be soft and warm. This almost feminine thought causes one to pardon this little lamented Florentine for another provision of his testament from which emerges the business like aspect of the testator's character: during the anniversary mass for his soul the monks should sing their prayers at the top of their voices so that the message could be clearly heard by God; if, on the other hand, the voices were weak, the compensation should be given to others.

In addition one should not forget the alms given to the poor on holidays which, during the Middle Ages, were one third of all the days of the year. And still more, there was the charity of the commercial companies which, at the time of their establishment, provided a sum for "Messer God" to be paid to the poor.

As a result, the Good Lord himself became a shareholder of the company and, when the books were balanced, the profits for his share were distributed to the poor. You will ask me: What of any eventual losses? They would not have been merchants had they not thought of dividing that, also. But they all hoped to gain and not to lose. Wasn't God himself one of the shareholders? Once He took a direct interest how could He allow the firm to be ruined? How could He hurt the poor?

In this case as well one could think that it was a matter of a joke. And in this case I should say: no. For in the intermingling of the two goals, the personal interest and the intent to perform charity, the latter prevailed. After all, when the company went bankrupt the poor were not called upon to share the responsibility of the management. From the status of shareholders they passed to that of creditors, and the archbishop withdrew the money that was owed to them as creditors. Thus, the property of the Church gradually expanded during the Middle Ages. For, in settling the accounts of the company the shareholders liquidated their social debts by selling their personal property and compensating their creditors. This practice, not required by law but rather performed spontaneously, is evident in all the commercial companies: from that of the Alberti del Guidice to those of the Bardi, Peruzzi and others.

I just talked of charity. In contrast to it I have already mentioned the harshness of the merchants toward their workers, and, if you consent to my using an anachronism, I shall call them the proletariat. These, by statutory provision, occupied a position of true inferiority. Not only could they not participate in public affairs, but they could not even form their own associations (today we could call them labour unions), and were constrained to accept the salary and all the harshest conditions of work dictated to them by their masters.

This contradiction, however, can be resolved with a certain facility. The greatness of Florence consisted in her industry: the guild of the Calimala imported from the Champagne coarse French cloth, refined it, and reexported it; and the Wool guild, having acquired sacks of wool from Spain and England, supervised the entire process of changing the wool into finished cloth. The fact that raw materials were imported from far away, and that the markets where the finished products were equally distant, constrained the Florentines to manufacture perfect cloth and sell it at the lowest possible price. Of all the various costs required for the production of their product the worker's wages was the only which could be easily manipulated.

The above statement should not be taken as an excuse for the capitalistic system. It is rather the affirmation of a fact, or rather the appreciation of the capitalistic system in a certain moment of its development.

* * *

The last aspect of the Florentine merchant which I should like to present contains no shadow, nor the possibility of doubts: it is the high cultural level which the merchant possessed, and his awareness that such a culture was necessary. Robert Davidsohn once said that the contents of the State Archives in Florence were written by the city's merchants. In fact, if we think of the commercial texts edited and used for the study of philology, and add the chronicles written by the Villani brothers, we must admit that the German historian discovered a truth. Let us see: Among the numberless personal diaries which have survived to our day, notable for the beauty and economy of language, for the sharpness of the spirit of observation, for a wealth of facts, the following were worthy of publication in modern times: those of Giulio dell' Antella, Lucca di Totto Panzano, Giovanni Morelli, Bonaccorso Pitti, Donato Velluti, Oderigo de' Credi, of the silk merchant Goro Dati, Guido Monaldi, Naddo di ser Nepo, of the pharmacist Luca Landucci, the wine merchant Bartolomeo di Michele del Corazza, of the coppersmith Bartolomeo Masi, the grain merchant Domenico Lenzi. Nor is it necessary to remind you that Giovanni Boccaccio and Franco Sacchetti were merchants by profession; that Dino Compagni, who at his death left a chronicle and a well regulated business firm, was a merchant, and the son of a merchant: that Leon Battista Alberti, belonging to one of the most eminent merchant families dating back to the 13th century, the author of a famous essay on domestic economy (a document widely used as a source for the study of the bourgeois spirit), was quite expert in matters of trafficking and merchandising.

I have mentioned published works. But before my eyes pass hundreds of account books, memoirs, and letters which in past years I momentarily withdrew from the dust of archival bins, examined with love, and restored to their place. A publication of this entire corpus would be impossible, even though it might shed so much light on a world that is only partly explored. The handwriting of these documents is extremely characteristic and easily distinguishable from the script of chancellors and notaries. The notary, bent over his desk, was reproducing his legal contortions, so to speak, with which he masqueraded the real business of his clients so that they might avoid the ecclesiastical condemnation on usury, evade the tax authorities, etc. The chancellor had an elegant and pompous calligraphy, in which one detects the dignity of the self-important man taking the minutes of the meetings in various councils, directing the diplomatic correspondence, and copying solemn diplomatic documents. The merchant, on the other hand, is sober, clear, incisive. He concluded his affairs with a good deal of agility demonstrating a decisiveness and clear mindedness, for in business matters he was sure of himself, avoiding redundancies, because he was not used to wasting time. He perceived the substance and penetrated to the heart of the matter: well-organized, self-sure, audacious and genial.

The uniformity of his handwriting (and I say uniformity realizing that there are differences in the various hands) confirms all that we know of the countinghouse [*fondaco*]: that specialized, postgraduate school which he attended after he had already completed his education in regular classrooms. It is clear that there he learned to perform complex mathematical calculations, even being able to compute the average maturity of several sums due at different dates, and to discount accurately. It is also evident that he moved effortlessly in that vast sea of international money exhanges; that he employed a complex accounting system which enabled him to know precisely what his costs were so that he could determine on that basis his yields, and calculate the gains and losses each time he closed his books. Master of the technical instruments; sure of himself in the use of the literary language, having served in his youth his apprenticeship in the shops of the various large companies, the Florentine merchant of the Middle Ages rounded out his personality by seeking contacts with the great men of the world. When Boniface VIII on the day of his coronation exclaimed that the Florentines were the fifth element of the world, because all the ambassadors sent to honour him by princes were Florentines, he discovered this truth: that the citizens of our city spread throughout the world, penetrated all the mercantile centers, prevailing everywhere by their intelligence, knowledge, will power, and the help of the gold florin which they proudly carried about because it represented, so to speak, their country, with the lily of the battle of Montaperti[3] incised on its one side, and the figure of St. John the Baptist, the city's protector, on the other.

[3] The famous battle (1260) celebrated by Dante in the *Divine Comedy* (Inferno, X, XXXI) in which an army of Florentine Guelf forces was defeated by the Ghibellines of Siena, thus establishing the short-lived Ghibelline regime in Florence.

THE CRISIS OF THE
FOURTEENTH CENTURY

11   *David Herlihy*
      Population, Plague and Social Change

The results of the Plague, which struck Europe in 1348, were dev-
astating and have been studied in some detail by numerous scholars.
Few historians, however, have sought to discern the factors in the
European social and economic structure that contributed to the fe-
rocity and destructiveness of the Black Death. In the following essay,
Professor David Herlihy of the University of Wisconsin raises just
these issues in the context of the contado *of Pistoia.*

The medieval Tuscan countryside, like the Italian countryside generally, has attracted comparatively little attention from
demographic historians. The great and culturally so brilliant
Tuscan cities have understandably dominated historical interest,
and research in rural matters has been further obstructed by
the peculiar elusiveness of the subject. Even in a region as rich
in archives as Tuscany, even for a period as late as the thirteenth
and fourteenth centuries, the historian of rural population must
work within a spotty, often vague and usually discontinuous
documentation. A gross picture of population movements in

SOURCE. David Herlihy, "Population, Plague and Social Change", *The*
Economic History Review, 2nd Series, XVIII (Oxford: The Economic
History Review, 1965). Reprinted by permission of the Economic History
Review and the author.

the countryside can still be constructed, as we hope to show. But the historian must then confront an even more difficult problem. He must seek to relate the often shadowy changes in the countryside to the broader trends of Tuscan economic and social history. How and how much, for example, did population factors support the growth and apparent prosperity of the Tuscan cities in the century before the Black Death? And did a population situation prepare the way for the plagues, famines and social troubles which darken the region's annals from the middle fourteenth century?

These are challenging questions, and responses to them have not been lacking. Perhaps the most vigorous of them has been presented in recent years by the Italian scholar Enrico Fiumi. In works distinguished by the author's seemingly indefatigable capacity for archival research, Fiumi has been developing a novel and even audacious explanation for the 'flourishing and decline' of the medieval Tuscan communes. He rejects, to begin with, the older interpretations of Salvemini, Volpe and others, according to which social conflicts, whether in the form of magnates versus *popolani*, new men versus old, merchants versus landlords, or the city versus the countryside, decisively influenced the pattern of urban development. For Fiumi, the stimulus which promoted the great medieval prosperity of the Tuscan towns was vigorous population growth in the countryside. By the middle and late thirteenth century, an exuberantly expanding rural population was forcing massive immigration into the cities and prompting entrepreneurship, experimentation and novel departures in all phases of urban life. As long as the challenge continued, the Tuscan cities remained large, strong and economically the wonders of Europe. After 1348, however, the demographic crash of the late Middle Ages dissipated that challenge, and decadence settled upon these once so thriving communities. Fiumi is unhesitating in assigning to population movements the decisive role in engendering the prosperity and then provoking the collapse of the medieval Tuscan economy. "The principal cause [of the decadence of Tuscan towns after 1348]", he writes, ". . . the exclusive cause, I would dare to say . . . lay in the impressive demographic impoverishment of the [Tuscan] cities and countryside."

No other economic historian, to my knowledge, is as forth-right as Fiumi in linking population growth with prosperity, and population decline with depression, although these equations are viewed with some sympathy by defenders of the thesis of an "economic depression of the Renaissance." Fiumi's reconstruction of the great trends of medieval Tuscany's economic history does, however, show one significant gap. If the economic decline of the late Middle Ages was the result of the demographic reversal of the fourteenth century, what explains the reversal itself? Fiumi does not consider this problem, and his silence implies that he holds the plagues, famines and accompanying demographic decline of the fourteenth century to be fortuitous interventions, pure acts of God, to which no social or economic factor substantially contributed.

Not all economic historians are content to write off the great demographic crisis of the late Middle Ages as simple accident, and many now discern a specifically human situation at the core of these catastrophes: excessive population, "overpopulation", too many people seeking to live on too tenuous means. The distinguished economic historian M. M. Postan has been a leader in advancing, although cautiously and with great concern for terms, the argument that the demographic fall of the fourteenth century was the consequence, even, as he says, the "nemesis," of the "inordinate expansion" of the earlier Middle Ages. J. Z. Titow agrees in discerning "acute land shortage and severe overpopulation" in parts of England before the Black Death. B. H. Slicher van Bath, in his recent *Agrarian History of Western Europe*, flatly attributes the high mortalities of the Black Death and other epidemics and famines to "prolonged malnutrition" brought on by excessive population growth. Georges Duby includes within his own general agricultural history a section entitled "overpopulation." And numerous studies have recently been calling attention to the high levels of population density reached in many areas of Europe on the eve of the Black Death.

We are, in other words, witnessing the emergence of an essentially Malthusian interpretation of the demographic crisis of the fourteenth century which, while cautiously expressed and far from universally accepted, still promises to remain a major interest of historians in the immediate future.

These then are the distinct and slightly paradoxical interpretations which recent historians of Tuscan and European demography have presented. Vigorous population growth, according to Fiumi, provided the essential stimulus for the expansion and prosperity of the Tuscan economy in the late thirteenth century. But that same population growth, according to Postan and others, eventually outstripped the means of subsistence and brought down upon the medieval community the plagues, famines and awesome demographic collapse of the late Middle Ages.

Do such interpretations really correspond with what can be known of demographic movements in medieval Tuscany, and especially in the Tuscan countryside? To answer this is first to reconstruct, as accurately as the sources permit, the movement of Tuscany's rural population before and after the Black Death.

The population decline in rural Pistoia in the late Middle Ages was of catastrophic dimensions. The population of Pistoia's countryside in 1404 was less than a third, only 29 per cent, of what it had been in 1244. This was also, we must remember, the countryside, supposedly less exposed to the ravages of the plague than the cities. In fact the *contado*'s population fell more drastically than the city's which seems, over a comparable period, to have dropped by a mere 50 per cent.

Moreover, this catastrophe followed upon a demographic situation in which the population density in the countryside had reached truly extraordinary levels. In 1244 the entire *contado* of Pistoia contained about 34,000 persons, settled within an area of about 900 square kilometres. This represents a destiny of rural settlement of about 38 persons per square kilometre. If we include the approximately 10,000 inhabitants of the city itself, the total population of Pistoia in the first half of the thirteenth century was about 44,000, representing a density of about 49 persons per square kilometre.

This may seem like dense settlement for medieval times, but it is not unusual for Tuscany. According to E. Fiumi's reasonable calculations, the density of settlement, both urban and rural, at San Gimignano had surpassed 50 persons per square kilometre already by 1227. By 1277–1291 it was more like 74 and by 1332 it had reached 85, making that area more densely settled in the Middle Ages than it is today.

For the Florentine *contado*, the largest in Tuscany, population densities can only be roughly estimated for the period before the Black Death. On the basis of salt consumption, Florence in 1318 seems to have counted about 25,000 families in the city and 30,000 in the countryside, exclusive of clergy and the rural nobles. On the assumption that the average household was 4.65 persons, this would mean a population of about 116,200 for the city and 139,500 for the countryside, or a total of 255,700 persons settled in something like 3,900 square kilometres. This is a density of about 65.5 persons per square kilometre. The density of settlement at Siena may have been even higher.

It is well to ponder briefly the implication of population densities which, as early as 1250, reached and surpassed 50 persons per square kilometre. If all Tuscany shared the same density of population that Pistoia had attained by 1244—and since fully one-half of the Pistoiese *contado* was thinly settled high hills and mountains, that is not unlikely—the Tuscan province would have contained an astounding 1,180,000 persons even before 1250. Not until well into the nineteenth century would Tuscany again attain that figure.

A catastrophic population fall, following upon a remarkable concentration of people—would not these unquestionable facts justify the conclusion that in Tuscany before the plague too many people were indeed trying to live on too little land? Must we not also conclude that the families, plagues and high mortalities of the fourteenth century were, in essence, Malthusian checks moving to reduce an inordinately swollen population? There can be no doubt that before the plague numerous Tuscans were living on the margin of subsistence. The Florentine chronicler Giovanni Villani was himself shocked to find that in 1330 the paupers of the city of Florence seemed to surpass 17,000. It is only reasonable to assume that these masses of ill-nourished people fell easy victims to epidemics and famines.

But it is one thing to recognize the existence of a precarious balance between population and resources on the eve of the

Black Death, and quite another thing to attribute the behaviour of our curve primarily to the impact of plague and famine upon an excessively swollen population. Rather a careful examination of our data gives several substantial reasons for doubting that our curve does indeed correspond to the simple outlines of a classical Mathusian crisis.

There is, to begin with, the pace and pattern of the population decline. The high mortalities of 1348 may with great plausibility be explained by malnutrition and by the inordinate numbers of consumers which caused it. But if Pistoia was over-populated in 1344, was it still over-populated in 1392, when the population was less than half its former size? Yet its population continued to fall, well beyond the point where one may continue to speak of inadequate resources.

There is this further and, I think, decisive fact for rejecting a simple Malthusian explanation for the depopulations of the fourteenth century. The plague of 1348 did not strike against a population blindly seeking to increase. At Pistoia the rural population had begun to decline at least a century before the Black Death. The rural population of 1344, four years before the plague, had already shrunk by a substantial 23 per cent from what it had been a century before. We have, to be sure, no full surveys of the countryside between 1244 and 1344, but much indirect evidence has survived to indicate that the curve which joins these two figures was sliding downwards. The Book of Hearths itself gives evidence of rural depopulations, in the many comments it offers concerning householders who were listed in an "Old Book", an earlier survey, but who had since disappeared without heirs or successors. The Book of Boundaries, redacted in 1255, shows that in eleven years the number of rural communes had already fallen from 124 to 109, and these "lost villages" are certain evidence that the rural population was declining markedly by the middle thirteenth century. The Statutes of the Podestà (1296) required all rural communes to pay taxes for their traditional number of hearths, even though the true number had fallen. This provision is understandable only in the light of a dwindling rural population.

This rural depopulation one hundred years in advance of the Black Death cannot be explained by the peculiarities of Pistoia's own history. Never before or since was the city to enjoy such importance as a commercial and banking centre as in the late thirteenth century. Moreover, for other Tuscan areas there is evidence that rural population was stagnant or declining well before the Black Death. At San Gimignano the density of rural settlement had apparently reached its height by 1290 and by 1332 had already diminished. It is more difficult to judge population movements in the Florentine countryside, for which surveys for only a few scattered rural communes have survived. But such surveys still convey the strong impression that the rural population was stable or even declining for at least a half-century before the Black Death.

Was rural Pistoia—and Tuscany—"over-populated" on the eve of the Black Death? Perhaps so, but it had been even more "over-populated" a century before. A precarious balance between population and resources, in other words, was a constant fact of Tuscan rural life for as far back into the thirteenth century as our sources permit us to discern. The plagues and famines of the fourteenth century cannot therefore be considered Mathusian checks brought into play by and operating against a vigorously expanding population. These blows, for all their ferocity, only accelerated a movement of rural depopulation long in operation.

But if external checks through plague and famine did not initiate this rural depopulation, how are we to explain it? The answer would seem to lie in an examination of the reproductive rate of Pistoia's rural population, and the impact upon it of the changing economic and social conditions in the countryside. This is an elusive but not unapproachable subject, thanks to the extraordinary wealth of Tuscany's magnificent archives.

It is sometimes assumed that the reproductive rate of pre-industrial agricultural communities was characteristically high, approaching the biological maximum, relatively stable and largely insensitive to economic and social influences. The Florentine Catasto of 1427[1] shows that this was hardly true in rural Pistoia. Because the Catasto gives the ages of most of the

----

[1] A detailed census and inventory of patrimonies compiled for the purpose of imposing taxes.

residents of Pistoia's *contado*, we can calculate the number of children fifteen years or under in Pistoia's households. We can further examine what relation, if any, existed between the wealth of a household as revealed by its tax assessment and the number of children it was supporting.

This conclusion is certain. A social group which was supporting substantially fewer than two children per household was inevitably breeding itself out of existence. Geographically considered, [the evidence] shows that the region of the middle hills possessed the fewest children per household, averaging only 1.52. In the middle hills also depopulations since the thirteenth century had been most pronounced. Inhabitants of that area comprised 44.5 per cent of the rural population in *c*. 1244, and only 26 per cent in 1427. Fewest children, highest rate of population decline—is there not a casual connexion between these two phenomena?

Equally revealing is the pronounced relationship between the wealth of these households and the number of children they were supporting. With an average of less than 1.5 children each, the poorer households of rural Pistoia were clearly not supporting enough children, and probably not producing enough to maintain their numbers. Comments in the Catasto itself partially explain why this was so. Daughters of the poorest families apparently had no hope of marriage. Those from slighly more prosperous backgrounds had to await a turn in their father's fortunes, perhaps a good harvest, before their dowries could be paid and they could join their husbands. In 1425 St Bernardino attributed the dwindling population of Siena and Milan specifically to the failure of thousands of young people to marry, and in this reluctance economic factors were undoubtedly a consideration.

And hard economic conditions seem to have forced married couples to refrain from having children. A Pistoiese chronicler even remarks how, for "a long time" before 1399 the women of Florence had been barren. Then in the plague years of 1399–1400 many became pregnant, presumably because the death of so many men had enhanced the economic opportunities of the survivors and the families they supported.

The Catasto of 1427 thus shows a close link between relative reproductive rates and the pattern of rural depopulation at Pistoia. It also leaves no doubt of the high sensitivity of those rates to adverse social and economic conditions. We have, unfortunately, no source of comparable explicitness for the thirteenth century. But it seems a safe assumption that reproductive rates in that century were every bit as sensitive to adverse social conditions as they were in 1427. And we can illustrate, precisely and statistically, what the lot of Pistoia's rural population was in the thirteenth century, at the time when this wave of massive depopulation was just beginning its chilling course.

In *c*. 1244, as the Book of Hearths shows, nearly a half of Pistoia's rural population (44.5 per cent) was settled not upon the *contado's* best lands—the plain and low hills—but upon the steep, dry and unpromising slopes between 500 and 1,500 metres in altitude—the area we are calling the 'middle hills'. According to a recent census—that of 1951—the region of the modern province comparable to the middle hills supported only 22 per cent of the agricultural population, while the plain and low hills accounted for 63 per cent—a division which would illustrate the true distribution of agricultural resources in rural Pistoia and how little the settlement pattern of *c*. 1244 corresponded with it.

It is sometimes assumed that, in the history of medieval settlement, the best lands were the first and the most intensely cultivated, and that only with population growth were the poorer soils sown. In fact, in the early Middle Ages other considerations —protection, for example, health conditions or ease of cultivation without substantial investments in time or effort—had primarily determined the choice of soils, and these factors had concentrated Pistoiese and Tuscan settlement upon the hills. For well into the thirteenth century, settlement upon the plain was obstructed by swamps and flooding, and poor drainage delayed the full agricultural exploitation of the fertile lowlands. The high mountains too were an area which the settlers of the early Middle Ages had largely avoided, but they also offered still substantial resources in chestnuts, wood, water and pastures.

Still largely concentrated upon the middle hills, Pistoia's peasants in the middle thirteenth century inhabited numerous, characteristically small villages (over 70 in the middle hills alone). As can be discerned in many surviving leases, they worked many small plots often scattered widely over the in-fertile slopes. They apparently made little use of cattle, or of the other aids in tools, fertilizers, seeds or outside labour which high capital investment might have secured for them. The land was typically leased for fixed rents usually for long terms, al-though, as we shall see, in the late thirteenth century the terms were getting shorter and the rents higher.

Largely concentrated upon the poor slopes and relying upon techniques which even in the thirteenth century were primitive, the peasants were nontheless supporting a staggering level of rents. Pistoia's rich archives have preserved hundreds of leases, through which the level of rents and changes in it can be precisely investigated.

Rents for a century before the Black Death were averaging two and one-half *staia* of wheat for each *stioro* of rented land. To support such a rent with any equity for the peasants would have required a harvest for him of five *staia* per *stioro* of land, or about ten to one on his seed. Ten to one on the seed was not beyond the technical capacity of the peasant working the good lower lands, aided by animals, utilizing the most intensive tech-niques and perhaps buying additional fertilizer outside his farm. But it can hardly have represented the average yields of all the cultivated lands of Pistoia's countryside, many of which were poor and poorly cultivated. These high rents may reflect par-tially the spread of better techniques and the better exploitation of better lands. But they primarily indicate widespread rent gouging in the countryside.

This situation is understandable enough. The peasants, crowded into their poor communes, desperate for land, had little choice but to take land on virtually any terms the owner might demand. Their negotiating position was weak, and it was made so by their own great numbers.

Much the same pattern is evident in regard to agricultural investments. The Pistoiese peasant who needed capital fre-quently established and sold a perpetual rent upon his land. Because this transaction did not violate the ecclesiastical pro-hibitions against usury, it was a common form of credit instru-ment at Pistoia, and a full series of such sales has survived in the parchment collections and notarial cartularies.

In the first half of the thirteenth century, with wheat costing about 5 *solidi* per *staio*, investors were already gaining the substantial return of 9 per cent. After 1250, with debasement of the coinage and a rapidly rising price of wheat, the value of perpetual rents also spurted, reaching their peak in the 1280's. Because of highly fluid grain prices and unstable coinage, it is difficult to assess accurately interest returns for these years, but they seem to have fallen off in this time of growing prices. The best years for investors were, however, those between 1290 and the onslaught of the Black Death in 1348. The cost of perpetual rents actually fell by 50 per cent in real value, while the cost of wheat was frequently at about 20 *solidi* per *staio* or better. The investors were regularly gaining 12.5 per cent and more upon their investments. This they received without sharing any of the peasants' risks.

Undoubtedly, the principal explanation for these large profits was the peasants' acute hunger for capital. Thus, the needs and even the plight of the countryside contributed substantially to the prosperity of the investor, who was characteristically becoming a city dweller. But it is undeniable that this system had some thoroughly unfortunate results. The peasant bore the entire risk of these investments, and agriculture in Tuscany is a peculiarly risky business. Some of these loans aided productive improvements in agriculture. but many others were purely consumption loans, which tided the peasant over one bad year, only to leave him weaker than ever in facing the next.

This was also fertile ground for the practice of usury on a massive scale. It is possible to find notaries whose business consisted in little else but redacting thinly disguised usurious contracts, which wrung from the peasant rates usually as high as 20 per cent and sometimes as high as 50. In this study of San Gimignano, Enrico Fiumi has concluded that usury more than any other economic activity contributed to "the development of the capitalistic economy and to the rise of the great private fortunes" in that city. Much the same may be said of Pistoia.

If the peasant suffered such harsh terms from the landlord and investor, he was similarly oppressed by the weight of city taxes. In spite of recent efforts to exonerate the town government of the charge of exploiting its rural citizens, it can be estimated that, in the 1280's, the countryside of Pistoia was supporting a tax six times as high as that paid by the city.

The Tuscan economy before the Black Death is full of para-doxes. The landlords and investors, city dwellers mostly, en-joyed high rents and high interest rates—a brilliant prosperity in sum, which in turn fed them the profits for use in other economic ventures. By measure of their size, wealth and splen-dour, the Tuscan cities, Pistoia among them, then indeed en-joyed their peak *fioritura*.

But the Tuscan economic and social system as it had evolved by the late thirteenth century was already carrying the seeds of future trouble. The high rents and rates of interest were based to a critical degree on the oppression of the poorer seg-ments of the population, especially in the countryside. The peasant, forced to meet high rents from his landlord and stiff rates from the money-lender, was prone to seek the highest, quickest return from the land. The prevailing system of high fixed rents unsupported by real productivity was an invitation to soil exhaustion and famine. Famines visited the Tuscan coun-tryside with dismaying frequency in advance of the plague, and they introduce a note of high instability into the apparently so prosperous preplague economy.

Destructive of the land, this social oppression of the country-side seems to have been destructive of people too. Poor people had difficulty supporting children in 1427. Undoubtedly, they could no more easily support them in the thirteenth century. The deteriorating social position of the rural population, in other words, more apparently than any other factor, seems to have launched the horrendous depopulations of the period 1244–1404.

Giovanni Villani once tried to explain the serried disasters which had struck the Florence of his day. Should they be attributed to blind chance, or to inexorable natural forces, set in motion by celestial conjunctures? Or were they divine retributions for the sins of the Florentines, among which figured prominently their avarice, greed and usury which oppressed the poor? He concluded that the sins of his contemporaries were responsible. Villani's society was indeed suffering from an acute imbalance in the distribution of its benefits, and on this basis at least the modern historian may agree with the chronicler's judgment.

And as long as these bad social conditions prevailed, so the reaction to them was depopulation. This would explain why the period of population decline was so extraordinarily protracted. Not until the early fifteenth century did the rural population at Pistoia begin again, although very slowly, to grow, after nearly two centuries of unrelieved decline.

But inevitably, these same depopulations were slowly bringing improved conditions for the peasant, whose labour grew more valuable as his numbers declined. The Catasto if 1427 is filled with references to farms and fields for which no tenants could be found. Rents tumbled by more than 40 per cent after the Black Death, as landlords had to compete in a depopulated countryside to gain labourers for their land. And with the high rents went also the *rentier*'s former great prosperity. The cost of perpetual rents, on the other hand, soared after the Black Death, as investors had to compete with good terms and low interest for takers of their capital. With grain prices sluggishly resting at 20 and finally 15 *solidi* per *staio*, the investor was lucky to receive 5 per cent upon his money. For him, too, the great prosperity of the thirteenth century had ended. The usurer also entered on bad times, at least in the countryside. Before the Black Death, notarial cartularies from everywhere in the Florentine and Pistoiese *contados* are packed with usurious transactions: fictious sales of land and leases, and particularly sales of grain well in advance of the harvest for artificially low prices. In later cartularies, such transactions diminish to the point of disappearing; in the countryside, the reign of usury was ending.

Simultaneously after the Black Death, the *mezzadria* or share-cropping was spreading in the countryside, and this too was all to the favour of the labourers. In 1349, for example, the monastery of Forcole, fearful "because of the plague" that a piece of its property would remain uncultivated, converted the rent due form it from 12 *staia* of wheat to one-half the produce. Several other similar conversions followed, as the monastery shifted its rent basis from high and fixed to flexible payments. One such abolition of a high, fixed rent is explained expressly, "because of the deadly pestilence which was and raged in the year of the Lord 1348 in the city of Pistoia and its *contado* and in very many other cities and *contados* of the province of Tuscany, because of which many places, possessions and properties have remained and continuously remain uncultivated."

Flexible rents would serve for this: "that [the labourers] may be more eager and efficient in working and cultivating."

The *mezzadria* committed the landlord to heavy investments, not only for the land and improvements upon it but for cattle, tools, seeds, additional purchased fertilizers and loans, interest-free and often in fact uncollectable, which the peasant needed for his labours. The landlord also assumed the chief burden of risk for bad harvests, and he also had to pay the direct taxes upon the land. His rent of one-half the harvest was still high, though he sometimes had difficulty getting his fair share. According to a *novella* of Franco Sacchetti, the wife of a goldsmith took as her lover her husband's *mazzadro*. "I did it," she explained to her irate husband, "for the good of the household . . . in order that he would make for us an accurate measure, and give us honest *staia*."

The Tuscan economy after the Black Death is full of paradoxes. The propertied classes, committed under the *mezzadria* system to high investment in the land, gained in return rents and profits which had shrunken by probably 40 per cent from what they had been in the thirteenth century. Their commitment to large agricultural investments also drained capital from other economic activities, and in those sectors of the economy there is an unmistakable aura of "depression" or at least of a dearth of enterprise and innovation. But in compensation, the new system of rents and tenurial relations was fairer to the land and to the people, and for this reason provided Tuscany's Renaissance society with a firm and stable basis for its political life and for its cultural growth. Indeed, to our own generation most Tuscan peasants have continued to live and work under an agricultural system which is essentially the product of the late Middle Ages.

12   *William Bowsky*
            The Impact of the Black Death

Of the disasters that through the centuries have inflicted untold misery upon Western Europe, the Black Death of 1348 must rank among the most devastating. Spreading from the Levant into the central Mediterranean and thence north and west, it left in its wake a decimated population and ruined economy. Professor William Bowsky of the University of California at Davis describes some of the effects of the Plague on Siena.

The Black Death struck Siena with tremendous force in the spring of 1348. Major industry ceased and most governmental activity ground to a halt. Men ceased bringing oil to the city for sale and the wool industry shut down almost completely. On 2 June the City Council recessed civil courts until 1 September because of the epidemic. The next regularly recorded council session did not take place until 15 August when regular sessions were renewed.

If at the onset of the disease Siena enacted sanitary legislation aimed at checking its spread, as did Pistoia, none has survived. The thousand florins allocated 13 June to succor the ill and poor in the city and *contado* could not check the ravages of the disease.

Though the plague occasioned renewed religious fervor and a desire to appease divine wrath—religious processions, promises to build churches and a hospital—only one piece of morals legislation was passed. And that was rescinded in December 1348 in order to increase income.

SOURCE. William Bowsky, "The Impact of the Black Death Upon The Sienese Government and Society." *Speculum*, Vol. XXXIX (Cambridge: Mediaeval Academy of America, 1964), pp. 14–18. Reprinted by permission of Mediaeval Academy of America and the author.

Men's preoccupation was with their own safety. Agnolo's[1] description has become classic:

"Father abandoned child, wife husband, one brother another; for this illness seemed to strike through the breath and sight. And so they died. And none could be found to bury the dead for money or friendship. Members of a household brought their dead to a ditch as best they could, without priest, without divine offices. Nor did the [death] bell sound. And in many places in Siena great pits were dug and piled deep with the multitude of dead. . . . And I, Agnolo di Tura, called the Fat, buried my five children with my own hands. And there were also those who were so sparsely covered with earth that the dogs dragged them forth and devoured many bodies throughout the city."

Especially hard hit were the clergy—exposed because of their calling or living in crowded monasteries, and not all in the prime of youth. But it is an ill wind that blows no good. While clerics may have suffered out of proportion to their numbers, judging from the results of investigations elsewhere, the legacies of the plague's victims and expectant victims enriched Siena's pious and religious institutions. *Contado* lands were willed to monasteries without regard for the communities to which they were liable for taxes. Evidence of this practice appears in a Sienese decision to permit the loss of needed revenue and allow the commune of the castle of Abbadia San Salvatore of Montamiata to pay only one-fourth of its annual debt of four hundred florins for 1349, and only two hundred florins a year for the following eight years, because during the plague many property owners had willed their possessions to the neighboring monastery and no longer paid taxes on them. So great were plague legacies that in October 1348 the Sienese City Council suspended for two years the annual appropriations to religious persons and institutions because these, formerly needy, were now "immensely enriched and indeed fattened" by plague bequests.

As might be expected, it is difficult to arrive at even a rough estimate of the plague's toll in any city. It is now well estab-

---

[1] Agnolo di Tura, a Sienese chronicler.

lished that the Black Death struck European cities with varying severity. Hamburg, for example, lost 50%–66% of its inhabitants in 1350, Bremen 70%. Italian cities are believed to have suffered particularly severely, but little modern historical research has been done that could confirm or deny such assertions as that of A. Doren that their losses ranged from 40% to 60%.

The *Reports to the International Congress of Historical Sciences* in 1950 includes the undocumented statement that "the plague in Tuscany caused the deaths of three-fourths to four-fifths of the population." In a recent ground-breaking study E. Fiumi reports the death rate in San Gimignano to have been about 58.7%. We may compare this with the claim of the fourteenth-century chronichler Matteo Villani (1, 2) that three-fifths or 60% died in Florence *and* its *contado;* and at the same time recall that, although very little has been done in studying plague toll in rural areas, it is generally believed that they suffered less than urban centers.

In an undocumented assertion Y. Renouard specifically designates Siena as an "urban hecatomb." The sole reference to the plague in an anonymous fourteenth-century Sienese chronicle states simply that "In 1348 there was a great pestilence in Siena and throughout the world, and it lasted three months, June, July, and August, and out of [every] four three died."

Agnolo di Tura offers a useful set of mortality figures, but they are generally ignored by modern authors who believe that they are not internally consistent. In actuality Agnolo's account is clear. The misunderstanding is due to the modern editor's arbitrary punctuation and capitalization.

According to Agnolo 52,000 "persone" died in the city, including 36,000 old persons ("vechi"). 28,000 died in the suburbs ("borghi"). Thus a total of 80,000 died in the city and suburbs combined. As a result there remained in Siena over 30,000 "men" ("homini"), and Siena, apparently not including the suburbs, was left with less than 10,000 men. It would not have been surprising for Agnolo to have distinguished between "persons" and "men" (adult males), especially if he was relying upon contemporary official documents.

Admittedly Agnolo claims as plague victims a number that was in fact probably close to the total Sienese population; but his account is not internally contradictory. Further, it is not improbable that he included as plague victims many persons who fled the city and only returned long after the scourge had passed. Nonetheless, Agnolo's estimate of an urban death rate of about 84% is high—a veritable "urban hecatomb."

Fortunately chronicles are not our sole evidence for Sienese population loss. By 9 September 1348 plague deaths were so common that the City Council imposed a heavy fine on all persons except widows who wore mourning clothes in the city or suburbs. Despite the fact that the city's governors lived and worked in more spacious and comfortable quarters than the great mass of urban workers the death toll was high among those who stayed at their posts during the epidemic. Of one group of IX[2] four died in office, as did two of the Four Provveditori of the Biccherna, one of the three Executors of the Gabella, one of the two captains of the mercenaries assigned to guard the IX, and Ser Matteo del fu Guido da Prato, the notary who for several decades had recorded the deliberations of Siena's major councils. The decisions of 30 August 1348 to reduce by one-third the size of the City Council (including the Council de Radota) and of the Council of the People, and to halve (or perhaps reduce by one-third) the number ordinarily needed to constitute a quorum in the City Council, may suggest a crude approximation of the toll among the members of the ruling oligarchy and great magnates.

The poor and the clergy may well have suffered greater losses. Men of lesser station filled the ranks of the military companies. These companies were reduced 51%. from forty-three to twenty-one, in the spring of 1349. This may be especially significant, for by that time persons who had fled the city during the plague—and hence might have been included among the dead in the earliest reckonings—would probably have returned home.

All told, it is not unreasonable to believe that the population loss in Siena was at least fifty per cent, and probably more. To be more precise would be to press our evidence beyond its limits.

[2] A high governmental office.

THE ECONOMY: 1350-1500

13   *Robert S. Lopez*
            Hard Times and Investment in Culture

*Robert S. Lopez, native Genoese and Professor of History at Yale
University, outlined in the following essay, first delivered as a lecture
in 1952, a revisionist view on the development of the European economy during the late* Trecento *and* Quattrocento. *His thesis, which
challenged the traditional interpretation of the synchronized economic
and cultural progress of the European society, has been discussed by
numerous scholars since its presentation. The most concrete result of
those discussions has been the fact that, increasingly, since Professor
Lopez's essay first appeared scholars have been investigating specific
problems of economic history in the 14th and 15th centuries in order
to provide evidence with which to substantiate or revise the "Lopez
thesis."*

When humanists like Michelet and Burchkardt accredited the
term Renaissance, a good many years ago, economic history
had hardly been born. Their lofty reconstruction of civilization
in the Renaissance was unencumbered by the suspicion that the
passions of Caliban might have something to do with the
archievements of Ariel. Then came the followers of Marx and
historical materialism, who trimmed the wings of the poet-
historians and inserted literature into the digestive process. We

SOURCE. R. S. Lopez, "Hard Times and Investment in Culture," *The
Renaissance A Symposium* (New York: 1953), pp. 19–32. Published and
copyright 1953 by the Metropolitan Museum of Art, New York. Reprinted
by permission of the publisher and author.

ought to pay our deepest respects to both schools, not only to set an example to posterity when our own turn in obsolescence comes, but also because both the brain and the stomach certainly have an influence on the movements of the heart.

Historians, however, after letting the pendulum swing fully in either direction, have labored to find an equilibrium and a chain of relations between cause and effect. The easiest way to link two unfolding developments is to describe them as parallel and interlocked at every step. The notion that wherever there was an economic peak we must also find an intellectual peak, and vice versa, has long enjoyed the unquestioned authority of mathematical postulates. In an examination book of a sophomore which I graded not so long ago, the postulate entailed these deductions: Doubleentry bookkeeping in the Medici Bank goaded Michelangelo to conceive and accomplish the Medici Chapel; contemplation of the Medici Chapel in turn spurred the bankers to a more muscular management of credit. But these statements, even if they were more skillfully worded, are quite misleading. There is no denying that many beautiful homes of the Renaissance belonged to successful businessmen—in Italy above all, then in Flanders, in southern Germany, and in other regions. Yet if bankers like the Medici and the Fuggers had been capable of conjuring up artists like Michelangelo and Dürer, then our own Rothschilds and Morgans ought to have produced bigger and better Michelangelos. And how could we explain the emergence of Goya in an impoverished Spain, or the artistic obscurity of the business metropolis that was Genoa? A minimum of subsistence is indispensable for art and a minimum of intelligence is indispensable for business. But this does not mean that great artists and great businessmen must be born in the same group and in the same generation.

What strikes us at the outset is the different relation between economy and culture in the high Middle Ages and in the Renaissance. I must beg leave to begin by a very brief description of what we call the "commercial revolution" of the high Middle Ages. This great economic upheaval, comparable in size only to the modern industrial revolution, surged from the Dark Ages at about the same time as the *chansons de geste* and early Romanesque art. It reached its climax in the age of Dante and rayonnant Gothic, after which a great depression occurred. Like the modern industrial revolution, it was a period of great, continuous demographic growth, of steady if not spectacular technological progress, of expansion both through increased production and consumption at home and through conquest of new markets abroad. It was an epoch of great opportunities and great hopes, of small wars for limited objectives, and of growing toleration and interchange of ideas among persons of different classes, nations, and beliefs. Its pace was, of course, slower than that of the industrial revolution, because progress traveled by horse and galley rather than by train, steamship, and airplane. The final results, however, were probably of the same order of magnitude. The medieval commercial revolution was instrumental in bringing about the momentous changes which bequeathed to the Renaissance a society not too different from our own, and was in turn influenced by all of these changes. It caused the old feudal system to crumble and the old religious structure to weaken. It all but wiped out slavery, it gave liberty to serfs over large areas, and created a new elite based upon wealth rather than birth.

A great expansion in all other fields occurred at the same time. The blossoming of a new literature and art, the revival of science and law, the beginning of political and religious individualism, the spread of education and of social consciousness to larger strata of the population, were concurrent and contemporaneous with the commercial revolution of the high Middle Ages. Though not all facets of medieval literature and philosophy were such as one might expect of an economic expansion, who will deny that there was a connection between economic and intellectual progress? It is also proper to suggest that the economic and social change of the high Middle Ages was an indispensable preparation for the Renaissance, even as it is safe to state that a man must have been an adolescent before he can become a father. But we must not confuse two different ages. Probably there would have been no Renaissance—or, rather, the Renaissance would have taken another course—if the Middle Ages had not previously built the towns, humbled the knights, challenged the clergymen, and taught Latin grammar. But the towns of the Middle Ages created the civilization of the Middle Ages.

Whether or not this civilization was as great as that of the Renaissance, it certainly was different.

Let us not say that the general coincidence of an exuberant civilization and an expansive economy in the high Middle Ages shows that great art and great business must always go together. Consider the different experience of different countries. Italy was to the medieval economic process what England was to that of the eighteenth and nineteenth centuries. It was the cradle and the pathfinder of the commercial revolution, which was on the move in several Italian towns long before it made its way through the rest of Europe. Like the industrial revolution, the commercial revolution did not spread evenly: here it passed by large areas or slackened its speed, there it gained impetus as it engulfed other generators of economic advance. In Flanders, for instance, the currents coming from Italy swelled a river which had sprung from local streams. But Ile de France, the home of so much glorious medieval art, literature, and philosophy, was a retarded if not quite a forgotten area. Its towns were small and sleepy in the shadow of the great cathedrals at a time when the Italian towns hummed with business activity and made great strides in the practical sciences of law, mathematics, and medicine, but had not yet produced a Dante, a Giotto, or an Aquinas.

With these three giants Italy concluded the Middle Ages in a thoroughly medieval way. Petrarch, another Italian, ushered in the intellectual Renaissance at the very moment when the economic trend was reversed. The exact span of the Renaissance is variously measured by historians of civilization. There was a lag in time between the Renaissance in Italy and that of the other countries. Moreover, the imperialism of certain lovers of the Renaissance has led them to claim as forerunners or followers men who would be better left to the Middle Ages or to baroque. I shall assume that, chronologically speaking, the Renaissance means roughly the period between 1330 and 1530, though the economic picture would not substantially change if we added a few decades at the beginning or at the end. Now that period was not one of economic expansion. It was one of great depression followed by a moderate and incomplete recovery.

Time alone will tell whether the economy of the age in which we live is the early stage of another "Renaissance" rather

than the prelude to another "Dark Age," or a mere pause before
another cycle of expansion. We shall see in a moment that certain resemblances seem to bring the Renaissance closer to us than
any other historical period, in the economic field as in many
others. But there was no resemblance in regard to population
trends. Following a great plunge in the mid-fourteenth century,
the population of Europe tended to stagnate at a far lower level
than that of the high Middle Ages. A number of epidemics, far
more terrible than any medieval contagion, whittled down the
population. Famines, birth control, and other causes which cannot
be enumerated here even in the most summary fashion, contributed to the same end. The decline was particularly pronounced in cities—the very homes of the essentially urban
civilization that was the Renaissance. The country suffered less
and recovered better, but it did not escape the general pattern.

The falling curve of the population was to some extent connected with other retarding factors. Technological progress continued, but, with the notable exceptions of the insurance contract,
the printing press and certain advances in metallurgy, it was represented by diffusion and improvement of medieval methods and
tools rather than by the invention of new ones. True, there was
Leonardo da Vinci; but his amazing inventions were of no avail
to his contemporaries, who were uninformed and probably un-
interested in them. Again, the Renaissance introduced a better
type of humanistic schools and of education for the elite, but it
made no sweeping changes in technical education and no significant advances in bringing literacy to the masses. In these respects
the Renaissance was less "modern" than the high Middle Ages.

A closer resemblance to our own times lies in the fact that the
gradual shrinking of political horizons frustrated the improved
means of transportation and the powerful organization of international trade which the Middle Ages had bequeathed to the
Renaissance. Shortly before the Renaissance began, a Florentine
merchant had described the road from the Crimea to Peking as
perfectly safe to westerners—a statement which we would hesitate to make today. But, during the Renaissance, East and West
were split deeply, first by the collapse of the Mongolian Empire in the Far and Middle East, then by the Turkish conquest

in the Near East. A medieval advance in the opposite direction
was nullified before its possibilites were grasped: the Scandinav-
ians abandoned Vinland, Greenland, and Iceland. Within Europe
each state manifested its incipient centralization by raising economic barriers against all of the others. To be sure, the twilight
of the Renaissance was lighted up by the greatest geographic
discoveries. But it was a long time before the beneficial effects of
the new round of discoveries were felt. The first telling result
was the disruptive revolution of prices through the flood of
American silver and gold—and even this came when the Renaissance had already been seized by its gravediggers, the Reformation and the Counter-Reformation.

War and inflation were as familiar to the Renaissance as they
are, unfortunately, to us. It is true that already in the high
Middle Ages a continuous but gradual and moderate inflation
of the coinage and a parallel growth of credit money had provided much needed fuel for the demographic and economic
expansion of the commercial revolution. But in the Renaissance
inflation was steeper and steeper. Soft money did not supply
larger means of payment for a growing number of producers
and consumers. It was chiefly turned out by monarchies and
city-states to pay for the largest wars that had afflicted Europe
since the fall of the Roman world—the largest that Europe was
to witness before the Napoleonic period, or perhaps our own
world wars. One thinks first of the Hundred Years War, which,
with some intermediate truces, lasted well over a century and
plagued most of western Europe. The Angevin-Aragonese contest was smaller in scope, but it desolated the whole of southern Italy and Sicily for almost two hundred years. The Turkish
armies inflicted still greater sufferings upon southeastern and
east-central Europe. In northern Italy the mercenaries may have
been gentle when fighting one another, but they were a plague
to private harvests and public treasuries. Germany was the
theatre of incessant local wars and brigandage, and Spain was
hardly more peaceful. It is true that in the second half of the
fifteenth century most of Europe had some respite. But then
came the wars between the Hapsburgs and France, with inter-
vention of the Turks, which involved the whole of Europe, used

artillery on a large scale, and renewed atrocities that had almost disappeared in the high Middle Ages. They had not ended when the wars of religion began.

Needless to say, disease and famine were faithful companions of war. Moreover, during the fourteenth century desperate revolts of peasants and city proletarians burst out almost everywhere from England to the Balkans and from Tuscany to Flanders. They also claimed their victims. In the fifteenth century a dull resignation seemed to prevail and banditism sprouted —sometimes even in the vicinity of towns. The early sixteenth century was marred by terrible peasants' revolts in Hungary, Germany, northeastern Italy, Switzerland, and northern France.

Then, as now, inflation was not enough to support the burden of war. Taxation rose to much higher levels than during the commercial revolution, when a booming economy could have borne it more easily. It fleeced peasants and landlords, but it skinned the bourgeoisie, which had greater amounts of cash. In France and England the Renaissance marked the downfall of town autonomy, largely though not exclusively because the towns were unable to balance their budgets and because the richer bourgeois, who could have come to the assistance of their poorer fellow-citizens, refused to bear even their own full share. In Italy the independent towns survived, at a price. They fell under dictators, who brought about some equalization of burdens through universal oppression; or under small oligarchies of very rich men, who could either bear or evade taxation.

Yet it would not be fair to ascribe to taxation alone the principal blame for an economic recession which was essentially caused by shrinking or dull markets. The markets had shrunk because the population had diminished or stagnated, and because the frontier had receded and had been locked up. Perhaps some compensation would have been found through a better distribution of wealth if the scattered revolts of the fourteenth century had grown into a general social revolution. They failed. The recurrence of wars and epidemics throttled whatever social ferment remained in the fifteenth century. In the general stagnation some of the rich men grew richer, many of the poor men grew poorer, and the others at best obtained security at the expense of opportunity.

The ominous signs are visible everywhere. Land prices and landlords' profits in the Renaissance were at their lowest ebb in centuries. The great movement of land reclamation and colonization which had characterized the centuries between the tenth and the early fourteenth was arrested. As early as the thirteenth century, to be sure, many landlords in England, in Spain, in southern Italy, and in northwestern France had transformed arable land into sheep ranges. Wool was a good cash crop and sheep farming required little manpower. The process continued throughout the Renaissance, but it became less and less rewarding as the demand for wool became stagnant or declined. Great patches of marginal and even fairly good land, which had been exploited in the Middle Ages, were now returned to waste. Fertile estates were sold or rented for nominal prices. But even these low prices were too high for many hungry, landless peasants who lacked even the small capital needed to buy seeds and tools. Fortunate was the peasant whose lord was willing to advance money in return for a share in the crop.

In the high Middle Ages the towns had absorbed not only an ever increasing amount of foodstuffs and industrial raw materials, but also the surplus product of the human plant. Noblemen, yeomen, and serfs, each one according to his capacity, could then easily find occupation and advancement in town. In the Renaissance, opportunities were usually reserved for those who were citizens of the town. Yet citizens, too, had little chance to improve their lot. The guilds formerly had accepted apprentices freely and assured every apprentice of the opportunity of becoming a master. Now they became rigid hierarchies; only the son of a master could hope to succeed to the mastership. Outsiders were either rejected or kept permanently in the subordinate position of journeymen. This trend also affected the guilds of artists. Occasionally, to be sure, a town encouraged immigration of qualified groups of countrymen on condition that they carry out the humbler industrial tasks at lower salaries than those of the lowest journeymen. Again, the old practice of putting out raw materials for peasants to work at home gained some ground, but the increase of manufacturing in the country fell far short of compensating for the decrease of industrial production in towns. It was not a symptom of economic growth but merely a means of depressing wages. Luxury industries alone maintained and perhaps increased their production. This reflects the decline of production for the masses and the growing distance between the very rich and the very poor.

The growing dullness of European markets and the loss of many eastern markets was bound to depress commerce. The leitmotif now was to offer for sale, not the greatest quantity and variety of goods, but—to quote a fifteenth-century manual of business—"only as much as one can sell in the place of destination." Nor was it always possible to buy as much as one desired. Wars and embargoes frequently interfered with trade. Increased duties in nearly every country from England to Egypt raised the cost of many wares to prohibitive heights. The age of rapid fortunes won in daring oversea and overland ventures was over. Sedentary merchants could still maintain their position if they employed many able and loyal employees and commission agents, if they planned every step carefully, and if they could wait patiently for their investments to bring hard-won profits. In Italy five to eight per cent was now regarded as a fair interest in commercial loans—a much lower rate than those prevailing in the high Middle Ages, although risks had not diminished. Banks improved their methods and often increased their size while diminishing in numbers. But they had to use a larger and larger proportion of their capital not for trade but for loans to the idle upper class and more frequently to belligerent states. Such investments usually brought high interest for a very short period and failure when the debtor was unable to pay the principal.

One business—insurance—boomed during the Renaissance. It bordered on gambling. Investors had no statistics to rely upon. Risky speculations on foreign exchange also drained capital away from commercial investments. Overt gambling attracted ambitious men who despaired of other gainful occupations. There were the extreme cases of scoundrels who staked their money against the life of an unknowing person and had that person murdered so that they could cash the bet. At the other extremity were many business men who abandoned trade and invested in land, not merely a part of their capital, as merchants had always done, but everything they had. Even when bought at the lowest prices, land was not very remunerative; but it could insure some reward for the owner who sank enough money in improvements and administered the investment in the spirit of business. The shift of production from butter to guns was reflected in the different fortune of merchants who exploited mines. After a long slump in mining there was a sudden boom in the late fifteenth and early sixteenth centuries. Metallurgy prospered: iron and bronze were war materials, and precious metals were the sinews of war. They also were needed to pay tributes to the Turks and increased custom duties to the Egyptians. But alum, a basic material for the declining cloth industry, was not in great demand. When the mines increased their output, the price of alum fell.

Italy, the earliest and most brilliant center of the artistic Renaissance, felt the impact of the economic recession most heavily. Its condition resembled somewhat that of England after 1918, or that of New England after 1929. Italy fell harder because it had climbed higher. It had exploited most of its possibilities, and it could not seek recovery by opening up many new fields of enterprise. Conversely, those countries which watered down their intellectual Renaissance with the largest proportion of medieval strains also seem to have felt the shock of the economic crisis less deeply.

Of course, we must not overstress the dark side of the picture. Contraction and stagnation had succeeded expansion, but the economic ceiling of the fifteenth century was still much higher than the top level of the twelfth, though it was lower than the peak of the thirteenth. The bourgeoisie preserved its commanding position in Italy and its influence in the western monarchies. The amazing progress of the commercial revolution in methods and techniques was not lost; indeed, the depression spurred business men to further rationalization and sounder management. Thanks to their accumulated experience and capital, the Italians not only defended their leading position but also quickened the recovery of other countries by investing capital and frequently establishing their resisdence abroad. Some countries which had formerly been retarded felt the full impact of the commercial revolution only now.

Finally, the depression and even the greatest disasters were sources of profit for some men. In many places food prices declined faster than real wages. Cheap land and cheap manpower made the fortune of many entrepreneurs. War enabled Jacques Coeur to grab fabulous riches. Inflation was a boon to the Fuggers, who controlled silver and copper mines. Southern Germany gained from the disruption of communications through France and, later, from the ruin of Venetian and Florentine banks. Barcelona inherited some of the trade which had slipped from Pisa. Antwerp fell heir to the commerce, though not to the industry, of other Flemish towns. Some of these successes were fleeting. Others lasted as long as the Renaissance. None of them, however, was as durable as had been the commercial and industrial blossoming of Italy and Belgium or the prime of English and French agriculture in the high Middle Ages. Qualitatively and quantitatively the compensations fell short of the deficiencies.

Economic historians are usually expected to back their statement with figures. These are not easily tested for a period which had not yet learned how to use statistics for the information of friends and the misinformation of enemies. Still what statistical data we have are reliable enough as indications of trends in growth or decrease, if not as absolute indexes of size. Here are some figures:

In 1348 the population of England was at least 3,700,000. In the early fifteenth century it plunged as low as 2,100,000. Then it rose slowly, but as late as 1545 it was still half a million short of the pre-Renaissance level. Yet England suffered comparatively little from war, and presumably was less affected by the economic slump than were some more advanced countries. Again, Florence in the time of Dante had more than 100,000 inhabitants, but no more than 70,000 in the time of Boccaccio, and approximately the same number in the time of Michelangelo. Zürich, a typical middle-size town, fell from 12,375 inhabitants in 1350 to 4,713 in 1468. Similar declines can be measured for the larger part of towns and countries. As for the

often cited compensating factors, Antwerp, the one Belgian
town whose population increased in the Renaissance while that
of all the others decreased, in 1526 had 8,400 houses. There still
were as many houses in Bruges, its ruined rival. Again, Cata-
lonia, one of the few countries which continued to grow after
the early fourteenth century, rose from 87,000 to 95,000 home-
steads from 1359 to 1365. But it declined to 59,000 in 1497, and
it was still down at 75,000 in 1553.

To turn to another kind of figures, the incoming and out-
going wares subject to tax in the port of Genoa were valued at
£3,822,000 Genoese in 1293. The figure fell to £887,000 in
1424. In 1530 it was still more than one million short of the
1293 level, in spite of the fact that the purchasing power of the
pound had greatly declined in the interval. Again, the aggregate capital of the main house and seven of the eight branches
of the Medici bank in 1458 was less than 30,000 florins, whereas
the capital of the Peruzzi bank in the early fourteenth century
had risen above the 100,000 florin mark. Yet the Medici company in the Renaissance towered above all other Florentine companies, whereas the medieval Peruzzi company was second to that
of the Bardi. Similarly, the combined fortunes of the three
richest members of the Medici family in 1460 were valued at
only fifteen per cent more than the fortune of one Alberti
merchant a hundred years earlier. As for the so-called compensating factors, it is true that in 1521 Jakob Fugger the Rich
obtained from Emperor Charles V an acknowledgment of debt
for 600,000 florins. But in the early fourteenth century the
English king owed the Bardi company an equal sum, according
to English documents, which probably underestimated the debt,
or 900,000 florins according to Villani, who may have overesti-
mated it. In addition, the English king owed the Peruzzi company a sum two thirds as large.

The woolen industry affords the best examples in regard to
manufacturing because it worked chiefly for an interantional
market. Without leaving Florence, we note that in 1378 the
weavers went on strike to demand of the industrialists that they
should pledge a minimum yearly output of 24,000 pieces of
cloth. Forty years earlier the yearly output had been between

70,000 and 80,000 pieces. Yet the depression did not hit Florence as hard as Flanders, her greater rival. The slow growth of English woolen industry, which occurred at the same period, was far from compensating the decline of production in the other major centers. Total export figures very seldom exceeded 50,000 pieces, and usually were not higher than 30,000.

It is harder to put one's finger upon agrarian figures. But we may regard as suitable examples the contraction of cultivated areas and the falling prices of agricultural products in a time of general monetary inflation. In Prussia the price of rye fell by almost two thirds between 1399 and 1508. In England the price of grain declined by forty seven per cent between 1351 and 1500, and that of cattle and animal products declined by thirty-two per cent. "Of the 450 [odd] English manors for which the fifteenth-century accounts have been studied, over 400 show a contraction of land in the hands of tenants." In Gascony after 1453 "thirty per cent of the rural villages were ravaged or seriously damaged." The plain of southern Tuscany, which had been reclaimed in the high Middle Ages, now relapsed to its previous condition of a malaria-ridden waste. In Castile the most powerful company of sheep owners in 1477 owned 2,700,000 sheep, or roughly a sheep for every other inhabitant of the country. Figures of this kind, and the frequent reports about starvation and vagrancy, more than offset what information we have on agriculture progress in some parts of Lombardy and the introduction of some new plants to France.

I hope I have said enough to show that the Renaissance was neither an economic golden age nor a smooth transition from moderate medieval well-being to modern prosperity. I have fired only a small part of the available ammunition; still less would have been needed but for the fact that the newer findings of economic historians do not easily pierce the crust of pre-conceived impressions. Is it necessary to add that nobody should jump to the opposite conclusion and contend that the coincidence of economic depression and artistic splendor in the Renaissance proves that art is born of economic decadence? I do not think it is. We have just seen that the peak of medieval economy coincided with the zenith of medieval art.

A more insidious path would be open to straight economic determinism if someone invoked the overwrought theory of cultural lags. Cultural lags, as everybody knows, are ingenious, elastic devices to link together events which cannot be linked by any other means. Someone might suggest that a cultural lag bridged the gap between the economic high point of the thirteenth century and the intellectual high point of the fifteenth, so that the intellectual revolution of the Renaissance was a belated child of the commercial revolution of the Middle Ages. What should one answer? Personally, I doubt the paternity of children who were born two hundred years after the death of their fathers. To be sure, the Renaissance utilized for its development the towns which the Middle Ages had built, the philosophy which the Greeks had elaborated, and nearly everything else that mankind had contrived ever since Neanderthal; but its way of life was conditioned by its own economy and not by the economy of the past.

There is no heap of riches and no depth of poverty that will automatically insure or forbid artistic achievement. Intellectual developments must be traced primarily to intellectual roots. But that does not at all mean that they are independent of economic conditions. The connection is not a direct and crude relation of cause and effect. It is a complicated harmony in which innumerable economic factors and innumerable cultural factors form together a still greater number of chords. That some of them are incongruous or dissonant should not surprise us. Every age is full of contradictions.

We have a unison rather than an accord when the literature and the art of the Renaissance make direct allusions to the troubled economic circumstances. Machiavelli in his *History of Florence* is well aware of the crisis, its causes and its manifestations. Martin Luther inveighs against the consequences of economic causes which he does not clearly perceive. The anonymous author of *Lazarillo de Tormes* embraces in his sympathetic irony the disinherited of all social classes. Agrippa d'Aubigné described in Biblical terms the terrible sufferings of France. Donatello and Jerome Bosch crowd their bas-reliefs and their paintings with portraits of starved persons. The enumeration could continue, but it would bring little light to the inter-relation of economics and culture. What we look for is not the direct image of economic facts, but the indirect repercussions of these facts on the development of ideas.

Of the many connections that might be suggested, some are too far-fetched and dubious for an earthly economic historian to take stock of them. For instance, some clever contrivance might be found to link together economic rationalization and intellectual rationalism. One might compare the clarity and symmetry of Renaissance double-entry books of accounting to the clarity and symmetry of Renaissance buildings. But the Renaissance also created such poems as that of Ariosto, which is anything put symmetrical, and such philosophies as that of Marsilio Ficino, which is anything but clear. Moreover, double-entry accounting was not a monopoly of the Renaissance. It made its first appearance in the early fourteenth century, if not earlier, and it is still used today. Perhaps we should leave these lofty comparisons to the examination book which I cited at the beginning.

More definite connections probably existed between specific economic factors and some themes or fashions in the literature, art, and thought of the Renaissance. Consider, for instance, the theme of the Wheel of Fortune, which is one of the refrains of the age. To be sure, the blind goddess at all times has exercised her influence upon all forms of human activity. But her sway has seldom been as capricious and decisive as in the Renaissance, when gambling was one of the principal means of making a fortune, and when ill fortune alone could unseat the fortunate few who were sitting pretty. Then consider the vogue of pastoral romance and the fresh interest in country life. The country always has its fans and its idealizers. Still its charm must have been particularly alluring to merchants who returned to the country after generations of rush to the city. They found there not only a better investment but also a healthier atmosphere and a more sincere way of life. Again, the list could easily be lengthened, but it might seem an anti-climax to those who are waiting for a comprehensive interpretation of the interplay of economy as a whole and culture as a whole. I shall not attempt to concoct a catch-all formula, which would only conceal the endless variety of actions and reactions. No harm is done, however, if the discordant details are grouped in tentative generalizations.

We have seen that the essential phases of Renaissance economy were first a depression, then stabilization at a lower level than the highest medieval summit. The implicit opposition between those two trends, depression and stabilization, may perhaps help us to understand a certain dualism in the general outlook of the Renaissance. Note that I said "may help to explain," not "explain." I am not postulating direct causes, but what my brilliant colleague, Mr. Ferguson, would call "permissive or partially effective causes." Some Renaissance men were pessimists: they thought of the lost heights rather than of the attained platform. Others, especially those who had managed to settle down in sufficient comfort, felt that they had definitely and finally arrived.

The pessimists may not have been the larger group, but they seem to have included some of the most significant personalities, ranging from Savonarola to Machiavelli, from Leonardo da Vinci to Michelangelo, from Dürer to Cervantes, from Thomas More perhaps to William Shakespeare. It would be useless to list more names without accounting for their inclusion, but I may be allowed, as an economic historian, to point out some of the intellectual aspects of depression. Some pessimists joined the medieval preachers in demanding an earnest return to God, or they imitated the pagan writers in exalting the golden age of primitive mankind. Others maintained that all human history, or indeed the history of the universe, is a succession of cycles in growth and decay, with no hope for permanent progress. Still others built political theories upon the assumption that men are basically gullible and corrupt, and that a statesman must adapt his strategy to human imperfection. Similar assumptions underlay many tragedies, comedies, and novels. Quite a few pessimists voiced the plight of the poor and the weak, or portrayed them in the background—but seldom in the forefront, because the forefront was reserved for the rich and the strong who purchased the work of art. A number invoked death or sleep, the brother of death. A larger number sought an escape from reality, not in Heaven but in a world of artistic, literary, philosophical, or even mathematical dreams. All of these diverse trends may of course be detected during any historical period, but they seem more pronounced during the Renaissance. It is easier to link them with economic depression than with any other economic trend.

The optimists in the Renaissance were not as different from the pessimists as one might think at first. Usually they shared with the pessimists a widespread belief in the flow and ebb of civilization, and a tendency to look for an ideal of perfection in the past and not in the future. Their standard, however, was nothing like the coarse emotionalism of the Middle Ages or the naïve primitiveness of the mythical Golden Age. It was classic antiquity—another age of stability and poise in aristocratic refinement. The optimists thought that antiquity had been one of the high tides in human history, and that their own time was another high tide, intimately close to antiquity and utterly unrelated to the recent past. Now was the time to stretch one's hand for the riches which the high tide brought within reach. One could be Horatian and pluck the rose of youth and love before her beauty had faded. One could be more ambitious and make every effort to comprehend, fulfill, and enjoy the greater wealth which was now accessible to men freed from instinct and ignorance. Private individuals and political leaders were equally impatient. Their drive for self-fulfillment was human-itarian and peaceful so long as they strove to discover and develop their own self, their own moral and material resources. But it had to become aggressive individualism and political ruthlessness when success depended upon conquest of resources claimed by other individuals or nations. All of these charac-teristics, too, can be found in other ages, but they seem to pre-dominate in the Renaissance. They are not surprising in an economic stagnation which still offers a good life to the elite but little hope for the outcast.

The moods of the Renaissance are so many and so various that they seem almost to defy definition. That is exactly why the Renaissance looks so modern to us—it was almost as rich and diversified as the contemporary scene. One important modern trait, however, was lacking. Most of its exponents had little faith and little interest in progress for the whole human race. Indeed this idea seems to be germane to economic expansion. The religious ideal of progress of mankind from the City of Man towards the City of God hardly survived the end of the commercial revolution and the failure of social revolts in the fourteenth century. In the later period, even the most pious men tended to exclude forever from the City of God the infidel, the heretic, and frequently all but a handful of Catholic ascetics or Protestant militant men predestined for salvation. The secular ideal of progress of mankind through the diffusion of decency and learning was seldom emphasized before the late sixteenth century, when economic stagnation began at last to be broken. In between there were nearly two hundred years—the core of the Renaissance—during which any hope for progress was generally held out, not to the vulgar masses but to individual members of a small elite, not to the unredeemable "barbarians" but to the best representatives of chosen peoples.

Contrary to widespread popular belief, the society of the Renaissance was essentially aristocratic. It offered economic, intellectual, and political opportunities to only a small number. But it lacked a universally accepted standard of nobility. The commercial revolution of the high Middle Ages and the social changes connected with it already had undermined the aristocracy of blood. The great depression of the mid-fourteenth century, and the stagnation which followed shook the security and whittled down the income of the aristocracy of wealth. Blood and money, of course, were still very useful—they always are—but neither insured durable distinction by itself. Too many landowners, merchants, and bankers had lost or were threatened with losing their wealth, and high birth without wealth was of little avail in the age which has been called "the heyday of illegitimate children." Neither was there any recognized hierarchy of states and nations. The Holy Roman Empire of the Germanic people had fallen to pieces; the Papacy had come close to total dissolution; France and England rose and fell many times; the Italian city-states witnessed a stunning series of *coups d'état* and mutations of fortune.

Perhaps this was why culture, what we still call humanistic culture, tended to become the highest symbol of nobility, the magic password which admitted a man or a nation to the elite group. Its value rose at the very moment that the value of land fell. Its returns mounted when commercial interest rates declined. Statesmen who had tried to build up their power and prestige by enlarging their estates now vied with one another to gather works of art. Business men who had been looking for the most profitable or the most conservative investments in trade now invested in books. The shift was more pronounced in Italy because in Italy business men and statesmen were the same persons. And it is in this field, I believe, that we can most profitably investigate the relation between economic and intellectual trends of the Renaissance. We ought to explore briefly the increased value of humanistic culture as an economic investment.

Quite probably the increase was relative and not absolute. It is doubtful that the Renaissance invested in humanistic culture more than any period of the Middle Ages. The precious metals which early medieval artists lavished in their works were a staggering proportion of the available stocks of gold and silver. The cathedrals and castles of the twelfth century probably absorbed a greater amount of raw materials and man-power-hours than the churches and palaces of the Renaissance. Medieval universities were far greater investments, in strictly economic terms, than the humanistic schools. But universities, cathedrals and castles were not built primarily—or, at least, not exclusively—for the sake of pure humanistic culture. Universities aimed at preparing men for professional careers, such as those of clergyman, lawyer, and physician. Castles were insurances against accidents in this life. It is not surprising that shrewd rulers and thrifty business men were prepared to invest part of their capital in functional works of art and in practical culture.

The investment, however, often was inversely proportional to the intensity of business spirit. We have noted that northern France, the home of most of the largest cathedrals, was one of the retarded countries in the commercial revolution. Let us now point out that cathedrals in northern Italy and Tuscany were usually smaller than those of France. Paris had the largest faculty of theology, whereas Italian universities stressed the more practical studies of law and medicine. Genoa, perhaps the most businesslike town in medieval Italy, had one of the smallest cathedrals and no university at all. Yet its inhabitants were pious and its merchants were quite cultured. Very many had gone to business schools and a good number had been graduated from a law school. But the state was run as a business proposition—and good management warned against immobilizing too many resources in humanistic culture, which was functional only to a limited extent.

The evolution from the state as a business affair to the state as a work of art, if I may still use the Burckhardtian formula, went together with the depression and the stagnation of the Renaissance. The decline of aristocracy and the recession of plutocracy left a gap through which culture, that other noblesse, could more easily shine. That culture was placed so high—higher, perhaps, than at any other period in history—is the undying glory of the Renaissance.

The transition was smooth because the seeds had been planted in the high Middle Ages. Already in the thirteenth century, culture was a creditable pastime to the nobleman and a useful asset to the merchant. It was then the fashion for kings and courtiers to write elegant lyric poems—or to have them written by the Robert Sherwoods of the time—on very subtle matters of love and courtship. So did the merchants who traded in and ruled over the Italian towns. They did still more: they elaborated a formula which vaguely anticipated the Renaissance notion that humanistic culture is the true noblesse. Real love, polite love—they said—can dwell only in a gentle heart. Though a gentle heart is not yet the well-rounded personality of the Renaissance, it resembles it in at least two ways. It is unconnected with birth or riches, and it is attainable by cultivating one's soul. Again, the Italian bourgeois of the thirteenth century were not content with building substantial houses with capacious storage rooms for their merchandise and with high towers from which to pour boiling oil on the lower towers of their neighbors. They embellished their homes as much as they could without diminishing the width of the storage rooms and the height of the towers. But a merchant of the thirteenth century would have been ill advised if he had neglected the expanding opportunities of trade for the pursuit of humanistic culture. He was too busy making money to consider lyric poetry and home decoration as a full-time occupation.

During the Renaissance many merchants were less busy—or, at least, thought they could spare more time for culture. In 1527 a Venetian merchant and ambassador was somewhat shocked at seeing that in Florence "men who govern the Republic sort and sift wool, and their sons sell cloth and engage in other work including the lowest and dirtiest." But this race of men was gradually dying out in Florence, as it had in Venice. More frequently the Italian merchant princes of the Renaissance had employees and correspondents who did the dirtier work for them.

Let us take a great merchant, indeed the head of the world's greatest financial organization in the fifteenth century, Lorenzo the Magnificent. He was at the same time the head of the Medici bank, the uncrowned king of Florence, a patron of art, and a poet in his own right. His record shows that, unlike his medieval forefathers, he was an amateur in business and a professional in literature. His mismanagement of the bank, or, rather, the mismanagement of the men he intrusted with running it, precipitated its downfall. But his patronage of the arts gave his illegitimate power a halo of respectability. His poems endeared him to his subjects—at least, to those who had not been involved in the failure of the bank—and made him famous among intellectual aristocrats throughout the world. Niccolo Machiavelli, the great historian of Florence, lauded Lorenzo for governing the state as an artist but blamed him for his poor conduct of business. Yet was this shortcoming not the inevitable counterpart of his artistic achievements? Today we no longer suffer from the ruin of the Medici bank, while we still are enchanted by the verse of Lorenzo de Medici. It is easier for us to be indulgent and to observe that business at that time was so bad that even a skillful management would not have brought many dividends. Perhaps Lorenzo may be forgiven for overlooking some opportunities to invest in trade at five per cent interest since he invested in art at a rate which will never be exhausted.

One might even contend that investment in culture drove the

Renaissance to untimely death. To obtain money for the building of Saint Peter's in Rome, the only Renaissance church that probably represented a greater investment in material and manpower than any of the Gothic cathedrals, Pope Leo X—another Medici—proclaimed a special indulgence. The sale of indulgences was the spark which ignited the Reformation. . . .

14   *Wallace K. Ferguson*
        Renaissance Economic Historiography

It becomes evident from the following selection that Professor Lopez's generalizations have not gone unchallenged. Professor Wallace K. Ferguson of the University of Western Ontario, Canada, outlines some of his objections to the "Lopez thesis" and suggests some alternate questions historians should raise in order to gain a better comprehension of the economic and secular trends of the Trecento *and* Quattrocento.

A serious problem for historians of the Renaissance, however, and particularly of the Renaissance in Italy, it seems to me, is that posed by a number of recent scholars whose statistical research has led them to depict the fourteenth and fifteenth centuries as, on the whole, a period of economic stagnation or decline. As Delio Cantimori pointed out in a recent article, students of the Italian Renaissance have found it disturbing to discover that the period which they think of as the Renaissance in literature, learning, and art is now depicted as one of economic decadence. English, French, and German cultural historians, accustomed to thinking of their national renaissance as beginning toward the end of the fifteenth century or in the

SOURCE. W. K. Ferguson, "Recent Trends in the Economic Historiography of the Renaissance," *Studies in the Renaissance*, VII (New York: The Renaissance Society of America, 1960), pp. 19–26. Reprinted by permission of The Renaissance Society of America and the Author.

early sixteenth, may be less concerned, as also may those who accept Huizinga's characterization of the fourteenth and fifteenth centuries as the waning of the middle ages. There may even be some medievalists who would welcome the idea with a feeling that an economic depression served the Renaissance right and was no more than could be expected. The thesis of economic stagnation or decline in the fourteenth and fifteenth centuries cannot, however, be so lightly dismissed by historians who, like myself, regard these centuries as marking one of the most important stages in the transition from medieval to modern civilization, not only in Italy but throughout western Europe. Whether we accept all the conclusions of the most enthusiastic proponents of this thesis or not, we must, I think, pause to reconsider the assumptions upon which our interpretation has in part been based, and to this subject I would like to devote the remainder of my paper.

A generation ago the assumption taken for granted by most historians was that the transformation of European civilization during this period was accompanied by—if not founded upon— a steadily rising prosperity, increasing wealth, and expanding commercial and industrial activity. As stated by E. P. Cheyney in 1936 in the opening chapter of his book, *The Dawn of a New Era, 1250–1453*, "the most fundamental of the changes that marked the passage from medieval to modern times was the increase of wealth, and the principal cause of the increase of wealth was the extension of commerce." An assumption of constantly increasing wealth during this period formed part of my own conception of the Renaissance twenty years ago. It was obvious, of course, that the mortality caused by the Black Death must for a time have reduced the number of both consumers and producers, and that the devastation which accompanied the Hundred Years' War must have materially reduced the wealth of a large part of France. But I think that there was a general assumption that the development of more efficient forms of capitalist organization of commerce, industry, and finance soon made good the losses caused by the Black Death in most parts of Europe. In any case, the predominantly institutionalist approach of the majority of economic historians in the prewar period focused attention on changes in economic organization rather than upon quantitative variations or trends in the volume of production and exchange.

Now, the first serious suggestion of which I am aware that this conception was open to question appeared in Henri Pirenne's *Economic and Social History of Medieval Europe* (1937). Here he noted that the beginning of the fourteenth century marked the end of the period of medieval economic expansion, that "during the early years of the fourteenth century there is observable in all these directions [of economic activity] not perhaps a decline but a cessation of all advance. Europe lived, so to speak, on what had been acquired; the economic front was stabilized." During the next few years this revisionist thesis was echoed in scattered articles which stated it more strongly and translated stability into decline, but it did not attract general attention until after the war, when scholars were once more able to establish contact with the work of their colleagues in other countries and when the volume of scholarly research, dammed up by the war, once more flowed freely into print. It dominated the debates of the section on late medieval economy at the Ninth International Congress of Historical Sciences at Paris in 1950 and again at the Tenth Congress held in Rome in 1955, and it was given the official sanction of those august bodies in the coöperative reports subsequently published. It also formed the central theme of the second volume of *The Cambridge Economic History* (1952). The effort to revise the traditional conception of the Renaissance as a period of expanding wealth has been international in scope. Among the most prominent contributors to it are M. M. Postan in England, Renée Dochaerd in Belgium, Edouard Perroy in France, W. Abel in Germany, Armando Sapori and Carlo Cipolla in Italy, and J. U. Nef and Robert Lopez in the United States.

The first question we have to ask in relation on their thesis, it seems to me, is: has it been proven? There have been some dissenting voices, and even its protagonists are not agreed as to either the intensity or the duration of the recession. Carlo Cipolla, for example, notes a rising secular trend in Italy, beginning toward the end of the fourteenth century and continuing through the fifteenth, while Robert Lopez states flatly that the period from about 1330 to 1530, with perhaps an additional decade or two at either end, was "one of great depression followed by moderate and incomplete recovery," and that Italy "felt the impact of the economic recession most heavily." Masses of statistical evidence have been produced, but the available statistics seldom form a continuous series or are sufficiently homogeneous to serve as a basis for accurate comparison. It is difficult to determine whether the decline of some old industries, like the manufacture of fine woolen cloth in Florence and the Netherlands, was not adequately compensated by the growth of newer industries like the making of silks, light woolens, linens, and fustians; or whether the decline of some old cities was not compensated by growth in others. To what extent did the growth of rural industry in England and the Netherlands make up for the losses suffered by the old industrial cities? These and other similar questions still call for further research.

Nevertheless, the weight of the evidence does seem to justify the conclusion that, taking western Europe as a whole, there was a general cessation of economic growth in the early years of the fourteenth century, and that this was followed by a long period of contraction in the volume of production and exchange. There seems to be especially convincing evidence of a prolonged agricultural depression in England, France, and parts of Germany. Land prices fell, and not only did the clearing of land for cultivation cease, but much marginal land that had been cleared during the thirteenth century was now abandoned, either because worked out or no longer needed. The demographic curve, which had been rising for two or three hundred years, apparently began to drop in the early fourteenth century, then fell drastically with the Black Death, while normal recovery was checked for a century or more by recurrences of the plague and by the devastation caused by war. It seems reasonable to assume, too, that commerce and industry suffered quantitatively from the reduction in population and hence in both labor supply and markets. And meanwhile, the European economy had ceased to expand geographically. The eastward drive of German colonization came to a halt, while the frontiers of European trade in the near east were beginning to shrink. The medieval frontier was closing, as A. R. Lewis argued in an article in *Speculum in 1958*, with results comparable to those which followed the closing of the American frontier at the end of the last century. The fourteenth century and the first of the fifteenth, in short, were plagued throughout by catastrophes and crises. But did not these very crises hasten rather than retard the transition from medieval to modern civilization?

With that question in mind, let us grant for the moment the thesis of the economic revisionists, and ask what effect it may have upon our interpretation of this period. In the first place, one of the major elements in the transition from medieval to modern civilization seems to me to be a shift in the center of gravity of economic, social, and cultural life from the country to the city, and this may well have been accelerated by the relatively more severe impact of the depression upon the land-holding classes—the nobles and the higher clergy—although, because of falling rents and rising wages, the peasants were in most places apparently better off than they had been. A second, and related, element, the disintegration of feudalism and the rise of centralized state governments, was undoubtedly hastened by the impoverishment of the nobility and by the disruption of the manorial system, the economic basis of feudalism, which accompanied the economic and demographic crisis of the fourteenth century and the first half of the fifteenth. Despite any possible reduction in total wealth, this period saw a rapid increase in governmental income through taxation, which enabled kings and princes to extend their military and administrative authority at the expense of feudal particularism, even though it aggravated the economic crisis, as Lopez has pointed out, by imposing a crushing burden on the economy of the state. In these centuries the church, which represented the universal principle in medieval civilization, also passed through a crisis that shook it to its foundations, but this crisis seems to have been caused less by economic recession than by the intrusion of too much money into the fabric of church government. When we turn to the economic and social development within the cities, we may admit as a reasonable hypothesis that there was a reduction in total wealth corresponding to the reduction in population. But was the *per capita* wealth reduced thereby? In any case most of the exponents of the thesis of recession are

agreed that shrinking markets, smaller profits, and keener competition accelerated the development of more rational and
efficient techniques of business enterprise, resulting in a qualita-
tive advance in the evolution of capitalism much greater than
that which took place during the rapid quantitative expansion
of the European economy in the sixteenth century. And if, as
has been suggested, one result of the crisis was that the rich
got richer while the poor got poorer, we must remember that
it was concentrated wealth rather than widely distributed prosperity that was responsible for the patronage of art, letters,
music, and all the higher forms of intellectual and aesthetic
culture. Nor, in this regard, should we forget the unprecedented
concentration of wealth during this period in the hands of kings
and princes which accompanied the growth of central government in territorial and national states. It was the wealth of the
Burgundian court as well as of the Flemish cities that furnished
the material basis for the flourishing art of the Netherlands in
the fifteenth century. And if, as Huizinga has so brilliantly
demonstrated, an air of decadence hangs over the literature of
northern France and the Netherlands in this period, this was
not the result of poverty but rather of the fact that under the
influence of the Burgundian and royal courts literary tradition
still expressed, with increasing aridity, the ideals and conven-
tional attitudes of a noble class whose economic, social, and
political roots had been cut off from the soil in which they had
grown during the middle ages.

But it is in Italy rather than the north that the relation of
economic to cultural growth poses the most serious problem
for the historian, for it was here that the culture which we
think of as specifically Renaissance grew in the midst of what
is now portrayed as a period of economic depression. So far as
patronage is concerned, I think the fruits of those years are
ample proof that there was still enough to go around. In Italy,
earlier than elsewhere, the concentration of wealth based on
taxation furnished princes with the means of patronage. If, moreover, there was any reduction in total wealth, it was more than
compensated by the growth of a tradition of culture which,
more than any quantitative variation in wealth, differentiates the
world of the Medici from that of the Bardi and Peruzzi. But

the economic factors which helped to condition the culture of the Renaissance were by no means limited to the mere existence of surplus wealth or the direct economic stimulus of patronage. The culture of the Italian Renaissance was different from that of the middle ages—though not, of course, completely different —because it was produced by and for a different kind of society from that characteristic of the greater part of medieval Europe. It was a society formed in large part by the early expansion of commerce and industry and the resultant growth of a wealthy urban society. One distinguishing characteristic of this society was the increasing participation in cultural activity of urban laymen, which broke the clerical monopoly of learning and the chivalric tradition in vernacular literature and which found expression in an increasingly urban and secular tone in literature, learning, art, and music. Now the growth of capitalism, was, it seems to me, an important factor in stimulating this development of lay culture, first, by requiring literacy of every one engaged in business and second, by offering opportunities for the passive investment of inherited income, which made it possible for a growing number of the upper classes in the cities to seek higher education, to qualify for the lay learned professions, and to form an appreciative public for the work of artists and writers. It seems to me, then, that the influence of capitalism upon the culture of the Renaissance depended rather more upon the evolution of its forms of business organization than upon the production of absolute wealth.

In conclusion, it seems to me that the recent tendency to concentrate attention upon the quantitative analysis of long-term trends in economic production and exchange, while undoubtedly important, tells us less that is of value in explaining and interpreting the civilization of this period than did the earlier studies of the structure of economic life, amplified, as they have been, by the more recent studies of individual business enterprises. It might be well to heed the warning of Armando Sapori not to ask of statistical data more than they can offer. Perhaps it is time now, with our increased knowledge, to return to the kind of question posed earlier in the century by Sombart, Weber, Pirenne, and others and to analyze once more the spirit which motivated Renaissance business men, to reconsider the relation between religion and business ethics, and to reassess the possible relation between economic individualism and the culture of the Renaissance. If we are to understand a civilization in which business men played an active part, it seems more important to know how they conducted their business, how they felt about it, what manner of men they were, and what were their aims and interests than to know whether the long-term trend of production and exchange was rising or falling. There may, indeed, be a point in asking whether the men of that age *thought* that things were getting better or worse, whether the psychological atmosphere was basically optimistic or pessimistic, but such subjective reactions are not susceptible of statistical analysis. Francesco di Marco Datini may have lived in an era of economic depression, but it is illuminating to know that he hopefully headed each of his ledgers with the inscription "in the name of God and of profit." Perhaps this was, after all, the spirit of capitalism.

15   *M. B. Becker*
Economic Change and the Emerging Florentine Territorial State

Professor Marvin B. Becker of the University of Rochester has written extensively on the history of Florence in the 13th and 14th centuries. In the following passage, he discusses one of the most important developments in the history of the Tuscan Commune: the growth of a new fiscal system that rendered the state the principal repository of the city's patrimonies. By the opening of the Quattrocento, *the new fiscal structure had been firmly consolidated, thus altering significantly not only the economic but also the political and intellectual currents of that age.*

SOURCE. Marvin B. Becker, "Economic Change and the Emerging Florentine Territorial State," *Studies in the Renaissance*, XIII (New York: The Renaissance Society of America, 1966), pp. 7–14 and 36–39. Reprinted by permission of The Renaissance Society of America and the author.

Even at the height of Florentine prosperity, the total income of the commune was barely sufficient to cover half of the republic's ever-mounting expenditures. This circumstance stemmed from the costly wars that Florence was compelled to wage throughout the fourteenth century. Earlier, the armies of Florence had been drawn from the populace, and the budget had reflected this fact. In 1303 the communal debt was a trifling sum, but within a generation it had increased to the grand total of 450,000 florins, and this was in excess of the amount that the city could hope to raise from all revenue sources over a sixteen-month period. Giovanni Villani tells us that the outlay for troops averaged 140,000 florins for the years between 1336 and 1338. As a bitter afterthought he adds that this exorbitant sum did not include the pay for those mercenaries hired by the republic to fight the disastrous campaigns in Lombardy. By 1342 this public debt had reached 800,000 florins. In that same year the number of mercenaries enrolled in the Florentine armies was twenty times greater than the citizen levies. These military expenses, more than any other single factor, brought on the formation of the consolidated public debt, and their continued incidence caused this debt, or *Monte,* to surge ever upward. By the end of the fourteenth century this communal debt totaled over 3,000,000 florins, and by the middle years of the fifteenth century, when Florence incurred new liabilities through the formation of the *Monte delle doti,* it climbed to the astronomical figure of 8,000,000 florins. The way in which this communal debt was accumulated, and its sharp ascent, remain neglected facets of Florentine history, and yet if we aspire to understand the emergence of new loyalties and the rise of a new political mentality, we must treat the *Monte* with the respect it merits.

An increase of public indebtedness from 47,275 florins in 1303 to 3,000,000 florins in 1400, and finally 8,000,000 florins just two generations later, did irreparable damage to medieval political and economic structures. New allegiances and bonds were created; private interests diminished in the face of a mounting concern with state affairs. In communal society, the church, the nobility, the confraternities, the *Parte Guelfa,* and the great guilds with their affluent burghers had provided capital and credit; money and credit were almost exclusively in the hands of these orders and medieval corporations, for the commune had little wealth. By the fifteenth century, however, the state had become the largest consumer of capital and a rentier class had invested heavily in the interest-bearing public debt. The movement was from a private system of multiple economies—lay and ecclesiastical—towards the formation of a unitary public fiscal structure. The management of this debt affected not only the fortunes of the citizenry but even the well-being of the Florentine business community which was using *Monte* shares as negotiable instruments.

The story of this funded communal debt occupies a central position in the writings of the most important of all the chroniclers of the second half of the *Trecento*, and it is not surprising to discover that the author was also a *Monte* official. The chronicler, Stefani, our best source for the events of the 1370s, believed that the reduction of interest rates on the debt was the single most important measure to be taken by the government in over a century. In the *Quattrocento*, when the communal councils spoke of the *Monte* as 'the heart of this body that we call city . . . [which] every limb, large and small, must contribute to preserving . . .', and described the same *Monte* 'as the guardian fortress, immovable rock and enduring certainty of the salvation of the whole body and government of your state', they were indulging in much more than ponderous metaphors. This was indeed an exact, if flowery, description of the economic heart of a new organism—the Renaissance territorial state. We might begin by asking this question: how much was the sum of 8,000,000 florins? The answer, if we employ the tax returns of 1427, would be that it was an amount of money approximately equal to the total wealth of the Florentine populace. In other words, the state debt had grown until it was equal to the entire capital of the Florentine citizenry; the entire state budget would not suffice to pay the carrying charges on this grand total. Next we might inquire into how and why this curiously modern system of deficit finance gained such momentum in the years just before the Black Death.

The medieval system of gabelles, or indirect taxes, was simply inadequate to underwrite the military expenses of the commune, and what is more, between 1339 and 1342, the years immediately preceding the founding of the *Monte*, the returns from the gabelles were decreasing alarmingly. It was evident that the days of the ever-expanding medieval economy were at an end. This is not to suggest, as several modern economic historians have done, that Florence was caught in the irreversible grip of a terrible depression. Nothing could be farther from the truth: rather it is to propose that the halcyon days of the medieval upswing were waning. It is important to realize that the economy remained viable, and was in fact to demonstrate an astounding capacity for resiliency. But beginning in 1339 we witness a general deterioration in the returns from the gabelles. The republic's revenue from her single most important impost, the customs toll, had reached 90,200 florins by the year 1337. Very soon, however, it tapered off and then plunged precipitously. In the following year it returned 83,500 florins and by 1343 the income had fallen to 68,000 florins. The city's second most lucrative tax was the levy on the sale of wine: it averaged 58,000 florins for the years between 1336 and 1338, but by 1342 it had dropped to 36,000 florins. The returns from the gabelle on contracts show a similar fluctuation during these critical years: for the biennium 1336–1338, it had totaled 20,000 florins annually, but within four years it had lost two-thirds of its value. The impost on salt averaged 14,450 florins for the interim 1336–1338; but by 1342 it had plunged to 4,679 florins. Comparable patterns of steep decline are evinced by the many other communal levies, and judging from these crucial indicators of communal well-being, we can conclude that the bottom of the curve of state finances was reached late in 1342:

The decline in public revenues is but one of the many indices that can assist us in determining the locus of the darkest part of the communal depression. As early as 1339 the Signoria had found it extremely difficult to farm out Florentine taxes. The auctions which were held annually had been able to turn up very few publicans willing to advance money to the treasury for the right to collect certain of the imposts. Moreover, many of those who had purchased this right were now unable to make payment because the yield had fallen far below its anticipated level. Therefore the Signoria was compelled to establish special commissions for the purpose of collecting those taxes that could no longer be farmed out. The yield from rural imposts was also dwindling, and the groups of tradesmen and shopkeepers, such as the vintners and butchers, tearfully petitioned the Signoria for tax relief. Villages and hamlets were likewise unable to fulfill their obligations to the commune, and their syndics railed against the evil times, lamenting the failure of crops and calling for a redress of grievances. The number of small landowners in the *contado* had declined, and as a result the commune acted to reduce the rural property tax by some 75,000 lire.

By 1341 it had become apparent that unless the fiscal structure of the Florentine commune was altered drastically the state faced bankruptcy. In January of that year the government announced that revenues from indirect taxes were no longer adequate to finance the republic's military ventures. At this moment it was suggested that lands and capital be taxed. The overwhelming resistance to this proposal is a fact of particular significance for an understanding of the economic mentality of the Florentines represented in the government at this time. Tradition and economic interest dictated a policy which was at the base of the formation of the Florentine Renaissance state. The elite—both new and old—held strongly to conservative communal fiscal thinking. The government must be financed through indirect taxes and *prestanze*. The latter were loans made by private citizens at rates of interest well above those realized from landed investment. Fifteen per cent, was not at all uncommon. Instead of paying taxes, then, an affluent Florentine lent money to the republic and gained a sizable income. The irony of the situation was that the government could not hope to repay the principal on these loans unless new sources of taxation were unearthed. Much has been made of the feeble efforts to discover these new sources, but the fact remains that even after they were found they were not tapped appreciably. This essentially is the way the *Monte* came into being and grew until it became the very "heart" of public life.

After 1345, when the consolidation of the public debt was achieved, this mountain of indebtedness came to dominate the formulation of public policy. As a result of its establishment, a new relationship emerged between the affluent citizen and the political community. No longer were his concerns explicable merely in terms of clan loyalty, guild affiliation, or membership in a tower society. Now he became involved—as he never had before—with the life of the republic. As the communal debt grew, so did his interest in politics, and in 1425, when the *Monte* for dowries was founded, his very progeny depended upon the ability of the state to weather the Milanese onslaught and Italian wars. At a time when a single dowry was a necessity, the winning of a husband depended upon the ability of the state to meet its commitments. It seems to me that the *Monte* had much to do with the creation of an audience for the civic humanists and the artists of the early *Quattrocento*. The Florentines wanted to believe in the durability and magnificence of this new entity—the state. The novel type of political discourse that comes to fruition with Machiavelli reflected the interests of men in the cult of the state. The citizen's well-being and his very economic survival were inexorably bound to this new organism, and if one views the enthusiasm with which increases in the value of *Monte* shares were greeted, and the grief when decreases were announced, then one comes to understand that the state was no mere abstraction in the *Quattrocento*.

In medieval Florence one's destiny was little influenced by government fiscal policy and the bonds of society were personal; at the upper level there was a bedazzling configuration of loyalties frequently in conflict. But with the rise of public indebtedness, these tended to be dissipated. In the thirteenth and early fourteenth centuries the republic could and did borrow money from the guild coporations and the *Parte Guelfa*, but now the sums that could be garnered from these sources were trifling in the face of the huge budgets that Florence was compelled to underwrite. Medieval corporations and political organizations lingered, but they contributed less and less proportionately to the state's fiscal problems. Private fortunes continued to rise and decline and, just as state consumption of capital increased, so too did the ratio of public to private expenditures—and the shift was inexorable.

To anticipate our story, it was to be the *Monte* and its management that became the single most important determinant of public policy. No longer could private citizens or medieval

corporations be called upon to alleviate substantially the now
perennial fiscal dilemma. During the 1360s, a system of deficit
spending insinuated itself into the scheme of budget operations. The Florentine treasury now began to borrow large sums
of money from the *Monte,* and this bookkeeping device was to
be resorted to with ever-mounting frequency over the next
century. Faced with staggering military commitments, the
Signoria would propose legislation authorizing the officials of the
Monte to make loans to the *camera,* and these credits were to
become the mainstay of the republic's budgetary program. By
the end of the century the Signoria was paying interest on the
debt only sporadically, diverting these funds to finance the
costly wars against the Visconti of Milan. Public life began to
center itself on the funded communal debt until the officials
of the *Monte* came to be numbered among the most important
of the republic's elected officers. The state had become a giant
corporation in which the citizenry had invested a very substantial part of its patrimony. Anything that adversely affected
the welfare of the republic would also deal a cruel blow to the
fortunes of the citizenry, for, in fact, the two were now
inseparable.

The late years of the *Trecento* and the early *Quattrocento*
witnessed acceleration of trends already prominent in the 1360s
and 1370s. During these war-torn years the government was
compelled to resort again to forced loans, and millions of additional florins were added to the public debt. The intake of the
treasury averaged slightly better than 300,000 florins a year,
while government outlays totaled some 800,000 florins annually.
Therefore the commune was obligated to borrow almost half a
million florins each year from the denizens of the city.

With such a heavy incidence of forced loans it was difficult
to set money aside for the amortization of the public debt.
Traditional revenues were already committed to the war effort,
and if monthly interest payments on the new forced loans were
to be made, additional sources of public revenue would have to
be unearthed. By the early *Quattrocento,* carrying charges on
these *prestanze* alone amounted to 280,000 florins per annum.
Communal councilors were still reluctant to levy direct taxes on
urban real estate or capital. Thus once again the Signoria

resorted to the stratagem of increasing the fiscal burdens of the *contado* and the subject domains. By the year 1402, the *contado* was contributing approximately 140,000 florins in tribute to the Florentine camera. Such a sum was equal to almost one half of the treasury's intake from gabelles and was much in excess of earlier receipts from rural imposts. The bulk of *contado* revenue was of course consigned to the treasurers of the *Monte*, and they in turn disbursed it to communal creditors in the form of interest payments. Over the next two decades the Signoria was also to extract substantial income from her newly acquired domains. Arezzo, Volterra, Pisa, and Cortona were each obligated to underwrite a part of the carrying charges on the public debt. In 1408, Pisa paid the very ample sum of 200,000 lire into the treasury of the *Monte*, and while it is not possible to make long-range assessments of the fiscal advantages won by Florence as a result of the domination of the seacoast town, certainly during these years it was a source of substantial profit.

Meanwhile, there was a continuation of the erosion of traditional medieval immunities. Now the Florentine clergy were regularly required to contribute large subsidies to the *camera*. Medieval guilds, religious confraternites, and a spate of other tax-exempt bodies also lost their antique privileges. In the 1380s the communal *estimo* was extended into the territories of the Counts Guidi and Ubaldini so that the last great Tuscan feudatories were now liable for state levies. Finally, by 1427, a single tax system had been forged for the whole of the republic's lands.

It was the government's desperate need for revenue that was weakening the private system of multiple economics—lay and ecclesiastical—and prompting the formation of a unitary public structure. Over the first quarter of the fifteenth century, greater sums of citizen money found their way—albeit reluctantly—into the Florentine treasury. The mounting pressures of warfare accelerated the flow of capital into the public fisc, until by 1427 virtually no Florentine with a modest patrimony (2,000 to 3,000 florins) was without holdings in the public debt. The number of *Monti* had multiplied, and now even the dowries of Florentine girls were invested in public stock. The state was rapidly becoming the proverbial economic Leviathan, and this trans-

formation cannot be overlooked by historians who would seek
for the boundary line between economics and intellectual life.
Private fortunes and personal prosperity were now linked with
the well-being of the body politic. Each time a Florentine military victory was announced or an important diplomatic advantage won, the value of shares in the *Monte* ascended. Every
chronicler, from the humblest *anonimo* to the most celebrated
humanist, was aware of the state's crucial economic role in civic
life. Sermons, letters, and diaries are replete with the anxieties
and the hopes occasioned by the effect of public policy on
private well being. Florentine chancellors and men of letters,
from Leonardo Bruni Aretino to Poggio Bracciolini, saw clearly
the connection between the affluence of citizens and the splendor, culture, and durability of the city-state. Moreover, they
encouraged the appetite for private gain since, in the end, such
an appetite must redound to the advantage of the state.

New loyalties, new concerns, and a new consciousness of the
rôle of the public economy had emerged. The historian
Francesco Giucciardini quotes the *Quattrocento* chancellor
Leonardo Bruni Aretino as saying that by the end of the fourteenth century the destiny of Florence and its denizens was tied
irrevocably to the *Monte*. Out of the communal chrysalis had
emerged a viable political entity—the Renaissance state—governed by an aristocracy whose private fortunes were dependent
upon the durability of the republic. Without such a dependency,
the audience for the pronouncements of the civic humanists
would not have been so ample, nor would Florentines have
been so appreciative of a civic art that extolled the integrity
and vitality of the state. That this state held powers and exercised a sway over an integrated territory made those who
thought on politics feel much closer to the *polis* of antiquity
than to that loosely-knit bundle of privileges—the medieval
commune.

THE COMMUNE

16   *Gene A. Brucker*
              The Pattern of Social Change

Professor of History at the University of California, Berkeley, Gene A. Brucker is the author of a significant monograph on the history of Florence in the Trecento. *Concentrating primarily on questions relating to the development of Florentine society, Brucker describes the dynamism generated in the 14th century due to the constant friction between the members of the various social strata, particularly the scions of the old, entrenched families and the ambitious newcomers who flocked to the city in the 14th century.*

THE PATTERN OF SOCIAL CHANGE

Historically, Florence's social structure had always been flexible, characterized by a constant shifting in the composition of its various classes. The extraordinary disturbances of the 1340's and the recurrence of plague, war, and economic crises after 1350 intensified the internal displacements and fluctuations making generalizations about social groups extremely hazardous. To construct a valid and useful picture of the social structure, one must employ several criteria for distinguishing between classes. These criteria may be listed as wealth, occupation, family antiquity, marriage connections, behavior patterns, and

SOURCE. Gene A. Brucker, "The Pattern of Social Change," *The Florentine Politics and Society—1343–1378* (Princeton: Princeton University Press, 1962), pp. 27–29, 40–42, 44–49. Reprinted by permission of Princeton University Press and the author.

attitudes. Applying these standards, Florentine society after 1350 may be divided into four groups: 1) the patricate; 2) the *gente nuova*, the newly enriched mercantile element; 3) the petty bourgeois artisan-shopkeeper class; and 4) the unorganized and propertyless laborers. These social groups each possessed distinctive characteristics: their members held certain common attitudes and beliefs and conformed to similar behavior patterns. Most important for the political history of the city, these classes maintained a sense of identity and common purpose which was often transformed into political programs.

It is legitimate to speak of a patriciate in *trecento* Florence, although its membership was not legally defined, as was that of the Venetian oligarchy. This patriciate was composed of individuals from families who had long been active and important participants in the city's history, whose ancestors had fought at Montaperti and Altopascio, had held major offices in the commune, and had acquired wealth and status. Membership in an old and eminent family was an essential qualification for high social standing. Florentines who compiled *ricordanze* invariably made reference to the *antichità* of their house, and the imposing role their ancestors had played in the life of the city. These evocations of family pride indicate that the blood tie remained the strongest and most durable link in the social structure. Families were closely knit units, their members banding together to form solid nuclei of wealth, political power, and social prestige. The visible evidence of their cohesiveness was the tendency of households belonging to a single family to cluster together in the same district, a vestigial practice from a past age when family vendettas were commonplace. Relationships formed by marriage alliances also served to bind together the families which constituted the aristocracy of Florence. United by blood, by community of interests, and by a shared tradition, this patrician class wielded a powerful influence over the destinies of the Arno city.

Within this group, and even within individual families, there were infinite gradations of wealth, status, and pre-eminence. The magnate families constituted roughly the upper stratum of this patrician class. Many of these houses were descended from the Tuscan feudal nobility, and several still possessed large estates in the *contado*. Through decades of intermarriage and close social, economic, and political contact, they had become so fused with the old *popolani* houses as to be scarcely distinguishable from them. Originally, the distinction between *magnati* and *popalani* had been an empirical one. The decisive criteria for magnate status were not antiquity and nobility; more important was the behavior pattern of the family, its reputation for violence and disorder, and the extent to which it constituted a threat to communal peace and security. The Cerchi, though not of noble descent, were designated as magnates in 1293 because they were rich, numerous, and dangerous; the Castiglionchi, though noble in origin, remained *popolani* because they were not sufficiently powerful to constitute a threat to the government of the guilds.

Although the origins of most of the *gente nuova* are shrouded in obscurity, the background of a few can be traced prior to 1343. Some received their business training as employees of the great mercantile companies, frequently serving aboard as factors or agents. Lodovico di Lippo Ceffini, a member of the Bardi firm from 1338 to 1342, later formed his own international trading company. Piero Bini, who had a long and successful career with the Bardi, became a partner of a banking firm in 1353, associated with two other parvenus, Roggerio Lippi and Jacopo Renzi. Several prominent businessmen began their careers as lower guildsmen engaged in retail trade. A dealer in used clothing, Giovanni Goggio, built up a thriving commerce in grain and cloth between Florence and Naples and amassed a large fortune. Included in the 1369 list of trading companies using the port of Pisa are the names of six lower guildsmen whose business activities had spread far beyond the local limits to which the affairs of the *arti minori* were usually confined.

Many of the *gente nuova* were immigrants or the descendants of immigrants who had moved into the city from the *contado* in the fourteenth century. Frequently, their names, as inscribed in guild matriculation records and prior lists, give clues to the location of their families' origin: Mugnaio di Recco da Ghiaceto, Filippo di Spinello da Mosciano, Niccolo di Ser Bene da Varazzano. A collection of Ghibelline accusations in the judicial archives provides information concerning the origin of several of these *gente nuova*. The Amadori, who were well represented in the Calimala guild between 1350 and 1380, came from the town of Ancisa. The ancestors of the Busini, five of whose members were enrolled in the Lana guild between 1360 and 1375, were originally *fedeli* of the Caponsacchi, a Ghibelline noble family with lands near Montereggi. Typical of the rise of these "new men" from poverty and obscurity to wealth and status is the story of a certain Gennaio and his descendants. Emigrating from Montecarelli where he had been the *fedelis* of a feudal lord, Gennaio established himself as a baker in the parish of S. Maria Bertelde. His descendants prospered: a grandson, Benedetto di Guccio di Gennaio, entered the Lana guild and was a member of the Signoria in 1332. Two of Benedetto's sons, Francesco and Alessandro, built a sizeable fortune from their profits in the Lana guild, and by 1378 had also become important political figures in the commune.

The Morelli, whose history was compiled in 1393 by Giovanni di Paolo, had resided in Florence for a century before they achieved a measure of distinction. Emulating his social superiors, Giovanni laboriously constructed, without any documentary proof, a geneaology for the Morelli dating back to the twelfth century. He admitted that his distant ancestors "were not rich but needy folk" when they emigrated into Florence from the Mugello, but he insisted that they were "honorable people." The cloudy past of the Morelli became clearer by the end of the thirteenth century, when they had become established as dyers of cloth and traders in dyestuffs. The family's energies in the fourteenth century were devoted exclusively to making money, and the tax records indicate a spectacular increase in their wealth between 1352 and 1378. Outside of the economic sphere, however, the Morelli made no substantial mark in the city.

The best-known representative of the *gente nuova* in this period of Florentine history is Francesco di Marco Datini, whose fame rests upon the great mass of surviving source material pertaining to his career. Datini was born in Prato in 1335 and was left an orphan by the Black Death. His tiny patrimony consisted of forty seven florins, a house and a piece of land, which he later converted into cash to finance a trip to Avignon. There he built the foundations of his fortune. His choice of a location was excellent; Avignon, owing to the presence of the papal court, was one of the few cities in Europe that were enjoying a burgeoning prosperity. Datini established himself as a merchant specializing in the trade of cloth and arms, the latter commodity in great demand in the 1360's and 1370's. After accumulating a substantial fortune, he returned to Tuscany in 1383 and made Florence the head-quarters of his business enterprises, which included a cloth factory in Prato and trading branches in Avignon, Pisa, Genoa, Majorca, Barcelona, and Valencia. When he died in 1410, he left behind him a large fortune of some seventy thousand florins, with which he endowed a charitable foundation for the poor in his native city of Prato.

Datini's career is a classic illustration of the self-made man rising from rags to riches through his own initiative and indus-try. His behavior and outlook were completely typical of the parvenu. He did not marry until he had already achieved con-siderable wealth, selecting for this bride a girl from a good family that had suffered misfortune and was therefore unable to provide a dowry. Datini's wife Margherita was descended through her mother from an ancient and noble Florentine fam-ily, and she frequently reminded her husband of the difference in their social origins. In one letter she wrote, "I have a little of the Gherardini blood, though I prize it not overmuch, but what your blood is, I know not." The most striking aspect of Fran-cesco's character is his overwhelming feeling of insecurity. His *angst* was only in part the consequence of the general insta-bility of the age; it was much more the expression of the parvenu's rootlessness and isolation. This insecurity was mani-fested in every aspect of Datini's behavior: his avarice, his pathological distrust of other men, his ostentation in clothing, house building, and almsgiving. It was reflected most poignantly in the terrible conflict raging within himself between his over-weening desire for wealth and material possessions, and his pro-found fear of damnation. Like many of his contemporaries, he sought to assuage the guilt feelings engendered by his usurious practices and his preoccupation with the things of the flesh by making lavish contributions to ecclesiastical and charitable foundations.

Francesco Datini's father had been a tavern keeper, a member of one of the lower guilds of Prato, and it was from this milieu that many of the parvenu merchants and industrialists had come. It was the world of the petty bourgeoisie, the men who provided for the local needs of the city's inhabitants: the bakers, butchers, and winesellers; the druggists and painters, the carpenters and stonemasons, the notaries and schoolmasters. This class occupied an intermediate position in the social structure, between the aristocracy of wealth and birth on the one hand, and the laboring masses on the other. But unlike Francesco Datini, these artisans and shopkeepers were securely anchored in the social hierarchy, fulfilling a role as ancient as the city itself.

Although the majority of these *artefici* were matriculated in the fourteen lower guilds (the *arti minori*), their numbers also included many from the seven greater guilds. In economic status, in business activity, in mentality and outlook, there was little to distinguish the lower guildsmen from the druggists, notaries and retail merchants of the *arti maggiori*. Their economic interests were predominantly local, in contrast to the Europe-wide activities of the big business class. The guild system, with its protectionist and regulatory character, was an extremely vital element in the lives of these *artefici*. They could not escape from its controls as readily as the international merchants, many of whose activities were geographically beyond the control of their guild. Although guild membership signified rigid control of the economic activities of the *artefici*, it also conferred substantial benefits: the protection which derived from association and a limited participation in the communal government. These guild members were distinguished from the unorganized laboring class not only by the possession of juridical privileges, but also by the fact that the majority were men of property on a small scale. This modest stake in the economy made them a less revolutionary force in the society than the mass of the *popolo minuto*, whose subsistence depended upon the chance of day-to-day employment.

The *artefici* of Florence lived in a circumscribed world of the shop, the guild hall, and the parish church. Their outlook was conservative and conformist, and they tended to accept without question the traditional modes of life and thought. In their behavior patterns they were not strikingly different from the upper classes: sanctity and piety existed alongside violence, brutality, and licentiousness. On rare occasions the even tenor of their lives was disturbed by a crisis or an exceptional event: the ravages of a pestilence; the outbreak of a riot or revolution; the preaching of an eloquent friar; the excitement and color of a civic spectacle, such as the reception of a cardinal or an ambassador; the punishment of a notorious crime, as that of the slave girl who poisoned her master and was carted through the streets of the city, her flesh torn by red-hot pincers before her execution at the stake.

The mentality of the artisan class is clearly reflected in the letters of Francesco Datini's closest friend, the notary, Ser Lapo Mazzei. From origins as humble as those of Datini, Lapo had been educated in Bologna, received his notary's diploma, and established himself in Florence. His professional conduct was without blemish; unlike so many of his colleagues, Lapo was not avaricious and was quite content with a modest livelihood, sufficient to maintain himself and his large family. The most noteworthy traits of his character were a sense of moderation and a genuine religious piety. The contrast between Lapo and Francesco Datini, as revealed in their correspondence, is a profound one, for the gulf between them separated two worlds: "on the one hand, a small enclosed society of craftsmen and shopkeepers, still wholly precoccupied with local interests, and on the other, a handful of men whose marketplace is the whole of Europe, and whose ambition and enterprise are as wide as their field of action. Datini's total preoccupation with gaining wealth was incomprehensible to the notary, who urged his friend to be content with less and to devote more time to religion. Ser Lapo's admonitory voice is that of the traditional, conservative, hierarchic "medieval" world; Datini was a prototype of the intensely competitive and materialistic world of the future.

Beyond the fact of guild membership, there was relatively little difference in the status and condition of many of the poorer *artefici* and the laboring proletariat. This mass of unorganized, unenfranchised, poverty-stricken humanity was the true *popolo minuto* of Florence. The bulk of this group, perhaps one-fourth of the city's population (including dependents) was made up of the *sottoposti* of the Lana guild, the wool carders, spinners, weavers, cutters, and fullers, upon whose labor the prosperity of Florence depended. Sharing their lowly condition was a host of other *minuti*) servants, market women *(trecce)* fishermen, apprentices, and prostitutes, living for the most part in misery and want, in hopelessness and despair.

Source material on the Florentine lower classes in extremely scanty. Only on rare occasions, when they were shaken out of their torpor by some crisis—famine, political upheaval, a wave of religious fanaticism—do they leave any substantial imprint upon the records of their time. The most frutiful sources of information on their life and activity are the records of the guilds, the tax commissions, and the courts. The guild records reveal that the laborers in the cloth industries were very strictly controlled, and that their position vis-à-vis the employers was similar to that of the workers in the Lancashire cotton mills of the early nineteenth century before the introduction of labor legislation. The tax returns contain the names of hundreds of these workers who were forced to pay their share of the *prestanze*, and they also identify the *miserabili* who were too poor to contribute even a pittance to the communal treasury. From this source, too, we can locate the slum areas where the lower classes were concentrated—in the quarters of S. Spirito and S. Croce. Through their depressing tales of violence and degradation, the judicial records throw some light on the conditions of poverty and misery in which these people lived. Precise details of their lives, however, are lacking. The notarial records, the source of so much information on the social life of *trecento* Florence, are generally silent concerning the laborers, whose rental agreements were usually too petty to be recorded by landlords, and whose possessions were too meager to necessitate the composition of a testament. Their infrequent appearances in the notarial registers usually pertain to those occasions when adversity forced them to resort to the money-lender.

There are no well-known representatives of the *popolo minuto* who can be utilized to portray the mores and attitudes of the entire class. However, fragmentary information about a few individuals does reveal certain general types within their ranks. The ugly figure of the racketeer who preyed upon the misery and weakness of his fellows is depicted in an accusation against a certain Niccolò Malefici, "a man of evil and base condition, who operates a gambling house, who is a pederast and a blasphemer against God and the saints . . . and who leads our sons into every sin." If the judicial records of the commune are worthy of credence, the Florentine underworld constituted a sizeable segment of the lowest stratum of the society, although examples of men of good character among the *minuti* are not lacking. The judicial deposition of one worker evokes an impression of honesty and candor: "I, Neroccio di Bartolomeo, a poor man, recommend myself to you. I do not know how to write properly." Neroccio complained to the judge that his wife, a mender of fish nets, had been assaulted by a magnate, and he asked for justice. Frequently, workers referred with some pride to the fact that they engaged in manual labor. "I am a poor man, and I live from the labor of my hands . . . I must follow my trade to live and to feed my family of four children, all of them small," was the simple but impressive statement of one individual, whose lowly condition had not destroyed his sense of human dignity and responsibility.

17   *Giovanni Villani*
        The Government of the Petty Bourgeois

In April 1345, the government of the petty bourgeois, instituted in Florence two years earlier, enacted a law directed against the large and old families of the city which, of course, were in firm control of

the Florentine ecclesiastical hierarchy. To a staunch and pious con-
servative such as Giovanni Villani, the government of the city and
the measures that it enacted were anathema and, in the following
selection, he levels some of his most bitter and devastating criticism
at the members of the lower classes who, with no deference to tradi-
tion and to their social superiors, seemed intent upon satisfying their
economic needs and social aspirations.

The cause for the enactment of this law and of all the provisions that it contains was that certain members of the great
and powerful families who were clerics, under the protection
of their exalted position, perpetrated evil and unfair acts
against powerless laymen. And in order to stop the opposition
to usurious contracts, and also because many banks had failed
recently, the government determined that it was no longer
possible to obtain privileges from the papal judicial representative. Though these were the reasons for this law, and though
they seem justifiable, it was universally condemned by the wise
men who said that even though Florence had the right to enact
such a law, she should not have legislated against the liberty
of the Holy Church. Whoever offered advice or supported that
law was excommunicated. If at that time there were in Florence
a brave bishop who was not a citizen of the state, as had been
Monsignor Francesco da Cingoli, the predecessor of the present
bishop, such a law would not have been enacted. But the present
bishop, a citizen of our city and a member of the Acciaioli
household, having become a weak man because of the recent
bankruptcy of his relatives, did not have the courage to act
against the iniquitous and unjust law . . . Please, reader, also
note what actions the governments of cities take, since the
masters of Florence then were craftsmen and manual workers
and idiots, for the greatest number of the governing body of the
21 gilds who were then ruling the city were labourers who

SOURCE. Giovanni Villani, "The Government of the Petty Bourgeoisie"
Cronica di Giovanni Villani, Book XII, Chapter 43 (Florence: Margera,
1823). Translated for this volume by Anthony Molho.

had recently arrived from the countryside, to whom the
republic matters little, and who know even less about governing
it. Willingly do they pass laws with much haste, and with little
consideration for reason. Those who turn the government of
the city over to this kind of men obviously have forgotten
Aristotle's advice in the *Politics* that the rulers of the cities
must be the wisest and most judicious men. And the wise
Solomon said: "Blessed be the state that is governed by wise
lords." And let this comment suffice on this matter, for, because
of the great mistakes of our citizens, and because of our sins
we have been governed badly by the important men, and even
worse by the middle classes. And now we have an abundance
of such small artisans, idiots, ignorant men with no discretion
who rule according to their wishes. May it please the Lord that
their government succeed, but I very much doubt that.

18 *Franco Sacchetti*
A Story About a New Knight

*Franco Sacchetti, one of the sternest Florentine moralists and ra-
conteurs of the second half of the 14th century, wrote a collection of
300 tales which serve as an interesting social and intellectual commentary on the two generations that separate the catastrophes of the
mid-14th century from the first flowering of the art of Masaccio and
Donatello. In the following tale of the crafty Sir Dolcibene, some of
the same feelings that were reflected in Villani's invective become
apparent: a deep resentment against the presumptuous and selfish up-
starts who, through the power of their money, ill-gotten at that, were
intruding upon the communal social hierarchy, thus undermining
hitherto stable traditions and customs. The habit of purchasing chivalric orders was one of these vices, scorned by Sacchetti, and Sir Dolcibene, the author's spokesman in this tale, makes sure to leave no
doubt about the ridiculously incongruous position of the new knight.*

This is a tale of how Sir Dolcibene, while going to visit a new knight, who was rich and avaricious, by using some trickery, manages to extract from him a present.

Now it is time to return to Sir Dolcibene, whom we encountered several times in the preceding tales for he was the greatest jester in his day, and for good reason the Emperor Charles [IV, of the house of Luxemburg] made him king of the buffoons and clowns of Italy. A rich man, who had amassed his fortune by loaning money on usury, and who, in addition, was old and suffered from the gout, had been knighted in Florence, and this was to the discredit and dishonour of chivalry which, as I see it, is being led to the stables and pig-pens. Whoever does not believe this statement may remember that in the last few years even mechanics, artisans and bakers have been knighted; and even worse, carders, usurers, and fradulent barterers. And because of this degradation one can call it "cacalry" and not chivalry.[1] It is well known that any judge, before he can become ambassador, has himself made a knight! I do not say that learning is not appropriate to a knight, but he needs real learning, without depending for his livelihood on it, or being in his study to offer advice, or even yet being a lawyer in the palaces of governors. What a beautiful chivalric practice! But there are even worse cases, when notaries are made knights, and even people of lower ranks, so that a pen-case is often converted into a sheath for a knife. Moreover, there is worse and worse, so that even he who commits a clear and perfidious act of treachery is often knighted. Oh, unhappy chivalric orders, to what depths you have now descended!

All knights are obligated to live by certain standards which would be too long to explain. Instead, however, all do the

---

[1] Here Sacchetti is indulging in a bit of word play. The original reads: *Si può chiamare cacaleria e non cavalleria.* Cacare, as a verb, in vulgar Italian means to excrete, but as a noun it may also mean a boaster or a *nouveau riche.*

SOURCE. Franco Sacchetti, "A Story about a New Knight," *Il Trecentonvelle* edited by Vincenzo Pernicone (Florence: Casa Editrice G. C. Sansoni, 1946), Tale No. 153, pp. 359–362. Translated for this volume by Anthony Molho. Reprinted by permission of Casa G. C. Sansoni.

contrary today. But, in any case, I should like to touch upon such items to illustrate to the readers how chivalry is dead. And, let me say it, is it not so that dead men have been knighted? What an ugly and foul chivalry is this! In such a manner one could knight a man made of wood or of marble, who is as sensitive as a dead man. But if this chivalry is valid why can't one knight an ox, an ass, or other animals who have the same feelings as men do, though they are not as rational? But dead men are neither rational nor irrational. Such a knight has a casket for a horse, while his sword, arms and banners precede him, as if he were going to fight Satan. Oh, vain glory of human power!

Now I return to the new knight already mentioned. Sir Dolcibene, going to him, as is customary, so that he might obtain a present of goods or money, found him sad and thoughtful, as if he were mourning the death of a relative, apparently little excited by the acquisition of the new chivalric honour. So that Dolcibene begins to ask:

—And what are you thinking about?

The knight was breathing as a pig. Since no answer seemed forthcoming Dolicibene said:

—Eh! Sir . . . Do not feel so depressed, for by God's own body, if you live any longer, surely you will see even worse men assume the knighthood.

The knight said:

—Allright, you've scored on me with one of your arrows.

Said Sir Dolcibene:

—If you're hit only by one, you'll be in good shape. But unless you change your tune you will be hit by four or more.

The knight just stands there, saying not a word, except to ask that biscuits and drinks be served. Nothing else happens. Finally, sir Dolcibene, seeing that this knight had no intention to offer presents begins to say:

—I have come to you because the Commune has imposed a tax of 10 lire on each bad man. And I have come to collect this tax for the Commune.

Says the knight:

—I won't complain if I have to pay this tax. But you should also charge this son of mine who is present with us, and who is twice as bad as I am. According to your reasoning he should pay 20 lire.

Sir Dolcibene turns to the youth:

—Do what you have to.[2]

To make a long story short, Sir Dolcibene, instead of the 30 lire he was to collect from both, obtained eight florins; and in addition, with great effrontery, ate at their table in those days, filling himself with all kinds of food.

And this knight, whether he was repentent for what had happened to him or not, was even less happy as a knight than he had been before. This is something that always happens, for he who is born evil can never correct himself.

19   *Jacob Burckhardt*
The Equalization of Classes

Whatever one's definition of an "historical classic" Burckhardt's essay on the Italian Renaissance, first published in 1860, deserves such a characterization, based as it is on a thorough and sensitive reading of numerous works of the Trecento and Quattrocento. It is no exaggeration to state that this book has been at the center of all scholarly discussion on the Renaissance in the last century. Intellectual, political, social, and art historians have been drawn to the generalizations of the Swiss scholar, many agreeing with his views, while others, even when disagreeing, being forced to direct their heaviest intellectual ammunition against his interpretation. One of Burckhardt's principal ideas was his view that society of the 14th and 15th centuries, having destroyed the corporate structure of the Middle Ages, made possible the creation of an aristocracy of merit. Thus, while in mediaeval Europe "man was conscious of himself only as member of a race, people, party, family, or corporation—only through some general

---

[2] Dolcibene is asking the youth, not only to bring the 30 lire, but also to do what the protocol requires on such occasions, by bringing him the present which the knight should have offered him spontaneously.

category," in Quattrocento *Italy "man became a spiritual individual and recognized himself as such."*

Every period of civilization which forms a complete and consistent whole manifests itself not only in political life, in religion, art, and science, but also sets its characteristic stamp on social life. Thus the Middle Ages had their courtly and aristocratic manners and etiquette, differing but little in the various countries of Europe, as well as their peculiar forms of middle-class life.

Italian customs at the time of the Renaissance offer in these respects the sharpest contrast to medievalism. The foundation on which they rest is wholly different. Social intercourse in its highest and most perfect form now ignored all distinctions of caste, and was based simply on the existence of an educated class as we now understand the word. Birth and origin were without influence, unless combined with leisure and inherited wealth. Yet this assertion must not be taken in an absolute and unqualified sense, since medieval distinction still sometimes made themselves felt to a greater or less degree, if only as a means of maintaining equality with the aristocratic pretensions of the less advanced countries of Europe. But the main current of the time went steadily toward the fusion of classes in the modern sense of the phrase.

The fact was of vital importance that, from certainly the twelfth century onward, the nobles and the burghers dwelt together within the walls of the cities. The interests and pleasures of both classes were thus identified, and the feudal lord learned to look at society from another point of view than that of his mountain-castle. The Church too in Italy never suffered itself, as in Northern countries, to be used as a means of providing for the younger sons of noble families. Bishoprics, abbacies, and canonries were often given from the most unworthy mo-

SOURCE. Jacob Burckhardt, *The Civilization of the Renaissance in Italy*, translated by S. G. C. Middlemore (New York: Harper Torchbook edition, 1958), Vol. II, pp. 353–360. Reprinted by permission of Harper & Row.

tives, but still not according to the pedigrees of the applicants;
and if the bishops in Italy were more numerous, poorer, and, as
a rule, destitute of all sovereign rights, they still lived in the
cities where their cathedrals stood, and formed, together with
their chapters, an important element in the cultivated society of
the place. In the age of despots and absolute princes which
followed the nobility in most of the cities had the motives and
the leisure to give themselves up to a private life free from
political danger and adorned with all that was elegant and
enjoyable, but at the same time hardly distinguishable from
that of the wealthy burgher. And after the time of Dante,
when the new poetry and literature were in the hands of all
Italy, when to this was added the revival of ancient culture and
the new interest in man as such, when the successful *condottiere*
became a prince, and not only good birth, but legitimate birth,
ceased to be indispensable for a throne, it might well seem that
the age of equality had dawned, and the belief in nobility
vanished for ever.

From a theoretical point of view, when the appeal was made
to antiquity the conception of nobility could be both justified
and condemned from Aristotle alone. Dante, for example, adapts
from the Aristotelian definition, "Nobility rests on excellence
and inherited wealth," his own saying, "Nobility rests on personal excellence or on that of predecessors." But elsewhere he is
not satisfied with this conclusion. He blames himself, because
even in Paradise, while talking with his ancestor Cacciaguida,
he made mention of his noble origin, which is but as a mantle
from which time is ever cutting something away, unless we
ourselves add daily fresh worth to it. And in the *Convivio* he
disconnects *nobile* and *nobiltà* from every condition of birth,
and identifies the idea with the capacity for moral and intellectual eminence, laying a special stress on high culture by calling
nobiltà the sister of *filosofia*.

And as time went on the greater the influence of humanism
on the Italian mind, the firmer and more widespread became
the conviction that birth decides nothing as to the goodness or
badness of a man. In the fifteenth century this was the prevailing
opinion. Poggio, in his dialogue *On Nobility*, agrees with his
interlocutors—Niccolò Niccoli and Lorenzo de' Medici, brother

of the great Cosimo—that there is no other nobility than that of personal merit. The keenest shafts of his ridicule are directed against much of what vulgar prejudice thinks indispensable to an aristocratic life.

"A man is all the farther removed from true nobility the longer his forefathers have plied the trade of brigands. The taste for hawking and hunting savours no more of nobility than the nests and lairs of the hunted creatures of spikenard. The cultivation of the soil, as practised by the ancients, would be much nobler than this senseless wandering through the hills and woods, by which men make themselves liker to the brutes than to the reasonable creatures. It may serve well enough as a recreation, but not as the business of a lifetime."

The life of the English and French chivalry in the country or in the woody fastnesses seems to him thoroughly ignoble, and worst of all the doings of the robber-knights of Germany. Lorenzo here begins to take the part of the nobility, not—which is characteristic—appealing to any natural sentiment in its favour, but because Aristotle in the fifth book of the *Politics* recognizes the nobility as existent, and defines it as resting on excellence and inherited wealth. To this Niccoli retorts that Aristotle gives this not as his own conviction, but as the popular impression; in his *Ethics*, where he speaks as he thinks, he calls him noble who strives after that which is truly good. Lorenzo urges upon him vainly that the Greek word for nobility means good birth; Niccoli thinks the Roman word *nobilis* —i.e., remarkable—a better one, since it makes nobility depend on a man's deeds. Together with these discussions we find a sketch of the condition of the nobles in various parts of Italy. In Naples they will not work, and busy themselves neither with their own estates nor with trade and commerce, which they hold to be discreditable; they either loiter at home or ride about on horseback. The Roman nobility also despise trade, but farm their own property; the cultivation of the land even opens the way to a title; "it is a respectable but boorish nobility." In Lombardy the nobles live upon the rent of their inherited estates; descent and the abstinence from any regular calling constitute nobility. In Venice the *nobili*, the ruling caste, were all merchants. Similarly in Genoa the nobles and non-nobles were alike merchants and sailors, and separated only by their birth; some few of the former, it is true, still lurked as brigands in their mountain-castles. In Florence a part of the old nobility had devoted themselves to trade; another and certainly by far the smaller part enjoyed the satisfaction of their titles and spent their time either doing nothing at all or else in hunting and hawking.

The decisive fact was that nearly everywhere in Italy even those who might be disposed to pride themselves on their birth could not make good the claims against the power of culture and of wealth, and that their privileges in politics and at Court were not sufficient to encourage any strong feeling of caste. Venice offers only an apparent exception to this rule, for there the *nobili* led the same life as their fellow-citizens, and were distinguished by few honorary privileges. The case was certainly different at Naples, which the strict isolation and the ostentacious vanity of its nobility excluded, above all other causes, from the spiritual movement of the Renaissance. The traditions of medieval Lombardy and Normandy, and the French aristocratic influences which followed, all tended in this direction; and the Aragonese Government, which was established by the middle of the fifteenth century, completed the work, and accomplished in Naples what followed a hundred years later in the rest of Italy—a social transformation in obedience to Spanish ideas, of which the chief features were the contempt for work and the passion for titles. The effect of this new influence was evident, even in the smaller towns, before the year 1500. We hear complaints from La Cava that the place had been proverbially rich as long as it was filled with masons and weavers; while now, since instead of looms and trowels nothing but spurs, stirrups, and gilded belts was to be seen, since everybody was trying to become Doctor of Laws or of Medicine, notary, officer, or knight, the most intolerable poverty prevailed. In Florence an analogous change appears to have taken place by the time of Cosimo, the first Grand Duke; he is thanked for adopting the young people, who now despise trade and commerce, as knights of his Order of St. Stephen. This goes straight in the teeth of the good old Florentine custom, by which fathers left property to their children of the condition that they should have some occupation. But a mania for title of a curious and ludicrous sort sometimes crossed and thwarted, especially among the Florentines, the levelling influence of art and culture. This was the passion for knighthood, which became one of the most striking follies of the day, at a time when the dignity itself had lost every shadow of significance.

Toward the end of the fourteenth century Franco Sacchetti writes:

"A few years ago everybody saw how all the workpeople down to the bakers, how all the wool-carders, usurers, money-changers, and blackguards of all descriptions became knights. Why should an official need knighthood when he goes to preside over some little provincial town? What has this title to do with any ordinary bread-winning pursuit? How art thou sunken, unhappy dignity! Of all the long list of knightly duties what single one do these knights of ours discharge? I wished to speak of these things that the reader might see that knighthood is dead. And as we have gone so far as to confer the honour upon dead men, why not upon figures of wood and stone, and why not upon an ox?"

The stories which Sacchetti tells by way of illustration speak plainly enough. There we read how Bernabò Visconti knighted the victor in a drunken brawl, and then did the same derisively to the vanquished; how German knights with their decorated helmets and devices were ridiculed—and more of the same kind. At a later period Poggio makes merry over the many knights of his day without a horse and without military training. Those who wished to assert the privilege of the order and ride out with lance and colours found in Florence that they might have to face the Government as well as the jokers.

On considering the matter more closely we shall find that this belated chivalry, independent of all nobility of birth, though partly the fruit of an insane passion for title, had nevertheless another and a better side. Tournaments had not yet ceased to be practised, and no one could take part in them was was not a knight. But the combat in the lists, and especially the difficult and perilous tilting with the lance, offered a favourable opportunity for the display of strength, skill, and courage, which no one, whatever might be his origin, would willingly neglect in an age which laid such stress on personal merit.

It was in vain that from the time of Petrarch downward the tournament was denounced as a dangerous folly. No one was converted by the pathetic appeal of the poet: "In what book do we read that Scipio and Caesar were skilled at the joust?" The practice became more and more popular in Florence. Every honest citizen came to consider his tournament—now, no doubt, less dangerous than formerly—as a fashionable sport. Franco Sacchetti has left us a ludicrous picture of one of these holiday cavaliers—a notary seventy years old. He rides out on horseback to Peretola, where the tournament was cheap, on a jade hired from a dyer. A thistle is struck by some wag under the tail of the steed, which takes fright, runs away, and carries the helmeted rider, bruised and shaken, back into the city. The inevitable conclusion of the story is a severe curtain-lecture from the wife, who is not a little enraged at these breakneck follies of her husband.

It may be mentioned in conclusion that a passionate interest in this sport was displayed by the Medici, as if they wished to show—private citizens as they were without noble blood in their veins—that the society which surrounded them was in no respects inferior to a Court. Even under Cosimo (1459), and afterward under the elder Pietro, brilliant tournaments were held at Florence. The younger Pietro neglected the duties of government for these amusements, and would never suffer himself to be painted except clad in armour. The same practice prevailed at the Court of Alexander VI, and when the Cardinal Ascanio Sforza asked the Turkish Prince Djem how he liked the spectacle the barbarian replied with much discretion that such combats in his country only took place among slaves, since then, in the case of accident, nobody was the worse for it. The Oriental was unconsciously in accord with the old Romans in condemning the manners of the Middle Ages.

Apart, however, from this particular prop of knighthood, we find here and there in Italy—for example, at Ferrara—orders of Court service whose members had a right to the title.

But great as were individual ambitions and the vanities of nobles and knights, it remains a fact that the Italian nobility took its place in the centre of social life, and not at the extremity. We find it habitually mixing with other classes on a footing of perfect equality, and seeking its natural allies in culture and intelligence. It is true that for the courtier a certain rank of nobility was required, but this exigence is expressly declared to be caused by a prejudice rooted in the public mind—"per l'op-penion universale"—and never was held to imply the belief that the personal worth of one who was not of noble blood was in any degree lessened thereby, nor did it follow from this rule that the prince was limited to the nobility for his society. It was meant simply that the perfect man—the true courtier—should not be wanting in any conceivable advantage, and therefore not in this. If in all the relations of life he was specially bound to maintain a dignified and reserved demeanour the reason was not found in the blood which flowed in his veins, but in the perfection of manner which was demanded from him. We are here in the presence of a modern distinction, based on culture and on wealth, but on the latter solely because it enables men to devote their lives to the former, and effectually to promote its interests and advancement.

20   *Lauro Martines*
     The Family: The Significance of a Tradition

With increasing frequency in recent years many of Jacob Burck-hardt's generalizations have been subjected to intense scrutiny. Based on careful examination of archival material, overlooked by the Swiss historian, this reevaluation has resulted in the revision of many of his ideas. Professor Lauro Martines of the University of California, Los Angeles, the author of an essay on Florentine social history in the first half of the Quattrocento, *is not alone in his belief that the "individualism" and the "equalization of classes," discerned by Burck-hardt in 15th century Italy, are misleading, possibly mistaken, concepts. The family, and family tradition, remained an extremely cohesive social force in 15th century Florence, and an individual's chances of succeeding and distinguishing himself depended, to a large extent, on his family's tradition and legacy.*

The family in fifteenth-century Florence stands between the individual and society. It mediates and determines his relations with the world at large, for he confronts the social system conditioned by his family's position in society, and his place in public life is governed by the political place of his family.

This is the underlying theme of this section. On it we shall build our account of the nature and importance of family traditions.

In Florence, the man who distinguished himself reflected honor on his family; behaving disgracefully, he disgraced it. By the same token, he could not be born into an illustrious family without concretely sharing in its distinction. He also shared its dishonors and shame. The great fourteenth-century lawyer, Bartolus, is said to have observed that "In Florence and throughout Tuscany liability for a crime committed by one of their member was imposed upon members of the family group. Furthermore, each individual's party affiliation was presumed to be that of the family group or its head." Finding himself legally embroiled in Rome or Venice, the simple Florentine artisan could make no effective appeal to Florence, owing to his political and social obscurity. But men with names like Soderini, Castellani, Peruzzi, Strozzi, or Guicciardini enjoyed the benefits of a family tradition, and traveled from one side of Italy to the other with the knowledge that their families would, if necessary, come to their aid through the diplomatic channels of the Florentine Republic.

The individual who stood out in public affairs bound his family to the state in a special and close relation. Often, indeed, family affairs and affairs of state were so closely bound that they tended to merge. Before Pisa surrendered to Florence in 1406,

SOURCE. Lauro Martines, *The Social World of the Florentine Humanists —1390–1460*, (Princeton: Princeton University Press, 1963) pp. 50–57. Reprinted by permission of Princeton University Press and the author.

the Florentines had to guarantee that they would live up to their promises by turning a group of hostages over to Messer Giovanni Gambacorta. The hostages, twenty youths, were the scions of leading Florentine families, the sons in fact of the architects of Florentine foreign policy.

Although the prominent Florentine family was not unique in deeply committing itself to political affairs, it seems to have had distinctive traits. For one thing, its intense political character was not diminished by the fact that its members often displayed a wide range of interests. Two typical families of the upper class will exemplify this.

The Corbinelli and Martelli families belonged to the inner circle of the oligarchy. In the first quarter of the fifteenth century there were five Corbinelli brothers and nine Martelli. Some of the brothers, cleaving to their traditions, deeply involved themselves in politics. In each case, however, the family's "allotment" of leading offices (e.g., *Gonfaloniere di Giustizia* or a seat in the *Decem Baliae*) tended to go to one of the brothers only. The others went into the cloth trade or banking, and occasionally one resided abroad. Giovanni di Niccolò Martelli, for instance, seems to have spent years in Spain. Antonio Corbinelli, on the other hand, at times invested money in commercial enterprise, but he was mainly interested in the Graeco-Roman literary classics; indeed, in the 1420's he owned one of the greatest collections of classical codices then in existence. Another Martelli, Domenico, was a doctor of jurisprudence. He lectured for a time at the University of Bologna and later became an important Florentine diplomat. But despite the diversity of their interests, each of the brothers was perforce a political individual. There was nothing strange in this: the necessity confronted all men of the upper class. At this social level, as we have said, the political action of the individual tended to implicate his family; for him, or for a brother, son, or nephew, to refuse this responsibility was both dangerous and foolish. The folly lay in the fact that the man who provoked the spite of the oligarchy or of a powerful house exposed his own family to persecution or disfavor; the danger was in being subject to grinding taxation, exclusion from public office, the rejection of private petitions, or a costly vulnerability in the law courts.

Clearly it behooved a man to take an interest in politics, but even then disaster was sometimes unavoidable. In 1411, when the oligarchy struck out at the Alberti clan for the third time, once more alleging a plot, it is difficult to see what might have been done to save the innocent. Citizen after citizen stood up in the executive councils, calling for the expulsion in perpetuity of the families of the conspirators: "Let all the Alberti be banished from the city." "Exile all their children and descendents." "Forbid even their women to live in the family houses." "No Guelf families related to them should be allowed to buy their houses."

Our theme is that responsibility in the patrician household was collective: all members of the family, whether they wished it or not, were associated with its reputation and political traditions. Yet there were significant departures from this system of "tribal" honor and guilt: the most remarkable fifteenth-century example involves the Albizzi family. When Rinaldo, one of the most impassioned enemies of the Medici, was banished in 1434, his brother Luca was permitted to remain in Florence, where, surprisingly enough, he even continued to enjoy the Republic's leading dignities. He was given numerous diplomatic assignments and in 1442 held the supreme executive office, Standard-bearer of Justice, a post for which Messer Rinaldo himself was never drawn. Luca's case, however, aroused the wonder of his contemporaries.

Since the nature of the upper-class family was such that each of its members gave moral qualities to the whole, and the whole to the individual, no man in this order of society could easily free himself from what was commonly supposed about his family. Consequently, contrary to one of Jacob Burckhardt's themes, the prominent Florentine did not enter society, nor circulate in it, as a "free individual," hurt or elevated purely by his own vices or talents. He was too closely associated with and rooted in his family background. Did it follow, therefore, that the man who came from a family of no importance was freer? Certainly not. For generally he could make no social or political claims: he had no environmental resources. Hence he abided in his obscurity, free to move only in the politically impotent world to which he was born.

The first requirement of the family type which enjoyed distinguished social rank was that it be old and established. Two factors produced this trait: wealth and public office, or better, honorably-acquired wealth and a long record of participation in the political affairs of the city. At the beginning of the fifteenth century, most of the dominant families could lay claim to these qualifications. They had entered the Priorate for the first time during its earliest years—the 1280's, 1290's, and the first years of the fourteenth century; or else they were connected by marriage with houses which had figured in public affairs even before the establishment of the Priorate. Furthermore, the wealth of these families antedated their rise to political distinction and often went back to the middle years of the thirteenth century. Leon Battista Alberti gloried in this aspect of his family history: "I say that the Alberti house is to be praised because for two hundred years and more it has never been so poor that it was not reputed to rank among the richest families of Florence: Both in the memory of our elders and in our family papers you will find that the Alberti were always great and famous merchants with distinguished reputations." But as we have said, the Alberti fell out with the ruling faction at the end of the fourteenth century, and although their civic eminence was partly restored after 1434, they never regained their political power of old:

This is the place to analyze a factor repeatedly mentioned but not yet discussed—tradition.

Neither wealth alone, nor civic eminence alone, normally sufficed to attain high social rank. The two, wealth and office, had to be combined; and being combined across a long enough period of time, they produced an entirely new factor—a family tradition. By dint of long association with the Republic's major offices, and by maintaining a solid position either as great landowners or in the area of banking and international trade, a family developed its specific reputation and authority in the city. This we call its tradition.

In the early fifteenth century, the Fortini (a branch of the Orlandini) were well-known as notaries, landowners, and merchants. Having a talent for dealing with administrative questions, they developed a powerful bureaucratic tradition. The

Medici house, renowned in business circles, enjoyed the special allegiance of the lower classes. The Panciatichi, on the other hand, once scorned as usurers, were respected and feared because they combined vast landed wealth and finance capital with an illustrious feudal past. By contrast with the Medici, the Albizzi and Ricasoli were deemed to be intransigeant oligarchs, along with the Peruzzi and Castellani. A final example: the Pandolfini, a family of prominent spice and silk merchants and landowners, were associated with traditions of political caution, wise counsel, and skill in diplomacy.

But in what did the essential strength of virtue of a family tradition consist? The social standing conferred by a tradition could not be achieved through wealth or public office alone. A tradition signified antiquity and stability; it denoted a certain recognized devotion to the Republic. It was associated with reliability, an excellent practical virtue both in politics and social life. Let an upstart—merchant or *scioperato*—exercise the authority of a given office with more severity than prudence, and he soon ran up against the resistence or vindictive action of the ruling families. A family tradition, on the other hand, permitted the individual to invest his administrative and executive posts with a special or higher authority.

Since the triumphant ideal of the old family produced various attendant fashions, it will pay to consider the one which best reveals the growing importance assigned to the claims of old lineage.

In the later fourteenth century, when Florence gradually came under the regenerate domination of the older merchant families, one concomitant feature was a growing and intense concern with family genealogies. Thus, the opening paragraph of Giovanni Morelli's memoirs announces: "Since this entry book hasn't been used yet, it occurred to me, Giovanni di Pagolo di Bartolomeo di Morello di Giraldo di Ruggieri, or rather Gualtieri, di Calandro di Benamato d'Albertino de' Morelli, to write about our ancient condition and ancestry, so far as I can remember, and also about our current and coming situation. I'll do this in order to pass the time and especially to let my sons and relatives know something about our origins and early condition. *For everyone today pretends a family background of great antiquity*, and I want to establish the truth about ours."

We find a similar theme in Buonaccorso Pitti's diary. He began to record his memoirs in 1412, "in order to leave a lasting account of what I have heard and discovered about our antiquity and about all our relatives both ancient and modern." An early example of this genealogical preoccupation appears in the domestic chronicle of the lawyer, Donato Velluti, who wrote in the late 1360's. Velluti's interest was shared by another lawyer of the period, the prominent Florentine statesman, Lapo di Castiglionchio. In a fascinating letter to one of his sons, written in the early 1370's, Lapo shows that he had leafed through the domestic papers of the Castiglionchi, clearly in search of the family's origins and early condition:

As we move into the fifteenth century, the self-conscious study of family trees grows at a rapid pace, until it seems to become the major "historical" interest of upper-class Florence. This throws light on the Florentine passion for family tombs, since we may suppose that they served, apart from their obvious function, as the tangible signs of a family's physical continuity. Seen in this light, we can understand why the ancestral crypt often set off angry disputes between different families over questions of burial priority on church sites. In these disputes, recourse to family papers was one of the ordinary procedures in the gathering of proof. The disputants also turned to parish records and early traces of armorial bearings on the site of the crypt.

The fashionable and enduring "obsession" with genealogies in upper-class Florence was a landmark on the way to the aristocratic society of the sixteenth century. Whatever this passion was to become under the principate, in pre-Laurentian Florence the esteem for antiquity of family stock was already a major ingredient in the formation of a new class consciousness.

A NEW ARISTOCRACY

21   *From the History of Milan of the*
Treccani degli Alfieri Foundation
Ludovico Sforza—New Ruler of Milan

In 1450 Ludovico Sforza became the ruler of Milan, the most im-
portant commune of northern Italy. Overthrowing the short-lived
Ambrosian Republic, which had been established in 1447 after the
long domination of the Visconti family, Ludovico proceeded to con-
solidate his political control by enacting a series of fiscal and social
policies meant to make his rule more palatable to his subjects.

The reconstruction of the Castle had revealed to his most
astute enemies Sforza's intent to use that fortress as a means of
intimidating his subjects, while at the same time making clear
his desire to return rapidly to the political situation prevalent
under the Visconti. Thus was to begin the most difficult experience for the new Duke: the reconstruction—after the destruction of the Ambrosian Republic—and the reorganization of
the new and vast domain. He had already given clear proof of
some qualities considered by Machiavelli as indispensable for
those who had become "princes through talent or fortune." He
had demonstrated, that is, "how to make himself secure against
enemies and win friends," "to be victorious either by force or
by fraud," "reverenced and obeyed by his soldiers," "disband

SOURCE. Franco Catalano, *Storia di Milano*, Vol. VII (Milan: Fondazione
Treccani degli Alfieri, 1953), pp. 17-21. Translated for this volume by An-
thony Molho. Reprinted by permission of Instituto della Enciclopedia
Italiana and the author.

an old, untrustworthy army and build a new one." Now he had to demonstrate that he could exercise those qualities which truly consolidate states: "to make himself loved and feared by the people," "refurbish old laws with new measures," "be severe, indulgent and liberal," "preserve the friendship of kings and princes in such a way that they will give assistance with pleasure and offense with caution."

Immediately after 26 February Sforza had sent an announcement to all the Italian princes and sovereigns informing them of his accession to the Duchy of Milan; from some he had received their congratulations, while from others (Venice, Frederick III, Charles VII) he got but a silent rebuke. Vainly had he attempted to mollify the hostility of the Emperor Frederick who was to have officially vested him with his new title. It was then that the problem of consolidating his state became even more urgent, for he had to be ready to oppose any possible foreign attacks, and he strongly wished to base his power on cordial and humane relations with his subjects—even make them love him. Without any doubt, his ability consisted precisely in his never taking punitive measures against one entire group, but rather always against single individuals; and he clearly kept in mind the knowledge that the force of the State was given by the "people," a term which he interpreted to mean the middle class whose members should be treated by the Prince with magnanimity and liberality. He should be feared (or one should better say respected) and at the same time be loved.

In fact, Sforza, after a short time during which he granted concessions and confirmed old privileges to the members of the nobility who had aided him to acquire the Duchy, quickly reoriented his internal policy toward the groups that were economically most active. Above all, he acted with great tact toward the exiles, suggesting to the secret council in August, 1450 to proceed against them with moderation. Moreover, he congratulated his lieutenant at Alessandria for the "good spirit" with which he had allowed them to return "home." He also demonstrated that he wished to protect his citizens from abuses of his employees, from the frequent lootings and thefts with which his soldiers tortured the populace. He addressed himself to his "dearest citizens," showing his willingness to protect them, ordering his lieutenants and commissaries to imprison whoever committed those crimes, encouraging them not "to pay attention as to who the criminal might be," and to fear no one but himself.

But this attitude does not necessarily explain his general political approach, for the above actions may only reflect Sforza's characteristically humane personality—something for which all contemporary chroniclers praised him. In reality, other decisions are more valid as clues to his political line. Among these, in particular, were his policies dealing with the gilds. In this field Sforza was anticipating Machiavelli's advice by "refurbishing old laws with new measures." In other words, he followed the policy of the Visconti who had based their power on the support of the affluent citizens, all of whom were members of the gilds. Sforza often took an interest in the affairs of the merchants, confirming privileges which had been granted to some—for example, to the navigators of Pavia, Piacenza and Cremona—or mediating the disputes between a city (Parma) and the wool merchants, rendering a favourable judgment to the latter.

It may well be that his policy toward the gilds was influenced by an acute industrial crisis in mid-1451, caused by various reasons such as the plague, excessive taxes, etc., and resulting in an intense emigration of artisans in search of better conditions of life. The survival of certain mediaeval theories regarding population should have contributed to Sforza's preoccupation with this exodus which decreased the population of the Duchy, thus diminishing the capacity of his subjects to pay taxes. Clear echo of such a preoccupation are the two edicts issued in January and February, 1452, according to which the Duke decreed that no artisan could be "harmed by his creditors because of his debts," while also granting a "valid safe conduct and absolute security" to all industrial workers wishing to return, and concurrently remitting repayment of all debts for the "future four years." All this, let one repeat, may have reinforced Sforza's favourable attitude toward the gilds, and may have in fact encouraged him to pursue such policies all the more avidly.

Sforza's policy with regard to the salt tax demonstrates that he constantly sought to modify his internal policies according to the exigencies and needs of a certain situation. This tax represented a substantial portion of his revenues, so that the Duke was always seeking to maintain it at a constant level, if not augment it when circumstances allowed it. In the beginning of 1452 he increased the price of salt from six to 17 pence per bushel, thus giving rise to many complaints and serious malcontent in all the cities. His enemies, of course sought to take advantage of the situation by spreading alarming rumors that the price of grain would be similarly augmented. Realizing that this policy of unrest and discontent threatened to alienate from him even the sympathy of the cities which he was trying to entice to his side, Sforza immediately restored the old price of salt.

Surely, one can best understand the above incident by keeping in mind the fiscal needs of the Duke. But this does not mean that he did not have a clear and resolute intent to aid the urban bourgeoisies. This intention must have become all the more urgent in the course of 1453 when it became apparent that periods of war strengthened popular and democratic tendencies: the revolt of Stefano Porcari broke out in Rome; in Florence the citizens were rejoicing at the democratization of the political process, while Genoa lived in a state of continuous agitation. These signs of popular unrest may have encouraged him toward an active policy in favour of the bourgeoisie whose interests, after all, coincided with his. This community of interests was evident in the efforts of the various cities to bring under their closer supervision the countryside surrounding them. Such a policy parallelled that of the Duke who was seeking to repress local autonomies in order to increase the administrative efficiency of the state.

Such changes in the orientation of his internal economic policy had important repercussions in the political attitudes of various social classes. Because of Sforza's original support of the nobles and feudal lords the first opposition to his rule had come from the cities which had followed the Duke's enemies by staging rebellions and revolts. By 1452–53, however, the feudal lords, who derived their strength from the peasants working their land, had become riotous and obstreperous. During these years these were continuous complaints of civil servants against the nobles who did not allow them to collect taxes in their domain, inspired the peasants to revolt, openly violating the Duke's orders, attempted to administer justice in their own lands, and usurped many of the state's rights. From Parma, for example, Sforza received in March, 1453 a communication informing him how the privileges of the nobles resulted in the total elimination of his authority: ". . . One grants himself an exemption, another awards himself a feudal right, yet another assumes some other privilege in such a form that it does not seem to me that Your Excellency is truly the master of Your domain. And with great pain, following a myriad of tricks, I have been able to convince them to obey me and let me exercise my office. And I have done all this in order to reinstate the jurisdiction of Your Lordship, which was all but lost." Another civil servant, Bartolomeo de Trovamalus, referring to Piacenza suggested to Sforza in July, 1453 to impose more stringent laws against the "minor" feudatories who refused to pay the taxes so that "the big ones will be convinced with real examples and not with words." On the other hand, the inhabitants of the cities had passed from an initially hostile position to one favouring the Duke, no longer offering their aid to Sforza's enemies.

This new economic and social policy culminated in September, 1454 in a vigorous and severe decree against the feudatories, now accused of wanting to reserve for themselves "almost a separate dominion, nearly a new monarchy, in which Our superiority does not exist." By now the new alliance with the elements of the bourgeoisie had been reinforced by the Peace of Lodi, so that the Duke could condemn even more vigorously the pretensions of the nobles. Certainly, the greatness and political sophistication of Sforza are revealed in this change of the social foundation of his domain, a change which in fact translated in practical terms Machiavelli's advice that the Prince should "become the friend of the people, and prevail over those who have power to be dangerous."

22 *Jacques Heers*
The Two Aristocracies—The Case of Genoa

Concerned with delineating the character of the Genoese aristocracy, Professor Jacques Heers has concluded that the ruling group of that ancient and powerful north-Italian port was neatly divided into the landed and enterpreneurial classes. In this respect, Genoa differed from other Italian cities, which we have already examined, where members of both groups had begun intermarrying from the 13th century, and where they were deeply involved in commercial affairs, while also maintaining close connections with the countryside. All this was different in Genoa. The entepreneurs and the seigneurs maintained different styles of life, pursued different interests, and retained a rigid separation between themselves. Thus, the Genoese society foreshadowed a similar dichotomy of Italian society that one observes in the early part of the 16th century.

In effect, the Genoese ruling class is divided in two: on the one hand, the lords who own fiefs and, on the other, the businessmen who do not. On many occasions I have had the opportunity to observe this division. It is essential. Several of the Doria have all kinds of dealings in Genoa but Andrea Doria, born in Oneglia, a lord and not a merchant, lives on his land.

Which of the two aristocracies is victorious in the period which we study? Without doubt, one can find large fortunes among the lords. No one could rival Giovanni-Ludovico Fieschi, a great lord—a vertiable prince. He owns lands, estates, men and beautiful houses in Genoa.

SOURCE: Jacques Heers, *Genes au XVe Siecle—Activite economique et problemes* sociaux (S.E.V.P.E.N., 1961), pp. 557–562. Translated for this volume by Anthony Molho. Reprinted by permission of Ecole Pratique des Hautes Etudes and the author.

Difficult as the differences in their fortunes may be to assess, what really separates these two Genoese aristocracies is their style of life, their ideals, the manner in which they approach the world and spend their money.

To begin with, even if the lords leave their castles occasionally in order to visit their palaces in Genoa, those who do not own fiefs remain continuously in the city. The Genoese merchant does not possess great landed property. The banker or business-man has a house in the center of town and, if fortune is kind to him, he also has a villa in the suburbs which, without doubt, is a nice house, surrounded by lands, vignards, olive groves, and all kinds of trees. The Genoese villas are already famous for their elaborate styles, their charming gardens, and parks. Situated around the gates of the city they make up that ravishing countryside which inevitably astounds all visitors. One took refuge there during the summer in order to forget the dark alleys and the crowded squares of the city. These Genoese suburbs along the coast are the Venetian equivalents of the banks of the Brenta river. Some pieces of property are large, some have forests and houses for the gardeners. But they re-main close to the city: the furthest points are Voltri on one side of the city, and Quinto on the other. Beyond these points the land belongs to the peasants, to the burghers of other cities or to convents. In the registers of the Genoese property tax [*gabella possessionum*] a house situated in Rapallo is a very rare find. The merchant's lands and houses are situated within the rather narrow confines of the suburbs.

Thus, the merchant does not possess great rural holdings—neither pasture nor farming land. He is not the lord of peasants; he only has a few house workers and gardeners. Piccamiglio [a prominent merchant] must hire day labourers to cultivate his vignard. Nor does he own any animals. He travels to Genoa on his mule, an animal which costs him dearly since he is forced to purchase its feed from Bisagno or Nervi. Whenever the merchant wishes to escape the plague to Savignana he must gather a small caravan of mules. All this lacks grandeur. For the Freschi and Fregosi own horses. Thus, on the one hand, one observes the grand seigneur with his entrouage travelling on horseback; on the other hand, the merchant who travels from the city to his vignard by mule. Nonetheless, this latter is wealthy. But his life is not the same as that of the lord. For he is an urban dweller. In any case, the desire of the urban bourgeoisie of other Italian cities to acquire great domanial holdings leaves our merchant rather cold, partly maybe because the possibility of satisfying such a desire does not exist in Genoa. The Genoese merchants may well have been similar to the Venetian gentlemen of whom Machiavelli said that they were noble "more in name than in fact, because they do not have large revenues from their land, their wealth being invested in enterpreneurial activities. Moreover, none has castles or enjoys jurisdiction over men."

The life of the lord is different and much grander. The luxury and high style of the Fieschi in Carignano was well known. These men know how to take an interest in the affairs of their age and, significantly, they were attracted to the arts and letters in the affairs of their age and, significantly, they were attracted to the arts and letters. Business matters did not confine their interests, for they were surrounded by·a small court of cultured and refined men. The Ligurian humanism, so vigorous and original, was forged in the palaces of the Freschi and Fregosi; Sarzana was the principal home of this literary movement. Ludovico Fregoso's secretary was the humanist Antonia Ivani. Raffaele Adorno, doctor of canon and civil law, writes in the purest Latin and, deeply committed to fine arts, receives several writers in his home.

Without doubt, the religious attitudes differ widely among members of the two groups. There is no question but that all, lords and bourgeois, sent their daughters to nunneries. Abbesses of such institutions bear the names of Fieschi, Doria, Spinola. But it is important to remember that the lord and the merchant could not entertain the same position vis-à-vis the Church. The lords enjoy privileges and benefices. To a great degree convents and bishoprics are their own monopoly. Moreover, they have remained deeply committed to tradition, as is shown by the very substantial legacies bequeathed to ecclesiastical institutions by the Fieschi. Eliano Spinolo of Luccoli had instituted a fund of 6,000 *lire* of which two thirds were "in honour of God, the indivisible Trinity, the most honoured Mary and St. Julien, protector of the said Eliano." This fund must distribute 200 *lire* per year to five monasteries of Genoa and the surrounding area and 50 *lire* to the poor of Serivia and Borgo Fornario. Here is another example of equally high sums, but of a drastically different testament: Frederico Centurioni subsidized the celebration of 1,000 masses, but assigned only 100 *lire* (of capital, not of income) for the poor, and 20 for a hospital. Nevertheless, he too was wealthy. But his mentality was that of a banker.

In sum, these two classes remain neatly separated. It may be relatively easy to accede to the class of the merchants or bankers, or to join an association [*albergo*] of nobles and assume a title of nobility. The class of the landed siegneurs, however, is tightly closed. With some rare exceptions the lords sell neither their lands nor their privileges to the merchants. Legal prohibitions against subdivision of land, and the practice of common, familial administration of such wealth reinforce the survival of old families.

Moreover, the lords intermarry and give their daughters only to men of their own rank. Both Giovanni-Ludovico and Matteo Fieschi married an Adorno. Let us, for a moment, study the Adorni: Giovanni, son of Raffaele (the Doge), marries Eleonora Sanseverino, the condottiere's daughter who had just obtained the castle of Silvano d'Orba from the marquis of Montferrat. Barnabo marries one of his daughters to Giovanni Malaspina, lord of Mursacco, and another to Leonello Spinella, lord of Busalla. Prospero, who also married a Malaspina, has five daughters. His sons-in-law are Alberto of Carretto, lord of Finale, Francesco Martelli, "Florentine nobleman," Niccolo Ocimano, lord of Incisa, Biagio Spinola, lord of Cassano, and Battista Colla who had fiefs between Asti and Alexandria. The Fregosi act precisely in the same manner. Spinetta gives his daughter to Pietro-Antonio Attendolo son of the condottiere, thus receiving the fief of Groparello; his other daughter is married to Michele Attendolo. As for Piero, the Doge who had been expelled from Genoa, he marries Bartolomea, daughter of

Giovanni Grimaldi, the new lord of Monaco. One could easily add to the above examples. The lord wishes to marry his children to other feudal lords—to men who own lands and fortresses, or who are condottieri. This is a matter of common interest, and of a common outlook. All are quite conscious of belonging to a world quite different from that of the merchants, they are proud of this fact, and often vaunt the title of knighthood. Finally, an alliance with a merchant was taken as a sure sign of the lord's failure. Indeed, this is a well-circumscribed world; mismarriage is not allowed.

The landed aristocracy, to which belong castellans and feudal lords. forms a distinct class which cannot be entered with facility. Its mode of life removes it from business matters and shops. The time when a lord of the Appenines might come to Genoa in order to invest his money in commercial enterprises is long past. Those capable of conserving or acquiring fiefs became increasingly entrenched and separated from the rest. These men were not necessarily wealthier than the great-bankers, the Centurioni and Guistiniani. But they manifest an *esprit de corps*, a sense of belonging to a cast, from which sense emanates their fear of failure by mismarriage or by an immoderate involvement in the affairs of the city.

The division between the two aristocracies is complete: the sources of their wealth, the manner of their lives, their ideals. Often, their interests also clash. So do their political conceptions. The one group wants a bourgeois commune, and in great part one can say that it was successful in realizing that ideal. The others wish to maintain their privileges. The opposition between these two ruling classes, each disposing powerful but diverse means, explains the political troubles of the city.

23

A. Ventura
The Triumph of the Aristocracy in the Veneto

F. Braudel in his monumental work[1] first published in 1949 and issued in a revised two-volume edition in 1966 addressed himself to an examination of a 16th century phenomenon which he described as the "treason of the bourgeoisie." Throughout the entire basin of the Mediterranean Sea, from Turkey to Italy and Spain, a new aristocratic class began emerging. This aristocracy, though it shared many of the ideals and aspirations of the old feudal aristocracy, drew its membership from the ranks of the urban, enterpreneurial elites that had flourished in Italy and other Mediterranean lands since the 12th century. In great part, the subtle social and cultural transformation wrought by the triumph of the aristocracy was a result of the fact that the members of the 15th century "bourgeoisie" did not have a conciousness of belonging to a class whose interests they strove to uphold; they lacked the espirit de corps *which 19th century middle classes were to exhibit. Thus, as Profesor J. Hexter suggested several years ago, it is important to remember that the 16th century was an age of aristocratic and elitist ideals, rather than an era in which, as numerous historians had suggested earlier in the century, the European middle class and the "bourgeois ethic" had triumphed.*

In the following selection, taken from a recent and very interesting study of the social history of the Venetian hinterland in the Cinquecento, *Professor Ventura outlines some of the processes which led to the creation of the aristocracy in that Italian region.*

---

[1] F. Braudel, *La Méditerranée et le Monde Méditerranéen a L'epoque de Philippe II*, 2nd ed., 2 vols. (Paris, 1966). An English translation will be published shortly by the London firm of Routledge and Kegan Paul.
SOURCE. A. Ventura, *Nobilta e Popolo nella Societa Veneta* del '400 e '500 (Bari: Laterza Publishing House, 1964), pp. 275–279. Reprinted by permission of Laterza Publishing House.

The *Cinquecento* is the century of the aristocratic triumph. Surely, the "failure of the bourgeoisie"—to repeat Braudel's fitting expression—had been manifest in this part of Italy two centuries before: the decisive game had been played during the era of the Signories, and it had been won by the nobility at the moment of the Venetian conquest. Only now, however, ridding themselves of the last vestiges of the communal era, the aristocracy consciously and unequivocally imposes its clear hegemony in the realms of communal laws, customs and ideas.

The rise of the nobility is a widespread and complex phenomenon, manifesting itself throughout Italy and Europe and generally becoming adapted to the peculiar social and political circumstances of each area.

The Venetian hinterland does not witness the triumph of the feudal aristocracy. It is true that in some areas, particularly in Friuli, there is a partial return of feudal forms. Undoubtedly, it is significant that the [Venetian] Republic, weakened by continuous wars, had to have recourse to the expedient of making a number of feudal grants in order to compensate some of its supporters, or more frequently, to raise some money. But these are only marginal and exceptional cases which do not alter either the political-administrative, or the social structure of the Republic. The "reaction of the nobility" (to use another of Braudel's phrases) is the work of the urban citizen patriciate and its character, therefore, is clearly urban. This aristocratic transformation, which comes to fruition in the principal centers of the hinterland, including all the communities which are not small, impoverished villages, penetrated deeply into the social texture, modified habits and ideals, altered the relations between classes and influenced the course of economic affairs.

The most clearly visible changes were in the realm of political institutions. In the course of the 15th century each city had witnessed the creation of a closed ruling class, an authentic aristocracy. But no laws yet existed which regulated the membership of this class, or even (with the exception of Brescia after 1488) which explicitly barred the accession of new men to the citizen assemblies and magistracies. Now, between the middle of the 16th and the beginning of the 17th centuries, every city saw the imposition of restrictive laws, meant to close formally entrance into the Councils. These new laws set up strict requirements, needed, it is said, to guarantee the "citizen-ship" *(civiltà)* of the subjects, but in reality meant to exclude from office members of the bourgeois class. The laws, however, did not stop at this point, but went so far as to establish the ruling group as a legally closed class, a privileged body.

With the formation of this hereditary aristocracy society as-sumes a definitive aspect which it will conserve essentially un-changed until the waning of the 18th century.

A carefully conceived series of legislative decrees over a period of three centuries defined with increasingly rigid criteria the privileges of the nobility in each city. The most distinctive sign of this class was the participation of its members in the affairs of the civic assembly which comprised, according to an elegant expression of the time, the "citizens of the Coun-cil." One deals, therefore, with a patriciate of officeholders, much more alike to the French nobility of the robe, than to the feudal nobility.

As all authentic aristocracies this, without excluding on prin-ciple the possibility of new elements joining it, was a hereditary one. The right of membership was transmitted from father to son (in the 18th century the nobility of the mother was also required), while rigorous procedures were established to safe-guard the purity of blood by ascertaining the legitimacy of individuals—a procedure guaranteed by the accurate registra-tion in appropriate ledgers of all the gentlemen who enjoyed this status.

Two additional discriminatory criteria were adopted in order to guarantee the "honour" of the ruling class, and exclude the new men. Above all, a candidate for a Council was obligated to prove his "original citizenship," that is, that his family had lived as citizens *("civilmente")* residing in the city and paying taxes for a number of generations—usually three—or for a long period of time. Moreover, the applicant, his father and grand-father should never have exercised the so-called "mechanical arts" *(arti meccaniche)*, which were interpreted to mean manual or servile labour, working for other men, or plying a com-mercial trade.

These norms—which would seem to guarantee a continuous

but slow accretion of new families into the ranks of the nobility —should be viewed within a political framework which was completely dominated by the citizen aristocracy. The magistracies and communal Councils were dominated by the aristocracy whose members formed a caste which did not tolerate the intrusion of outsiders. Thus, the small crack which had been left open could be penetrated, and then only with difficulty, by those families which had enriched themselves after the middle of the *Quattrocento*. In practice, such accretions to the ranks of the aristocracy occurred only when economic necessities—such as those created by the war in Crete—forced the ruling patriciate to admit within its ranks a few wealthy citizens who were willing to acquire this honour with the power of their money.

THE MERCHANT AND HIS WORLD

24   *Hans Baron*
        A New Attitude Toward Wealth

No scholar has contributed more to our understanding of Quattrocento *Florentine humanism and of the far-reaching and subtle intellectual transformations wrought by the advent of that movement than
Hans Baron. In the following selection, extracted from an essay first
published in 1938, Professor Baron discusses the important changes in
the manner in which 15th century humanists viewed wealth and material possessions. Abandoning the stoic notion that riches corrupt
man and that the individual pursuing wisdom will shun them, this
new breed of intellectuals, whose following among laymen was exten-
sive, advanced the notion that wealth and material possessions edify
and enoble men. Thus, work and its fruits assumed a nobility in the
eyes of these intellectuals and their followers that it had lacked before.*

THE FIFTEENTH CENTURY

The ultimate reason why Italian citizens did not begin to
participate in humanism till the turn of the fourteenth century
can be explained only by a thorough examination of the internal
development of the Italian city-states. But it is evident that the
citizen could not take a personal share in humanistic literature

SOURCE. Hans Baron "Franciscan Poverty and Civic Wealth as Factors
in the Rise of Humanistic Thought," *Speculum*, Vol. XIII (Cambridge: The
Mediaeval Academy of America, 1938), pp. 18–25. Reprinted by permission
of The Mediaeval Academy of America and the author.

nor even communicate his spirit to humanists belonging to civic circles, until the fourteenth-century tradition had been intellectually abandoned, and humanists were able to look upon life not with the eyes of the "sage" but with those of the citizen proudly acknowledging work and self-acquired possessions as the foundations of his morality and the greatness of his city.

At this stage in Renaissance history a new perspective was opened up. The participation of the citizen in intellectual life explains the suddenness and the depth of the change which took place in the character of humanism in the fifteenth century. From its very first decades, the ancient cry of *paupertas*[1] was drowned both in Florence and in Venice by the voices of the citizens who were at home in the world of active life and earthly goods.

In 1408 the philologist Guarino was still attempting to convince Francesco Barbaro, the rick and noble Venetian, of the stoic rule that a truly moral life requires poverty. The little book *Concerning Marriage (De Re Uxoria)* which Barbaro himself wrote a few years later (1415) for the wedding festivities of his Florentine friend, Lorenzo de' Medici, is almost an answer to this challenge. It is the first time that we meet with expressions of the genuine civic spirit in humanistic literature. Taking very little notice of old or new philosophical theories, the rich Venetian citizen, envisaging the duties and habits of his own life, declares that gratitude, charitable sentiments, and the joy of giving remain without true value "if we are unable to prove our feelings by deeds." But such deeds require possessions, and these are, therefore, "exceedingly useful for many things"—if not for ourselves, then in order to help friends or others and thus to awaken gratitude which might become useful to our descendants. Moreover, rich possessions enable us to give our children the best of educations. Thus we much cherish our wealth in order that later generations may not one day look upon us as merely self-gratifying egotists who have not increased our riches for the benefit of those under our care.

Such is the other, the civic view of morality, in which the meaning of life is rooted in activity for family and community,

---

[1] Poverty.

and moral value is found in that which increases man's power of action.

The greatest progress in this civic philosophy was made on Florentine soil. But even in the minds of the Florentine citizens the fourteenth century ideals were so firmly anchored that at the beginning of the new century men of the old school felt the spirit of the young generation to be alien and dangerous. About 1405 Francesco Rinuccini, a good citizen and patriot, gave vent to his indignation that young Florentines ascribed to Cicero the opinion that human happiness is not independent of the possession of worldly goods. We know that such a view (already anticipated by the aged Petrarch) was far truer to Cicero's meaning than all previous interpretations of his philosophy as a warning against wealth. Thus Rinuccini's protest from the past achieved nothing. Shortly after Barbaro the Venetian had written his little book on marriage, civic intellect gave birth to an apology for "riches" in Florence. Its author was Leonardo Bruni Aretino, the pupil of Salutati, and later his successor as Florentine Chancellor.

Bruni, born of an Aretine family, was not originally a Florentine citizen, and did not settle on the Arno till about 1415, after long years of wanderings as a secretary of the papal Curia. But in his youth, in the years decisive for his education, he had lived in Florence in Salutati's circle and had become a Florentine in thought and feeling. After his long sojourn in the international world of the Curia, and owing to the fact that he had only become a citizen and attained civic rights in Florence from inclination, he had a much clearer perception of the peculiarities of the civic sphere than citizens who knew nothing but the atmosphere of the city on the Arno. "Civic" thrift and strivings after property were qualities which even in the opinion of his own contemporaries distinguished this voluntary Florentine from the usual type of humanist of the chancelleries. A humanist in literary circles like Poggio Bracciolini, in spite of his personal friendship with Bruni, was unable to suppress the reproach that Bruni's "pedantry and thrift" ("morositas parcitasque") were more strongly developed than was permissible within the spirit of humanist students. But Bruni's Florentine fellow-citizens praised this quality because it enabled him, though his origins were poor, to bequeath a considerable fortune to his son.

Thus nobody was so well endowed as this humanist with civic instincts to pierce the defence of the "poverty" doctrine of older humanism. Bruni, who was the first to reveal Aristotle to the fifteenth century as an ally in the citizen's struggle for the "vita activa politica," was also the first to re-discover the other "civic" characteristic of Aristotelian ethics, the doctrine of the moral value of wealth. Studying the *Economics* (probably attributed to Aristotle in error, but in any case Aristotelain in conception) Bruni first recognized a kindred spirit. In 1419–20 he translated this book for the greatest merchant prince and richest man of Florence, Cosimo de' Medici, and wrote a commentary on it. He then defended his own activity by saying that if (as the existence of this little book shows) it is a philosopher's task to study the State, the family, and even the administration and increase of property, then this alone proves that possessions and riches should not be regarded by the wise man with sovereign contempt. Bruni considered the quintessence of Aristotelianism to be the doctrine that only the possession of external goods "affords an opportunity for the exercise of virtue" —especially in the case of liberality and munificence. Like Barbaro, he did not forget to add that "divitiae" make a social and political career easier for one's children. He then discovered the same opinion in the poems of Juvenal. The Roman poet who, two centuries before, had provided Brunetto Latini with the picture of the man trembling for his possessions, now bequeathed to the fifteenth-century humanist his dictum (III, 164 ff.) that it is not easy for a man to rise if penury at home restricts his virtues ("quorum virtutibus obstat res angusta domi, haud facile emergunt").

This discovery of Aristotle as an ally of the civic mentality was rendered even more important by the wide publicity given to Bruni's translation of the *Economics*. For the first time the stoic and Franciscan ideals of poverty were seriously threatened. In the conflict which now began to rage, Bruni reached complete clarity as to what Aristotle had to offer to the new epoch. In his defense of Aristotelianism, he did not fail to refer to Aristotle's realization of the harmony of human nature, that is to say, of body and soul, to that aspect of Aristotelian philosophy, therefore, which had already been appreciated to a certain extent in the century of St Thomas Aquinas. "As the soul, although it is much more valuable than the body, yet has need of the body in order that the human being may exist, thus the goods of the soul may be by far the more valuable and yet need corporeal and external goods to produce man's happiness"—that is the principal sentence which Bruni, in a polemic pamphlet, takes from Aristotle. In his hands it becomes a deadly weapon against the doctrine that virtue is self-sufficient even where there is a lack of all external goods. The stoic rule, the humanist of the fifteenth century replies, cannot be practised by 'human beings' but only by "soulless blocks" that have cast aside their "humanity"; the Aristotelian doctrine, however, considers human beings in their capacity as human beings. From the *Nicomachian Ethics* Bruni, as a humanist, takes the sentence: man needs external prosperity "because he is a human being"; as a citizen, he adds that these external aids are the condition of virtue in "active life." In hac civili vita in qua versamur," he states, referring to Aristotle, the condition of liberality is money; of justice, possessions; of courage, power; of munificence, riches. "Taking it all in all, in order to accomplish deeds we need many external goods, and the greater and more excellent the acts pf virtue are, all the more do we depend upon these means." Let the stoic opponents say that this Aristotelian and civic combination of virtue with material things makes the heart petty and narrow. In truth it is they themselves whose education leads to pettiness. "If goods are instruments of virtue, and great and noble things have need of them, because they cannot be achieved without their help, who then is it who renders hearts narrow and petty? . . . Which of us has the more noble goal in view? I who intend to attempt great things and acquire what I need therefor, or you whose thoughts are not directed to anything great and noble?"

With Bruni the path had been cleared for a free development of civic experience and ideals. Boccaccio who in the Florence of the fourteenth century had been the most pronounced advocate of the ideal of poverty, was now submitted—in a biography by Bruni's younger friend, Gianozzo Manetti—to a later compatriot's scrutiny of what lay behind his painfully acquired

and painfully borne mask of stoicism. Manetti's conclusion is
that in Boccaccio's own life "poverty" was in truth not a good,
but a very serious hindrance to virtue, that it forced the poor
poet to earn the means for his studies by the troublesome
process of copying classical texts at night and to confess to
himself with sighs the truth of those words of Juvenal "haud
facile emergunt quorum virtutibus obstat res angusta domi."[2]
Even Boccaccio's idealization of the Roman soldiers who were
satisfied with a little flour, cured meat, and fresh water now met
with opposition. Stefano Porcari. a young Roman, who in 1427
as the Florentine *Capitano del Popolo*[3] so excellently expressed
the moods and convictions of the Florentine citizens that his
public speeches were soon widely circulated in Florence, boldly
declared that such wretched frugality might only be assumed
of the warriors under Caesar and the Emperors when the power
of Roman citizenry had been destroyed by tyranny and a healthy
Respublica was no longer in existence. This interpretation was
ventilated on the Piazza in Florence in a speech of which the
climax was a real hymn of praise for the blessings brought to
citizens by wealth. "Let us contemplate the requirements of
private life," Porcari cried challengingly. "Whence are our
houses and palaces procured . . . ? From riches! Whence come
our clothes . . . ? Whence the meals for us and our children?
From riches! Whence the means to educate our children and
make them virtuous . . . From riches . . . These consecrated
churches with their decorations, the walls, the towers, the defences, . . . your palaces and dwellings, the most noble buildings, the bridges, the streets, with what have you built them,
whence do you obtain the means of preserving them, if not
from riches?

Civic funeral orations of that time breathe the same spirit.
They praise the deceased no longer on account of his renuncia-
tion of vain worldly goods, but rather for his acquisition of
wealth by labor and industry, and for the praise-worthy use he
made of his possessions. We have already seen how, after his
death, Bruni was praised for having left a fortune to his son in

---

[2] No one hampered by poverty at home can easily attain to virtue.
[3] A high judge.

spite of his own early indigence. When Matteo Palmieri, the citizen closest to Bruni in thought and feeling died in 1474, the picture drawn of him by Alamanno Rinuccini, his fellow-citizen, contained the following unvarnished statement: Palmeri, who had been obliged to work his way up out of poverty-stricken circumstances, had "realized how much riches contributed to a civic life led with dignity"; he had therefore so much increased his small inheritance by lifelong industry that it was not only sufficient for his needs "but sufficed for a brilliant life, for fame, for ever-increasing honors, . . . for magnificent buildings in the city and in the country, for his personal needs . . . as well as for foundations in honor of God."

Matteo Palmieri, of whom these words were spoken, was the Florentine who had set the crown on Bruni's thought with a perfection only attainable by a citizen whose own life was devoted to mercantile transactions and political activity for his native city. About the middle of the 1430's, Palmieri, in a book entitled *On Civic Life (Della Vita Civile)*, undertook an adaptation of Cicero's *De Officiis* which went far beyond Cicero's recognition of wealth. Cicero, though in *De Finibus* he defended the Aristotelian doctrine of worldly possessions, in *De Officiis* followed the stoic maxim that only what is virtuous is 'useful' for mankind, wherefore true philosophers should not regard external goods as claiming a sphere of their own in moral philosophy. The citizen of the fifteenth century—in openly expressed opposition to the stoic view—added to his presentment of a civic doctrine of morals a special book concerning "the Useful," a large-scale picture of all the public and private values which lent to the life of Renaissance Florence its strength and its splendor. This description dealt not only with marriage, friendship, and health, but with the importance for the individual of money and economic acquisition; it emphasized the advantage to the community of a favorable geographical situation, of a citizenry proficient in arms, of honorable riches possessed by the higher classes and of the dignity of public buildings. All this was here displayed with the same naïve self-confidence that we have observed in Porcari's speeches.

Aware of not having received these rich treasures in vain, the citizen was in a position to say that morally mature human beings "must not despise usefulness and their own advantage," that "it is blameworthy to despise useful things which one can acquire rightfully, and that such contempt is in no wise in conformity with the nature of a man of virtue." Like Bruni, Palmieri referred to Juvenal's view that no one hampered by poverty at home can easily attain to virtue; like Bruni, he adopted the Aristotelian maxim that "the true commendation of every virtue is to be found in action." For capable men (for "valenti huomini") the *Vita Civile* says, riches and abundance are instruments in the exercise of virtue, and there are many virtues which have need of such help and which remain "weak and fragmentary ("deboli et manche") without them and never attain perfection." The charitable man, the patron of arts, must have money to spend; the temperate man must prove himself in the temptations of life; "he who passes his life in solitude and is neither experienced nor skilled in important matters, in public offices, and in the business of the community, will never become just and courageous." Here the main idea of the citizen is developed in complete clarity, that is, the belief that man is destined for active deeds, and that everything may be looked upon as good which increases his power of action. "Virtue will never become perfect if it is not challenged; fidelity cannot be recognized in those whose shoulders carry no burden, but in those to whom great matters are entrusted." One might set these words as a motto under the whole period in which the victory of the Renaissance citizenry was gained over the ideals of 'poverty' dominating the late Middle Ages.

After the discovery of Aristotelian civic ethics by Bruni and his group had dispelled the prejudices of the fourteenth-century humanists, it became evident that Aristotle was not the only classical writer who could be cited in support of the rehabilition of worldly goods and the economic sphere of life. Leon Battista Alberti, a scion of an old Florentine family who had grown up in exile and was accustomed to a life of deprivation, was unable to share the proud belief of the wealthy merchants on the Arno that rich external possessions are a condition for full development of the moral life. When he returned late and temporarily to his native city, he did not, therefore, follow the civic Aristotelianism of his Florentine compatriots. He found support

in those stoic treatises of Seneca which at all times have lent
assistance in misfortune to strong natures dependent on themselves alone. But even as a Stoic, may, because he was one,
Alberti did not deny the far-reaching transformation of intellectual life which had been accomplished by Florentine citizens.
The stoic independence of fortune striven for by this fifteenth-
century Florentine was no longer associated with mediaeval contempt of the world and its goods, but made renewed contact
with the true Seneca who did not forbid riches to the wise man,
but only demanded that possessions should be taken not into the
heart but merely into the house. It was rather a reawakening of
Seneca's spirit than a superficial literary imitation when Alberti
in his *Libri della Famiglia* (1437–41) proclaimed that riches
bring to a noble spirit not servitude but inner freedom and
cheer. 'Virtus,' he taught in this book, needs external possessions
in order to appear dignified and beautiful; wealth is a source of
fame and reputation because it renders possible the creation of
great and noble things. On the other hand, proud spirits regard
the necessity of making requests to others as servitude. "We
should therefore not despise riches but remain lord over our
desires when we live in the fulness of possessions and in super-
fluity." Seneca's belief in the power of the wise man to bear
both fortune and misfortune without succumbing to the temptations of wealth thus gained the victory in the Florentine of the
Quattrocento over the mediaeval fear of worldly temptations
which had still been present in the stoicism of the fourteenth
century. "Have no fear," Alberti advised, "of what *Fortuna*
may bring you, neither must you long for her. If *Fortuna* grants
you riches, employ them in great-hearted and honorable things.
If *Fortuna* is sparing and miserly towards you, do not therefore
spend your lives in disquiet." And if *Fortuna* deprives you of
her gifts, bear that also with inner "peace and fortitude."

The counterpart to this Renaissance of the true, the pre-
mediaeval Seneca, was the re-discovery of Xenophon's *Oecon-
omicus*, probably of all classical works the most kindly disposed towards economic acquisition, and the closest to the
capitalistic spirit. Its influence, too, began with Alberti. It had
not been known in Italy till, in 1427, Aurispa brought the
Greek original from Byzantium. About the middle of the cen-

tury the book was translated into Latin by Biraghi, the Milanese, and dedicated to Pope Nicholas v. From then on, Xenophon's work furthered the positive attitude of the Renaissance to the world of material goods and industrial acquisitions, in the same way as the pseudo-Aristotelian *Economics*, newly revealed to his contemporaries by Bruni, had influenced thought in the previous decades.

25   *Frederick Antal*
Florentine Painting and its Social Background

There is little doubt that until his recent death Frederick Antal was the outstanding Marxist art historian in the English speaking world. Few are the American and English historians, and even fewer those dealing with the history of art, who in the last few decades have organized their material strictly in terms of Marxist categories. Antal was one of these few. It is interesting to compare his description of the Florentine society with Gene Brucker's analysis and to relate his version of the economic and social stratification of that city with his examination of the 14th and early 15th century collective psychological motivation which gave rise to the art of that era. Committed to an ideology though he may have been, Antal's essay merits close study, particularly for his interesting and often illuminating insights into the psyche of the Florentine patriciate, whose patronage was directly responsible for many of the artistic masterpieces of that age.

THE ART OF THE FOURTEENTH CENTURY: THE OUTLOOK ON WHICH IT IS BASED

A decisive new factor in the fourteenth century which affected these arts, as it did all other forms of culture, both in

SOURCE. Frederick Antal, *Florentine Painting and Its Social Background— The Bourgois Republic Before Cosimo de' Medici's Advent to Power: XIV and Early XV Centuries* (London: Kegan Paul, Trench, Trubner & Co. Ltd, 1947), pp. 117–122 and 288–291. Reprinted by permission of Boston Book and Art Shop, Inc. and Routledge & Kegan Paul Ltd.

Italy and elsewhere, was the increasing independence of outlook of whole classes of the laity, in particular of the ruling
upper middle class. The works of visual art were now no longer,
as in the early Middle Ages, of an esoteric, monastic nature,
unintelligible to the majority of the layfolk and created with
little desire to appeal to them. These works were now produced
not only *for* the laity as well, but more and more exclusively—
in the fourteenth century almost entirely—*by* them, and they
increasingly reflected their point of view. This new outlook, and
the new art that followed from it, necessarily appeared in its
most vigorous form in Italy, the country of the new middle
class *par excellence*. Central Italy, with its highly advanced
Tuscan city republics was, in this respect, of paramount importance for all future development, the smaller city republics,
such as those of Umbria, playing in the earlier phases a minor
role. Outstanding among these Tuscan towns were Florence
and Siena, each having its special outlook in accordance with
its social structure and reflecting this strongly in its art.
Florence had a uniquely powerful oligarchic upper bourgeoisie,
whereas Siena was more of a petty-bourgeois democracy; nowhere, therefore, was an art to be found so pronouncedly
upper-middle-class as that of Florence.

In Florence ruled the export merchants and the financiers, a
self-satisfied bourgeoisie capable of unlimited expansion who had
overcome the nobility with the aid of their financial resources,
and had also won a position of economic and political supremacy
over the petty bourgeoisie and the workers unique in the
Europe of the time. They were prepared to exercise this power
to the utmost in whatever way seemed material to their interests,
and without sentiment; in this their alliance with the Church and
their close and purposeful relations with the great mendicant
Orders assisted them. In the outlook of the fourteenth-century
Florentine upper bourgeoisie, whose commerce embraced the
whole world and whose calculations were far-reaching, there
necessarily ruled a kind of rationalism, a desire and a capacity
for giving full weight to material relations. This factor was
more pronounced than it could be in any other part of the
Christian world at that time. It implied a manner of thinking
which—to put it briefly—followed naturally from the essence of

capitalism, of monetary economy, a manner of thinking by which the world could be expressed in figures and controlled by intelligence. But as we have seen, there were many factors tending to obstruct the free economic development of the Florentine upper bourgeoisie, and these also must be taken into account, for they show themselves in the mentality of this *early* capitalist class as a tendency towards a pure speculation and irrationalism. The early capitalist *enterpreneur* possessed a very definite makeup; side by side with his faith in God went a firm belief that the world could be controlled by rational thought, and a serene confidence in his own power to multiply capital; he also exhibited much irrationality, many almost feudal-aristocratic elements, such as a love of adventure, and even courtly traits, for he still felt himself to be and in some respects actually was related to the nobility.[1] This "irrational" factor is highly complex. It was very evident in the early revolutionary

---

[1] To call the sum of these qualities "individualism" does not get us much further. It is necessary, in each case, to define the particular kind of "individualism", for as a mere general concept the word is valueless. J. Burckhardt (*The Civilisation of the Renaissance in Italy*, Eng. trans., London, 1929) saw in "individualism", in the development of the personality, the foundation of Renaissance culture. In his view, the political conditions at the time of the Renaissance—the rise of the tyrants and *condottieri*—were favourable to individualism, and this development of one's own personality made it possible to recognise what was individual in others. But in my opinion the unrestricted individualism of the types just mentioned is rather a continuing form of feudal individualism, deriving from the social system of orders and characteristic of the knighthood of the Middle Ages, which recognised no restrictions except those imposed on it by its order. In the *condottiere* there is also something of the early capitalist *entrepreneur* and of the adventurer-type. It is the revolutionary merchant, breaking through social barriers with the help of his wealth and creating a new and recognised class, or being accepted into an old one who paves the way for a bourgeois individualism. It is this economic calculation with which he must operate (even though in this early period it is rarely found in its pure form) which may be considered as the strongest contrast to the uncontrolled aristocratic individualism. Refutation of Burckhardt's theory of the heroic individualism of the Renaissance are to be found, though developed exclusively from the standpoint of the history of ideas, in Troeltsch (*Renaissance una Reformation*) and Burdach (*op. cit.*). For the relation between the individualism of the Renaissance in Burckhardt's sense and that of the feudal knights of the Middle Ages, cf. Huizinga, *op. cit.*

period of the upper middle class of Florence during the thirteenth century, and although its intensity diminished in some directions during the fourteenth, it is felt all the more clearly in others, even if continually fused with the rational factor. It shows itself in various ways; sometimes in a reckless adventurousness, sometimes in an emphasis on sentiment, sometimes in a hankering after the seigneurial manner of life; according to the different spheres in which it appeared, diverse names can be given to it. Its variations are many, and it can only be brought, by a rough generalisation, under some sort of common denominator. During the period we are considering these two components of the attitude to life, the rational and the irrational, are in a continuous state of conflict and adjustment; no strict line of demarcation can be drawn between them, for they blend with one another to form the most varied compromises; some touch of adventurousness, for instance, is indispensable to even the most calculating of great merchants. Among the upper bourgeoisie, the rational factor ultimately proved the stronger; in its own way it absorbed the irrational, whose elements were nevertheless continuously existent and clearly recognisable even if they tended to vary in intensity.

In the field of religious sentiment, it goes without saying that even this powerful class sought to feel themselves close to God. But they now drew much exterior support from the Curia, effectively grasped the practical use of the mendicant Orders, and of good works, and no longer retained a belief emotional enough to require, in their relationship to the Almighty, the element of personal ecstasy. A composed, self-confident aloofness sufficed, while at the same time the cult of the saints as mediators was fully allowed for. This sobriety, this religious detachment, as it were, was supported by the Church with her emphasis on dogmatic faith and aided by the diversion of the mendicant Orders into paths useful both to the Church and the upper bourgeoisie.

We have already considered the numerous compromises the Church made with the upper middle class in economic, social and political matters; we have seen that at the same time she upheld in principle her own ideals, generally in the form of reservations. For, given the close relations between these two parties, the maintenance of ecclesiastical-religious ideals in a pure form was of the greatest importance, as they had to hold sway, even if only ideologically, over the practical difficulties relentlessly presented by everyday life. The upper middle class believed on the one hand in practical everyday life, in which they ruthlessly exacted their claims, and on the other in the religious ideal—yet each on a different plane of thought. Though the upper bourgeoisie were perfectly realistic in their recognition of the definite advantages which accrued from their alliance with the Curia and from the activity of the mendicant Orders, their own religious ideals, that is, those of the Church, were nevertheless an ever-present factor. The alliance with the Curia naturally prompted an emphasis upon the ideal of the immunity of the Church as an institution. Furthermore, the privileged position accorded to the mendicant Orders by the middle class sprang from the firm belief that in this sinful world their pious ascetic life was essential for the salvation of the laity; the upper middle class strove, in making this ideal of life possible by their large bequests to monasteries, to save their own souls, and no acts of impiety or lack of asceticism on the part of the friars could have made them waver in their belief. Similarly, behind the practical collaboration of the Church and the upper middle class in good works lay the desire of this prosperous social section to obtain salvation—in other words, the ideal of charity. But, in accordance with their general views and interests, even these religious ideals of the upper bourgeoisie were free from any trace of exaggerated emotionalism; they were sober and moderate. They approved the ideal of an ascetic, but not of a truly propertyless, monasticism. Only if the mendicant Orders accepted this monastic ideal were the upper bourgeoisie ready to support them; for only then would they be supporting themselves.

The Church and the mendicant Orders used to the full their close relationship with the upper middle class (and indeed with the middle class as a whole) to exercise a cardinal influence on their private lives, on their manner of thought, and to a great extent on their culture. In the fourteenth century this was in its essentials an ecclesiastical culture. Everything in the last resort was subordinated to religion, even though in a temperate and rational manner. It is characteristic of the complex mentality, embracing different levels of thought, among the members of this section that they felt no consciousness of any opposition between the Church's interpretation of the world, the inter-relation of all phenomena in terms symbolic of the coming Kingdom of God, and their own ways of thought, which recog-nized the causal relationship of individual events. It is merely a question of a shift of stress; of whether we emphasise the fact that the Church became, to a high degree, secular and adapted herself to the bourgeois-capitalist mode of thought, or that the new bourgeois laity became ecclesiastical by taking up ecclesias-tical culture and winning a share in it themselves. Either state-ment would be equally true.

How did this general outlook of the Florentine upper middle class affect their art? As their thought centered round religion, their art was, perforce, above all religious. But it is natural that this religious art, all over Europe, and especially in Italy, should no longer have the mere symbolic, dogmatic and didactic char-acter it had assumed when produced in isolated monasteries before town life had really begun to flourish; as the urban bourgeoisie became pre-eminent, the purpose of art tended to gravitate towards a humanisation of the Divine. The Florentine upper middle class of the fourteenth century, however, now firmly seated in the saddle and more or less rationalist in out-look, had already passed beyond the early revolutionary phrase of middle-class art, which aimed chiefly at bringing God emo-tionally close to man. It was natural that this class should still need a devout art, but—and it is this that is essentially new—a tranquil art, not so devout as to be too emotionally disturbing. In such a manner did they wish to have their objects of wor-ship and veneration represented. Similarly, they liked to have their own religious ideals portrayed—for example, the pious friar (usually in the guise of a friar saint), charity (often in the form of good works)—by which the justification of their own everyday life was elevated into the stable, religious sphere. Such representations helped to make these ideals convincing and binding for the other social classes as well. Obviously, a class which, despite all its religious sentiment, was so sober-minded and so close to reality as was this could find satisfaction only in a religious art which already showed a considerable degree of fidelity to nature. So much only need be said here of the formal side of their artistic requirements.

As the Church's fundamental views roughly coincided with these, it was not difficult for her to adapt herself to these artistic demands, just as she did in numerous other fields. It is true of Europe generally that with the rise of the urban middle class an increasingly worldly Church took earthly life far more into account, and correspondingly changed her attitude to art. So did the Church come to participate in the formation of an art that humanised God and brought him nearer, even though she still preferred, as the conservative partner, symbol and allegory. Here again, however, the Church and the upper bourgeoisie compromised by adapting symbolical art to the latter's practical needs. The Church now generally laid increasing emphasis on this world as the scene of meritorious acts, as an effective preparation for the world beyond. She was therefore increasingly ready to permit art to incorporate earthly objects as God's creations, and even moderated her proscription of the portrayal of the human body. These various concessions were nowhere taken up and exploited so vigorously as in the art of the Florentine upper middle class, the most progressive in Europe and the most closely allied to the Pope.

Very different from the relationship between the upper middle class and the Church, which grew out of mutual dependence and expressed itself in the field of art in mutual voluntary concessions, was that between the same class and the lower bourgeoisie. From the upper bourgeoisie, keeping themselves in power by the crudest means, artistic concessions to the lower classes—concessions to their religious sentiment at once emotional and symbolically restricted, and to their cultural deficiency—could be expected only for very cogent reasons. Sometimes they were compelled to make them simply on account of the conservatism and lack of culture of certain of their own strata. This occurred rather on the part of their collective associations, such as guilds or fraternities, than with individuals. For—since general ideological changes are necessarily slow—the culturally conservative elements were, as a rule, in the majority. The upper bourgeoisie also inclined to accommodate themselves artistically at times when the political balance was tilted in favour of the petty bourgeoisie. For at such times their own lower levels, culturally closer to the lower middle class, usually made their influence felt. In these situations, therefore, their own security induced, or forced, the upper bourgeoisie to give way—for example, in the period between the collapse of the big banks and the revolt of the *ciompi*, and again immediately after that revolt. On the other hand, they were wont to give artistic expression to their increasing social and ideological sympathy with the now harmless nobility; but since the nobility at this period were culturally rather backward, the effects of such an approximation were not always to be distinguished from those of the approach towards the lower middle class.

If this is true of religious, it is even more so of secular art, now slowly emerging to an independent life. For the full share which the bourgeoisie took in ecclesiastical culture in no way precluded, during the fourteenth century, the growing secularisation of the cultural needs of their higher strata. So long as was possible, this secularisation took place within the old ecclesiastical and religious boundaries; and indeed, long after secular culture had achieved a certain independence, no marked contrast is to be discerned between it and religious culture. Here again it is a question of accent—of whether we emphasise the degree of secularisation or the degree of subordination to religion. The concrete desires and interests of the upper middle class in purely mundane spheres (economics, politics) can be linked up with the religious sphere through a "secular" art: they can be represented as equally desired by Heaven and so, as ideals, enjoying Heaven's sanction. Anything resembling a really widespread secular art could spring up only in a city as large and as economically advanced as Florence, with her highly developed upper bourgeoisie; it was less possible in Siena, still less in, for example, Perugia. Yet just at the very time when the worldly-cultural and hence the artistic needs of the upper bourgeoisie became particularly pronounced, at the end of the fourteenth century, both the speed of their development and the possibility of their consistently following their own bourgeois way were to a certain extent hindered, as we have seen, by a marked propensity for the old feudal ideals of chivalry.

The predilection for classical culture, on the other hand, which helped to sustain the self-confidence and national feeling of the new bourgeoisie was confined in the fourteenth century to an upper-bourgeois intellectual élite, and even then had not penetrated their consciousness sufficiently to receive distinct expression in the visual arts.

THE ART OF THE EARLY FIFTEENTH CENTURY: THE OUTLOOK ON WHICH IT IS BASED

In the first decades of the fifteenth century the oligarchy of the upper middle class, composed of a few wealthy families from the greater guilds, was at the zenith of its power. In this period of formal democracy, actual power was concentrated in these few families, particularly the Albizzi, the Uzzano and the Strozzi. By the year 1434 their rule had been broken by the wealthy Cosimo de' Medici, who at first made use of the support of the popolani and the lesser guilds. At the beginning of the fifteenth century, as we have seen, the upper bourgeoisie were already in a state of disintegration owing to the intense economic competition from abroad, even if to all appearances they were stronger than ever, with nothing to fear from the classes below. These few decades, during which the political power of Florence reached its highest point despite incipient economic decline, also saw the ideology and art of the upper middle class at their peak.

The rationalist element in the general outlook of the upper bourgeoisie, of which we spoke at length when dealing with the fourteenth century, was now most pronounced. The mentality of this class, particularly in its topmost ranks, was marked by an almost puritanical sobriety, accompanied in the political field by a "democratic" republicanism, and by great stress upon action. Hand in hand with this general attitude went an intense interest in antiquity—a clear sign of the awakening national feeling of the new bourgeoisie. In the first decades of the fifteenth century this interest was much keener than during the fourteenth, and the approach more understanding and scientific particularly as regards the rationalist elements of antique culture, produced in the heyday of the Greek and still more of the Roman middle class (that is, the time of the late Republic and of Augustus, and partly also the time of the enlightened absolutism of the first two centuries A.D.) In all ideological fields, particularly in the sciences, antiquity provided support for and accelerated their independent, organic development. We have already seen in sufficient detail that for the upper middle class there was no contradiction between the cult of the antique, a scientific spirit, on the one hand and religious sentiment on the other. Even the most far-reaching knowledge of empirical facts then possible was still quite compatible with religious feeling. But among the intellectual élite of the upper bourgeoisie, religious sentiment was now more dispassionate in tone than ever before. And these intellectuals, even if no others, carried their rationalism and their search for new legitimacies to the length of rejecting scholasticism and its casuistic "realism of detail," although in practice they were far from being hostile to the Church. The city chancellor Bruni is the typical representative of this endeavour to gain a systematic understanding of the world, with the help of classical knowledge. Nothing indicates more clearly the spiritual attitude of the moderns than the words Bruni places in the mouth of Niccoli in his *Dialogi ad Petrum Paulum Histrum:* "All things are wonderfully linked with one another, and the particular cannot be properly known without perception of the abundance out of which it has been taken." In their advance towards a casual comprehension of nature, the upper middle class made increasing use of the secular sciences which they had themselves created, particularly mathematics. Another indication of a more mundane spirit was the new attitude to literature among the most modern intellectuals. Hitherto value had been accorded only to the religious content. Now a new appreciation of form began to appear, and a preference for simplicity and clarity of style, which signified not only the possibility of a profane content, but even more that the religious content was now receiving a more worldly interpretation.

An art in accordance with the outlook of the intellectual élite of the upper middle class was bound to be very novel in character. More than ever before, it became secular and life-affirm-

ing, expressed action and energy, was sober, logical and cal-
culated; in religious art these new tendencies were particularly
strongly marked. Even in this period of extreme rationalism
in art we cannot speak of an irreligious spirit, but only of a
relatively secular interpretation of the religious content. The
achievements of the profane sciences, of mathematics, such as
linear perspective, were now applied to art, religious art included. The study of antiquity also encouraged in art the exact
study of nature and facilitated the search for rules and laws,
for new principles of arrangement.

But, as we have already seen, this highly developed rationalism
was to be found only among the most progressive intellectual
élite of the upper middle class, the most secular, the most self-
confident. And, as the economic and social basis necessary for
this ideology was very soon to change, this scientific world of
ideas, dependent as it was on the help of antiquity, could expand
in a really consistent way, that is, in a modern, bourgeois sense,
only during a very short period.

Moreover this élite represented only a comparatively shallow
stratum at the summit of the upper bourgeoisie. Beneath the
surface, the class as a whole was undermined and no longer
capable of organic development; all their enterprises were increasingly dominated by the speculative factor. This inner sense
of insecurity, as a result of incipient economic decline, found
ideological-religious expression among the majority of the upper
class in a greater or lesser degree of emotionalism, even though
rationalist elements were undoubtedly still active. Since the
upper bourgeoisie were now on the down-grade and shrinking
in numbers, the culturally conservative majority of the class
involuntarily drew spiritually nearer to other bourgeois sections
beneath them, which equally stregthened the tendency towards
the emotional. The Observance movement, so influential in this
period, also illustrates the approach of the various sections to
one another; it did not appeal only to the lower sections, like
the "Poverty crusade" in the previous century. Another cardinal
factor acting in the same irrational direction was the adoption
by the middle class of an aristocratic manner of life—again as a
result of their lack of certitude.

The self-assurance of the puritanical upper bourgeoisie increasingly lost its power of resistance to the preciosity and splendour of the aristocratic and courtly. The upper middle class, under the actual economic and ideological conditions, regarded the old feudal standard of life of the knights as a distinguished corollary of the actual calling by which they had made their money. Intermarriage and fusion of the wealthy middle class with the nobility also had an influence. Furthermore, the transference of weight from the woollen to the luxurious silk industry strengthened this tendency. But, of course, for all this, it was not simply a question of a mere revival of the mode of life of the landed, feudal nobility, which had previously developed naturally and inevitably out of the conditions of the time. The new inclination of such a conduct of life, for imitating feudal habits, originated in a yearning after nobleness, was parvenulike and necessarily playful in many respects. Nevertheless, the upper middle class, who built their villas in the surroundings of Florence, enjoyed nature with a new, more conscious intensity unknown to the feudal nobility.

So both factors, the antique as well as the neo-feudal, had greatly augmented among the upper bourgeoisie at the beginning of the fifteenth century. Though opposed in principle, these two ideologies could very well be reconciled in practice. In general, the two outlooks, that of the ideologically most progressive and that of the less progressive sections of the upper middle class, struggled against, interpenetrated, formed compromises with each other. The resulting mentality of the average member of the upper bourgeoisie was a "fantastic" transposition of antiquity, a kind of ideological middle way, a feudal-"antique" outlook with the main emphasis on the feudal.

The conflicts and compromises of these ideologies, the bourgeois-"antique" and the neo-feudal, condition the increasingly independent secular art of the upper middle class and also redound upon the general character of their religious art. This is strongly affected by the cultural approximation, now inevitable, of the conservative part of the upper bourgeoisie to its less advanced sections. These latter strata, still largely constrained by the habit of symbolic thinking, were now, of course, in this period of their complete political impotence, more then ever inclined to religious emotionalism, which also found expression in art, so far as their passive situation allowed. In particular, the emotional religious ideals of the Observance movement, equally popular both in upper and lower sections, will now frequently be represented. The artistic result of the cultural approach of the upper middle class to the lower sections of the bourgeoisie—a process much more apparent in the early fifteenth than in the fourteenth century—was similar to that of their approach to the aristocracy: for both the aristocracy and the lower bourgeoisie, relatively backward culturally—their affinity in outlook consequently expressed itself in art as well—were prone to greater irrationality in their attitude than the upper bourgeoisie, though in varying nuances. So, apart from the art of the most progressive group of the upper middle class, there will occur between the other sections a certain equalisation within the framework of a more or less irrational, emotional art, into which, however, individual rationalist elements continuously penetrate from above. In spite of this equalising process considerable shades of difference will still appear according to the different strata—as this follows from their whole world of ideas. Emotionalism will show itself, on the aristocratic side, rather in a lyrical delicacy of mood, sometimes approaching preciosity; on the bourgeois side, in a greater animation, sometimes even in passionateness.

26   *Giovanni Rucellai*
A Quattrocento Father Advises his Sons

Visitors of the great cathedral Santa Maria Novella in Florence may have observed the name Giovanni Rucellai recorded on its façade by the architect Leon Battista Alberti. One of the most successful merchants of his day, Giovanni was instrumental in commissioning the construction of numerous monuments in his city. In the following selection from his diary one catches a glimpse of the interesting and often tumultuous world in which the great merchant princes of the Quattrocento lived. Above all, a reading of Giovanni's diary leaves one with the unavoidable impression that the very center of his universe was his family, and that all of his interests and concerns were subordinate to his uncompromising commitment to the welfare of his family. In his thumbnail biographic sketch of Palla di Nofri degli Strozzi, his own father-in-law, Giovanni betrays many of his ethical and practical commitments.

I do not advise you, Pandolfo and Bernardo [the author's two sons], to seek or desire public offices or a high political position. There is nothing which I consider less worthy or honourable than finding one's self in these public offices. Do you know why? They should not be prized or desired because of the dangers, the dishonesty, the injustices which go along with them, and because they are not durable and lasting, but rather bring infamy to those who do not deal properly with them. I do not say that it displeases me to see you honoured by being included in the lists of eligible officeholders, if for no other reason but to demonstrate clearly that you are not a political outcast. Yet, any other kind of life, every other condition has appealed to me more than the public life which must displease everyone: A life full of injuries, hatred and insults, replete with uneasiness, troubles and headaches; full of servitude, enmity, subject to every passing fad. What do we expect from those who labour and give their whole selves to the state? To advise, deliberate, beg this one, answer someone else, please yet another one, compete, inflict injuries, prostrate yourself while all this time never acquiring friendships but rather an infinity of enmities. A life of lies, of fiction, vanity and false pomposity, because the friendship of the people lasts only as long as does your service to them, and when you need help you can never find someone willing to live up to his word and promise. Thus, all one's hopes, beliefs and labour produce nothing but one's dam-

SOURCE. Giovanni Rucellai ed il suo Zibaldone, Vol. I, *Il Zibaldone Quaresimale*, edited by Alessandre Perosa. *Studies of The Warburg Institute*, Vol. 24 (London: The Warburg Institute, 1960), pp. 39–42 and 63–54. Translated for this volume by Anthony Molho. Reprinted by permission of The Warburg Institute.

age and ruin. Suppose that you enjoy a commanding position in the city. Of what use will it be to you? You will say: "I shall be able to surpass and excell over others, I shall steal having the law on my side, lighten my tax burden." Oh! What an iniquitous and cruel thing for you to wish to enrich yourself by impoverishing others! How may one, in fact, enrich oneself from the state except by robbing the commonweal and the individual citizens and subjects of the state? Not wishing to pay one's own tax and instead to impose it on others, always caring for one's own private gains without a thought to the public and individual damages one inflicts? You will always be in the midst of petitions, grievances, accusations, unjust, avaricious, quarrelsome men who fill your ears with suspicions, your soul with cupidity, your mind with doubts, fears, hatreds, and enmities. You will then be compelled to leave your own shop and your affairs in order to follow the wishes and ambitions of others. Now you have to staff offices, enact laws, provide for the city's income, its expenses, taxes, wars, treaties, discords; and always related to these are numerous deliberations and counsels which, however, never allow you, or anyone else, to do precisely as you wish. Each wants his desire and judgment to be sanctioned, insisting on the wisdom of his opinion. You, a politician, following the ignorance and arrogance of others, will acquire men's bad will, for if you please one man you are bound to displease a hundred others. Oh! Perilous ambition, misleading desires, not escaped and hated by everyone as they should be. All this happens because this kind of servility seems vested in a few honours. How stupid are men who appreciate such vaporous things, going about with trumpets preceding them, that they are willing to abandon their own true repose and freedom. Oh! They are mad, avaricious, and tyrannical for they cannot tolerate that others be their equals; they do not wish to live without pushing and surpassing the weaker and those who are nobler and more meritorious than themselves. As a result they want an exalted political position. In order to obtain control of the government they subject themselves to every imaginable danger, and even expose their persons to the risk of violent death. They consider it honourable to partake of conspiracies with other presumptuous and arrogant men. They do not know how to live with good people, appreciating neither honesty nor justice. They consider it more important to become wealthy by appropriating the wealth of the Commune. What bestiality! Men worthy of every contempt, who seek to improve your position and wealth with so much perversity, while causing untold damage to others. Certainly, whoever devotes himself so wholeheartedly to the administration of public offices should be considered the worst kind of citizen; nor can he ever be content, or acquire a peaceful soul, for chances are that he already is of a cruel disposition. What sort of satisfaction can a politician have, forced as he is all day to look at thieves, spies, detractors, perpetrators of every kind of scandal and falsity? You, therefore, being a pious man, will you still desire an eminent political position? Will you go searching for it? You will say yes, because you will consider it honourable to suffer these disadvantages in order to punish the evildoers and to favour the good men. Will you then, in order to punish them, become the most evil one yourself? According to my way of thinking he who is not content with his own condition is not a good man; he who aspires to acquire that which belongs to others is even worse; and the worst man is the one who desires public offices in and of themselves, without considering any individual or communal damages which he may be inflicting.

I do not deny that participation in the republic's affairs is not a most worthy enterprise, nor do I castigate him who, because of his excellence and his good works, honours his country by being just and honest. In fact, I say that a true honour is one which is appreciated by all citizens. But to do as they do: submit to this one, line up behind that one, form alliances, factions and conspiracies in order to surpass the most sagacious citizens; to desire to administer the state as if it were one's shop, appropriating its wealth and considering it as dowry for one's daughters, competing with one group of citizens while despising another; all these are dishonest things in a city. Therefore, my sons, I wish that you never desire an important political position in order to convert the treasure of the state into your own, for such an action is not good and I shall not approve it. He who aspires to a political position with this goal in mind has always been destroyed by the state itself regardless of the power of ingenuity which he might command. Everyone who has tried to ride this horse has always fallen from it, and the higher his position, the greater his blow and the more complete his ruin. All of history is replete with such examples. Oh! Misguided citizens, why are you ruining yourselves pursuing as you do with so much labour, attention, skill and dishonesty a high political position in order to amass wealth? And to whom do you wish to leave your patrimony? The greater the inheritance you leave for your children, the greater will be their burden, for nothing is more fragile than wealth. One must first teach children to comport themselves, limit their passions, solicit not only their own well being but also that of others and of their country, without ever neglecting their own affairs. Always you should wish to be benevolent, honest and just and never will you be dishonoured. Let others enjoy the ceremonies and the public offices, but also suffer exile and punishment. You, content with your own position desiring neither to elevate yourselves nor to acquire that which belongs to others, will not be upset by the fact that you do not enjoy political power. My dear sons! Leave alone all those who aspire to high political position. Curtail your ambitions and make sure to be wise and good providers, be happy with your family, and use the goods which fortune may have given you. Those living without vices, pursuing an honest and free life are appreciated and honoured sufficiently. Whatever fortune may concede to you should make you content.

Let me repeat that the act of governing is notable and praiseworthy. He is a true citizen who assumes office not of his own will, nor for his own advancement or grandeur, but when guided by reason, justice, prudence and has the approval of the good citizens—not with a view to becoming an overlord and superior to others, but in order to be of greater service. The good citizen wishes the good of all, he loves peace, equality, honesty, humility, the tranquility of the entire city, is happy in the pursuit of his own affairs, scorns avarice and uncontrollable passions and seeks to advance good understanding in his household and even more in his country. None of these qualities can be observed in those who are strong and who wish to be superior to others. The wisest men have said that the best citizens must take into their hands the government of republics and must bear the pains and inconveniences in order to serve the country, advancing the common weal and honouring the state. If, on the other hand, the good citizen stands on the sidelines the evil and ignorant men will be able to prevail with impunity and will pervert the rightful and just mode of life, administering poorly private and public affairs, causing the eventual demise of the state. I am of the opinion that in order to merit fame, a good name, and to be honoured with public dignities by one's fellow citizens, one must not renounce the state primarily so that he does not become the victim of some wretched citizen's envy and enmity. I should also say that I consider it necessary and salubrious for the city that abusers and thieves of public revenues and all those in general who maltreat the citizens of the government be exterminated. But because, as I have already said, one man alone cannot accomplish such a goal, and many are never in agreement on how to do it, I advise you to leave the affairs of government and the pursuit of high political office to whomever wishes to have them.

My dear sons, I would not advise you anything less than that with every effort and action you desire to be praised and honoured, to be useful to the republic so that, when the government is good and renders justice, your reputation will be such that the old, modest and solemn citizens will consent to having you in their company as a member of the highest public offices. I do not consider it an act of servility that the young men act as they must, by honouring their elders, following their counsel, seeking to amass name and dignity. Nor do I think that he who is solicitous of his country's affairs, as tiresome and exhausting as these may be, has a tyrannical outlook. Only by having such interests can a man acquire fame and glory. Man is not born to spend his life sleeping, but in order to act. Ingenuity, judiciousness, memory, reason, good counsel and all the other powers which we have are not given to us so that we may neglect them. All wise men agree that man's nature lends itself to doing and acting, so that he is indeed the measure of all things. Certainly, it is not in private hatreds but in public experiences that fame is born, the flame of virtue lit, and the glory of good men illuminated. So that, I do not blame him who by virtuous operations, with care and solicitude, with regard for good advice and the examples of the past, while also leading a good life, attempts to attain a public position equal to that of honest and upstanding citizens. It is in this manner that I should like you to live, and I fully expect and hope that you will do so. I also remind you that in order to attain honour there are many things which you will have to neglect, but these should not be of a substantial nature so that you will avoid neglecting your private interests while governing others. Do not overlook your own affairs for the sake of public concerns, for he who does not have enough at home will find even less outside of it. Public affairs, when administered honestly, are not substitutes for the needs of the family, nor do public honours feed the family at home. Make certain to conserve your private patrimony, so that you will have enough to meet your needs. Finally, seek public offices not when desire lures you, but rather when virtue and the recognition of your fellow citizens will allow you to do so.

THE HAPPIEST MAN IN THE WORLD

I was married only once, to Iacopa, Palla Strozzi's daughter. When I married her, which was in the month of May, 1428, messer Palla was the most powerful and outstanding citizen of our land. He also was the richest, and it was thought that in all of Christendom there was not a man wealthier than he. His holdings of Florentine government bonds were 200,000 florins, which at that time were negotiable at 51% of their face value; in addition, he had numerous possessions amounting to 80,000 florins, in addition to cash, houses and household effects including silver, books, and jewels both in the city and in his country estates. He collected more than 15,000 florins from rents, while his farms brought in 600 bushels of grain a year. All this patrimony was dissipated within a short time for two reasons: First, because in a ten year period, from 1423 to 1433 he paid the Commune for taxes, needed to finance the wars of those times, 660,000 florins; secondly, because of his exile to Padua in November, 1434, a result of the divisions which then existed among the inhabitants of the city.

I shall always remember that once, when preparing for my wedding, I met in the street that famous poet, messer Leonardo [Bruni] of Arezzo; being a kind man, he came to me, congratulated me as is customary on such occasions and said: "Best wishes to you." Among other things he said: "You have become related to the happiest man, not only of our city, but of all time, because he is endowed with all seven parts of happiness; all other happy men in the world have always lacked at least one." He recounted to me these seven parts, and I shall note them below in the order in which I heard them:

First, for having been born in as noble and worthy a country as there is in the universe.

Secondly, for being of noble blood. The house of the Strozzi is most worthy, his wife was a Strozzi herself, his mother a Cavalcanti, his sisters and daughters married into the most distinguished Florentine families.

Thirdly, for having a beautiful family of female and male members.

Fourth, for being well-built and healthy. It had been 50 years since he had a fever. His countenance was so gentle that all men who met him immediately were attracted to him.

Fifth, for being rich, and having a legitimately earned patrimony.

Sixth, for being thoroughly well versed in Greek and Latin.

Seventh, for being well-loved and very highly esteemed as a result of his own goodness and excellence, his reputation extending far beyond the city.

27   *Alessandra Macinghi negli Strozzi*
          A Mother's Advice

In 1422, Alessandra Macinghi married Matteo Strozzi, a member of one of the most illustrious Florentine households. Exiled from Florence in 1434, widowed the next year, Alessandra assumed the difficult task of bringing up her seven children, deprived of her husband's support and plagued by difficult financial conditions. Throughout her life (d. 1470), she maintained a steady correspondence with her eldest son, Matteo, a successful merchant in Naples. In the letters of this simple and not well-cultivated woman, one has a chance to observe much the same phenomenon one discerns in the pages of Giovanni Rucellai's diary: the family was the center of the spiritual and practical world in which the merchants and their families existed during the entire 14th and 15th centuries.

To Filippo Strozzi, in Naples.
In the name of God. On the 24th day of August, 1447.

Dearest son, I had one of your letters dated 16 July recently, and I answer you with this. To begin with, I inform you that, with the grace of God, we have promised our Caterina to the son of Parente di Pier Parenti, a 25 year old youth, only son of a good family. He is rich, sober and conscientious and owns a silk manufactury. They [the Parenti] are moderately prominent politically, the father having been a member of a College[1] only a short time ago. I am giving her a dowry of 1,000 florins: that is 500 florins which is due to her in May, 1448 from the *Monte delle Doti*;[2] the other 500 I shall give her in a combination of cash and presents when she gets married which I hope will be in November, if it pleases God. This money is partly yours and partly mine. Had I not chosen this husband for her she could not have gotten married this year, for whoever takes a wife wants money, and I could find no one willing to have part of the dowry in 1448 and the rest in 1450. Since I am giving her

---

[1] One of the two important offices whose members advised the priors of the city.
[2] A system, instituted in 1425, whereby parents of young girls deposited a sum of money at the Communal Treasury, collecting the capital and interest when the girl was married. In the case of Caterina, half her dowry of 1,000 florins was due to her in 1448 and the other half in 1450.

SOURCE. Alessandra Strozzi, *Lettere di una gentildonna fiorentina del secolo XV ai figliuoli esuli,* edited by Cesare Guasti (Florence: Casa Editrice G. C. Sansoni, 1877), letter No. 1, pp. 3–9. Translated for this volume by Anthony Molho.

now 500 florins in cash and presents, I shall collect the money in 1450 provided she is still alive then. Surely, we have concluded this affair all to the better, for she is 16 years old and it was not advisable to wait any longer to marry her. We tried to place her in a nobler and politically more powerful family but we would have needed 1400 or 1500 florins, and this would have meant our ruin. I do not know if the girl is pleased, for it is true that, with the exception of political advantages, this marriage has little else to recommend it. I, having considered everything, decided to prepare the girl and not be too fussy, for I am sure that she will be as happy as any other girl in Florence. Her father- and mother-in-law, being overjoyed, think of nothing but how to please her. Oh! Not to speak of Marco, her fiancé, who always tells her: "Ask me what you want." When she became engaged he gave her a brilliantly red cape made of heavy silk and velvet and a matching dress, both made of the best material available in the city. He had it prepared in his shop. Also, he had made a necklace of plumes and pearls which cost 80 florins. To go under it there is an arrangement of two strands of pearls costing at least 60 florins so that, when she leaves the house, she will be wearing clothing more than 400 florins worth. He is ordering for her a red velvet dress with large sleeves with heavy lining which he will give her when they get married. And he is also having made a pink petticoat decorated with pearls. He is never satisfied having things made for her, for she is beautiful and he wants her to look at her best. In truthfulness, there is not another girl in all of Florence as beautiful as she is, and in the opinion of many she has all the requisites of beauty. May God grant her health and favour for a long time, as is my wish.

As for sending Matteo away, I do not desire to do so now. Not only is he too young, but he also keeps me company and I can ill afford to stay alone without him, particularly after Caterina gets married; then I would be too lonely. As of now I do not have the courage to send him. If he wants to be good I shall keep him here. In any case, he is not subject to being taxed until he is 16, and he was only 11 last March. He has already learned his arithmetic and now he is learning to write. I intend to place him as an apprentice in the shop, and he will spend the winter there. Then we shall see what he wants to do. May God grant him the excellence which he will need.

Of the communal affairs I advise you that I have a debt of 240 florins and I have been pestered by no fewer than four different offices charged with collecting for the Commune. In the last six months I have done nothing but go from one office to another. Now, with the grace of God, I have been able to reach an accommodation with them, so that beginning in February I have been paying about 9 florins a month. It is thought that the new tax will be issued in October. If they do as they say and do not impose a tax on estimated income of widows and minors I shall have to pay a maximum of two florins, and maybe not that much. With the Duke's death[3] it is thought that we shall not have to pay many taxes, provided that the king of Aragon[4] does not bother us. But he has already started moving near Monte Varchi, occupying a castle called Cennina. When they took it we thought that we would have had it back the next day. They have already been there for three weeks and will stay longer because inside the castle there were many peasants with supplies to last them for one year. Before we can reconquer it we shall probably have to spend more than 40,000 florins. May God provide for our needs.

Caterina asks that you send her a bit of that soap; and if you find some special water or any other good cosmetic, she begs you to send it soon by a trusted person so it does not get lost or spoiled on the way.

Do not wonder if I do not write to you often, as I am immersed in Caterina's affairs. I shall compensate for my silence when Matteo learns to write. You should not emulate me. Send me a letter with every courier, even if you say no more than that you and Niccolò[5] are well. I do not know how you are conducting yourself in your affairs. God knows of my unhappiness when I learned that you could not come to see me while visiting Livorno; such displeasure can only be expressed orally

---

[3] Filippo Maria Visconti, Duke of Milan, who died on 13 August, 1447.
[4] Alfonso of Aragon, king of Naples.
[5] Matteo's cousin who had offered to Alessandra and her family much valuable help during their exile.

and not in writing. May it please God that I see you again in good health before I die. Above all, my son, make certain to behave well so that, while last year you caused me so much grief by your poor behavior, now you may give me consolation. Consider well your position, and reflect upon all the benefits that Niccolò has rendered to you. You will then realize that you should kiss the earth on which he walks. You are more obligated to him than to your father and mother for all that he has done for you; no one else would have done the same. You should not be ungrateful to him for his past and present favours. I do not wish to say anything more, for you must be able to understand. You are not a little boy any more, as last July you were already 19. Enough. Above all, save some money. You will need it because your conditions are even worse than you think. Nor do I wish to say anything more in this letter. May God keep you from evil. I am not writing to Niccolò since he has already been notified by Giovanni and Antonio. Greet him for us. And if you are the treasurer of your company behave honourably, keep your hands clean so that I may not suffer more pain than I already did in the past.

28   *David Herlihy*
 Civic Humanism at Pistoia

Frederick Antal had ascribed the development of the 14th and 15th century art to the "rationalism" and sophistication of that city's upper bourgeoisie. David Herlihy, in examining the development of humanism in Pistoia, one of Florence's subject cities, came to the conclusion that this new intellectual movement, far from having its roots in the self-confidence, optimism, and "rationalism" of the Renaissance, was deeply embedded in the unsettled social and economic conditions of that age. The notion of excellence attained in the midst of civil society, encouraged by humanists such as Salutati and Bruni, served as a diversion and an outlet to men whose lives were constantly threatened by

*physical calamities, while their well-being was made even more un-
certain by excessive taxation and the vagaries of an unpredictable and
often arbitrary government.*

CIVIC HUMANISM AT PISTOIA

One of the colorful customs of fifteenth-century Pistoia was
the summoning at the birth of a baby of an expert to predict,
apparently through consulting the afterbirth, the child's future.
Antonio Rospigliosi secured such analyses twice, at the birth of
his sons Iacopo in 1461 and Tommaso in 1466. Commercial
success and brilliant marriage were the common ingredients of
such predictions, but the expert said also concerning Iacopo
that the boy would not die a "bad death" but would grow up to
be a "beautiful speaker," a fortunate man and a "spender."

Beautiful speech and a willingness to spend may not appear
the most appropriate virtues for sons of a mercantile family, but
Iacopo's father was pleased to hear this future foretold for his
baby; "may God grant it to him" he wrote in his *Richordi.*

Good speech and spending, an admiration of rhetoric and of
splendid living, are indeed two of the outstanding characteristics
of the lay culture of the fifteenth century.

Rhetorical skill and a magnificent presence were useful if not
essential to a patrician son for three reasons. The defense of his
family and friends and the upholding of the dignity of his house
still required, in the fifteenth century, participation in communal government even in a subject city such as Pistoia, and
rhetoric and magnificence helped make that participation effective. Moreover, for many patricians, particularly from the older
families, government service offered a honorable and remunerative career at a time when other professional opportunities
were few and unrewarding. Finally, for the patricate as a whole,
rhetorical theory was at the basis of a new concept and standard
of nobility, to which the great families could aspire, in spite of

SOURCE: David Herlihy, *Mediaeval and Renaissance Pistoia* (New Haven:
Yale University Press, 1967), pp. 258–261 and 263–268. Reprinted by permission of Yale University Press and the author.

their disparate backgrounds, and which in turn could offer them justification for the privileges they enjoyed and the distinctions they claimed.

For beautiful speech, according to traditional theories of rhetoric, included not only verbal dexterity, *eloquentia*, but learning and wisdom as well, *sapientia*. In humanist thought, the most useful and honorable of men were those who could apply abstract learning to particular human situations, convince their fellows of the proper course of actions to be taken, and so serve their communities. They were the experts in politics, the moral philosophers, and the lawyers, who combined their general knowledge with the persuasive rhetoric needed to make it socially beneficial.

"For how great is the dignity of those who judge or govern others or who assist the governors, who teach the judges, and how great the dignity of patrons, who prosecute or defend in cases, is clear to all."

Moral philosophy and law, made effective by rhetoric, assured the conservation of human society, the formation of good citizens, and thus embraced all virtues.

The great dignity attached to community service could also be used to justify the position, privileges and distinctions of the fifteenth-century patriciate. As we have seen, that patriciate, while largely stable, had been recruited from disparate origins, from old magnate houses, from old *popolani* families, and was still in the fifteenth century not entirely closed to new men. Claims of birth and lineage alone could not confer distinction upon such a group, particularly since many originally noble families were abandoning their former status in order to assume the politically more advantageous position of *popolani*. But the humanists were simultaneously developing a concept of nobility which applied to and appealed to such men. In the early fifteenth century a humanist of Pistoia, Buonaccorso da Montemagno, stated that ideal as well as any contemporary writer.

The history of Buonaccorso's own family was itself fairly typical. It had originally been a magnate house. But it adopted popular status in 1332 and thus, like many other once noble families, consciously abandoned the pretense that blood or birth along brought social superiority. Buonaccorso himself produced, among many writings, a tract "On Nobility." It was posed in the form of a debate between two Romans of the classical period, both arguing before the Senate for the hand of the beautiful Lucretia. One of the suitors, Publius Cornelius, spoke of his distinguished ancestors; the other, Gaius Flaminius, described only his services to Rome:

"For when I understood that human skills are so much the more glorious when placed at the service of the Republic. I gave myself entirely to my fatherland. Never thereafter did I cease to think of its safety and prosperity, fearing no labor and no danger, which might bring it glory and security."

Gaius' public service thus proved his superiority as a man, and of course he was given Lucretia's hand.

All this, of course, has the redolence of oil, and Buonaccorso's views were no more than a humanist commonplace. But the strength of its appeal to the social and professional pride of the patriciate is understandable. When Antonio Rospigliosi died, the chief consolation for his sons was not even so much his religion and piety, but the gratitude shown by the city for his public service. In other words, the patricians, most of them now of relatively assured position, were given an ideal to justify their privileges, and the best of them were not remiss in living by it.

The high prestige accorded by the humanists to public service seems to have been something more than a reflection of their own social and professional associations. May we not also discern in it a parallel with the contemporary changes in religious piety? One of the most marked developments of the age was, as we have seen, the growth of social conscience, the effort to define Christian responsibility in the light of existent social conditions. In secular culture too, there is evident an effort, through the art of politics, to apply another body of largely traditional, abstract learning, philosophy and law, to the concrete problems of social life. The culture of the Renaissance, in both its religious and secular manifestations, included a common effort to place the accumulated knowledge and wisdom of the Middle

Ages at the service of the community, in the interest of achieving a higher, more ethical, more virtuous and more rewarding form of civic life.

This fundamental idea, that the end of learning should be the service of men in their present world and society, was expressed with some passion by Coluccio Salutati:

"I, however, to speak the truth, would say boldly and freely admit that I would leave you and to those carrying speculation up to the sky all other truths without envy or argument, if the truth and reason of human things would be left to me. You may be full of speculation, but I would abound in the goodness by which I may be made good. . . . I would always be engaged in doing things, I would consider the final end: whatever I do, am I helping myself, my family, my relatives and (what above all is to be preferred) am I helping my friends, am I useful to the fatherland? And I would so live that I would contribute by both example and works to human society. In all these things I shall always think is that supreme happiness, which we cannot but wish for, and which we cannot desire for any reason other than itself."

The secular culture of the Renaissance also shares with the religious a pronounced taste for splendid display. This is the age when the commune of Pistoia, along with the governments of other cities, waged an uneven battle againt the luxurious fashions of its citizens, especially its women. In 1332, 1360, 1439 and 1558 sumptuary laws were passed to restrain the lavishness, each one sterner, though apparently no more successful, than the last. According to G. B. Tedaldi, the women of Pistoia were among the worst offenders in Tuscany.

The great events in the history of the patrician families—births, knightings, marriages, even funerals—were all occasions for public exhibitions of magnificence. In April 1388 the celebrations accompanying the knighting of Giovanni Panciatichi lasted seven days. Weddings were no less lavish. Agniola, one of Antonio Rospigliosi's daughters, was married in a multiple wedding the like of which, her father recorded with satisfaction, Pistoia had never seen before. Agniola's groom and his three brothers were all married on the same day, and all conducted their brides to the same house. At the principal tables at the wedding feast, there were seated no fewer than 94 men and women, "not counting some of their brothers, because they did not sit at table." At the lower tables 300 persons and more "of every type" ate and drank to the health of the spouses. The festivities lasted a week, and Antonio had reason to call this a "dengnio paio di noze" [a fitting pair of weddings].

In 1415, the scion of one of Pistoia's most distinguished patrician families, Lotto di Gualfredi Cancellieri, made an accounting of his own wedding expenses, which well illustrates the extravagant façade a great household presented to the world. The context in which this document has survived is itself noteworthy: it was part of Lotto's tax declaration. His motives in listing these large expenses for the benefit of tax assessors are less than clear. To present one's self as wealthy and a great splender is rarely advisable at assessment time. Was it sheer pride that prompted Lotto to reveal the fortune that his wedding had cost him? It is more likely that Lotto believed that the assessors would recognize that these were necessary expenses for a great family, without which it could hardly expect to maintain its station.

To present a proper appearance at his bride's house when the wedding agreement was signed, Lotto needed a company of eight horsemen, and this and other visits made to the girl cost him in all 18 florins—more than a year's salary for a well-paid artisan. Clearly, Lotto did not appear casually at his fiancée's home. In wedding gifts he gave his bride six dresses, some embroidered with silver and lined with fur, and all—he carefully noted—of excellent cloth, a petticoat, doublet and cloak, several chests filled with girdles and garlands, a silver chain, rings of diamond, sapphire and pearl, an inlaid bedstead, mattresses, bed clothes, towels, pans and other bedroom furnishings, and additional girdles, which his bride gave as gifts to her relatives.

The culminating ceremony in a Renaissance wedding, following a Mass in the morning (the "messa dei congiunti"), was the procession of the bride to the house of the groom.

"Also I spent [Lotto related in his ungrammatical statement] in the marriage when I brought her when I made the marriage of my own expense in sending for her and on the way and through the rooms and for horses in all I spent 65 florins."

The cost of bringing Lotto's bride to her new home would have paid the salaries of perhaps six servants for an entire year. The total cost of his marriage, not including celebrations afterwards, was 574 florins. Such a sum would have made a man wealthy according to the Catasto of 1427.

This public extravagance of Pistoia's great families is the more remarkable, as it often concealed a mean existence behind the locked doors of their homes. Lotto Cancellieri, describing how he had embellished his bedroom with new furnishings for his ride, stated that there had been "gran bisogna"—"great need"—for the refurbishments. His furniture had been lost when soldiers were garrisoned in his house during the "war of Sambuca." But the war of Sambuca had been fought more than a decade before his declaration, in 1401–03! For all the intervening time, his bedroom and house had apparently been left in shambles.

Public exhibitions of splendor were, for many of Pistoia's patrician families, quite clearly a matter of social and even professional need. A magnificent presence might influence the decisions of councils, upon which family welfare could depend. And men who wished to represent cities and princes in high public office had to cultivate a brilliant appearance. When messer Bartolomeo Bracciolini journeyed to Perugia in the early fifteenth century, apparently to assume public office, he had to borrow 500 florins from Florentine merchants, to assure himself a dignified and impressive "andata" and entry. Messer Giovanni Panciatichi, whose knighting in 1388 had been celebrated for seven days, similarly spent 500 florins while serving at Ferrara, undoubtedly to maintain a splendid household, and comparable sums in the other cities where he held office. At another point in his colorful career, he was robbed of "money, horses, cloth, silver and arms" worth more than 600 florins.

Moreover, this love of magnificent display, which parallels a similar taste for a sumptuous liturgy in the age's religious life, may also be considered a kind of diversion and escape, not only for the patrician families themselves but for the populace which witnessed their processions and often participated in their feasts. In spite of frequent plagues, the young adult of Pistoia did not need, as we have seen to be excessively troubled by the prospect of his own imminent demise; children and the aged accounted for the bulk of the population's tremendous losses. Still, his life was led in the midst of death, and could this have failed to impress him? Not terror of his own immediate departure, but awareness of death's ultimate, inevitable triumph, of old age and decrepitude which would prepare its way, seems to have weighed upon his thoughts. The psychological antidote for this melancholy experience was to be a fortunate man and a spender, to live, in pretense and imagination if not in reality, a magnificent life. And so, for example, in Giovanni Boccaccio's *Decameron*, the young narrators sought solace from the plague by telling tales largely concerned with youth, nobility, love, wit, humor and success. Franco Sacchetti, in his own preface to the *Trecentonovelle*, similarly stated that people wished to hear pleasant tales which would "bring comfort" amid so many human miseries. Italian life as depicted in the abundant *novelle* literature of the fourteenth and fifteenth centuries, for all its earthly flavor, remains an idealized reconstruction. in which the cruel realities of the age, the appalling death of children, the *maninconia dei padri*, the ravages of time, the ill-concealed miseries, the harshness and the violence, find scant attention.

In the fourth part of his great book, Jacob Burckhardt defined the essence of Renaissance culture as "the discovery of the world and of man." When measured against the experience of this one small town of Pistoia, the phrase has a certain validity, although only in part. Pistoia's citizens (or at least, the more sensitive of them) showed in their charity and service a new commitment to the welfare of their fellows and their community. By their actions they were implicitly accepting the humanist proposition that both religion and learning imposed a primary obligation to benefit society. To this extent, it may well be said that they showed a new consciousness and awareness of their social surroundings. But at the same time, in their festivals and ceremonies, their literature and art, they strove not to depict the world as it was, but rather to construct diverting and refreshing visions of an idealized, sublime and splendid life. And, in cultural history, it is for their imaginative and enchanting explorations of ideal worlds, rather than for any supposed rediscovery of the harsh nature which surrounded them, that the men of this age deserve to be remembered.

THE COURT AND THE COURTIER

29   *Lodovico Alamanni*
          The Making of a Courtier

*After an 18-year period of republican rule, Florence, in 1512, fell
into the hands of the Medici family. Shortly thereafter, the head of
that powerful and eminant clan was elected to the Papacy assuming
the title with the name of Leo X. Control of the city, therefore, was
relegated to a younger Medici, Lorenzo, Duke of Urbino, who was
immortalized by his compatriot and contemporary, Michelangelo
Buonarrotti. Obviously, one of the most pressing problems confronting the new ruler was the creation of the social and political conditions
that would render the rule of one family palatable to men not accustomed to living under tyrannical governments. Lodovico Alamanni, a
member of the Medici faction, addressed himself directly to this issue
in the letter which he sent to Lorenzo in 1516.*

So that it may not be said that I am one of those better at
criticizing the views of others than offering my own advice, I
wish to suggest in what manner Your Excellency will be able to
maintain more securely and govern more efficiently the Florentine state. First, having considered everything, whoever wishes
to maintain that state must do so with the aid of the Florentine
citizens by governing with their support. Every other way is

SOURCE. Lodovico Alamanni, "Discorso sopra il fermare lo stato di Firenze
nella devozione de' Medici," in Rudilf von Albertini, *Das Florentinische
Staatsbewusstsein im Ubergang von der Republik zum Prinzipat* (Bern:
Franeke Verlag, 1955), pp. 368–371. Translated for this volume by Anthony
Molho. Reprinted by permission of Franeke Verlag.

much too difficult and dangerous, for in case even of a small
war Your Excellency would need three armies: one to oppose
the citizens of Florence, one to fight the enemies, and one to
defend the state of Urbino. If, on the other hand, you have a lot
of citizens who were your supporters, particularly if they are
those with spirit and brain, without preoccupation for any
internal matters, Your Excellency would be able not only to
defend the city from outsiders, but could also assault all your
offenders suffering no embarassment in the process.

I know that when discussing the question of governing the
city, the men who supported actively the older Lorenzo the
Magnificent suggest that you use the ways employed by him
to govern the city peacefully and with honour. I also know that
others object by suggesting that times and conditions being
different one must devise novel ways, for the old ones will no
longer be adequate. For my part, I insist that, from that time to
the present, though the problems have increased in number,
they have not changed in substance. Surely, the ways of Lorenzo
being best for the older problems will also be best now. For new
problems there are always secure remedies, so that it should
be as easy to control the government now as it was then. As for
those who disagree and insist that those were easier times than
ours, they may say what they wish; reason should clarify all
questions.

They will say that the Magnificient Lorenzo the elder was
able to base his power on the support of the citizens who stood
by his family in 1434, '66 and '78. I respond that the present
government could sustain itself even better on a similar foundation, for there are numerous citizens who supported the Medici
not only then, but who have remained their friends in the
course of all adversities. If these men are not sufficient, His
Excellency the Duke will be able to earn the support of as many
citizens as he wishes, and these will embrace his cause even
more ardently than they supported Cosimo [de' Medici], his son,
or his grandsons, for you, being in a more advantageous position
than they were, will be able to grant more important benefits
than they could in the past.

These detractors will also say that in the times of Lorenzo
the Council was larger than now and that the citizens then

could identify more easily with the government. But I insist that this is a difficulty which can be overcome easily, for Florentine citizens can be divided into three categories: first, those men who are held in highest esteem, who are the most intelligent and the noblest, whose aspiration is to control the state and the government; the second group comprises those who are content to enjoy the honours of the city, occupying government posts without being worried about really governing the state; the men who make up the third group are entirely satisfied when they do not fear the imposition of extraordinary taxes, when the city is affluent and they can find work. It is my view that the potential of the present government is such that one will be able to satisfy more fully these three kinds of men than one could with the large Council. First, those who aspire to govern the state will be much more satisfied with the present form of government because now they will have a much greater amount of authority and reputation than they had in the past when they were considered the equals of dozens of other men. The second group, whose members are interested in possessing offices and acquiring honours, will also be satisfied if the public offices are filled by lot, for they have learned that scrutinies[1] treat them much more kindly than does a large Council. Moreover, the honours of the state, if Lorenzo's old methods are followed and if they are distributed justly, will appear to be much greater than those given by the large Council. Moreover, by dividing the honours in the following manner: once to this family, then to that other, always to the eldest and to the heads of families, those who are so honoured realize that they are contracting an obligation while the rest wait patiently for their turn. When, however, the honours were granted by lot in the Council, only fortune had her way: often all the honours were given to one family, all the rest having none, while frequently fortune quite unjustly favoured minor to elder brothers, and other such extravagances were current. Therefore, things will always be better regulated in Florence, to the greater satisfaction

---

[1] Lists of eligible officeholders; the names of all the individuals included in the scrutiny were placed in a bag, and when a vacancy had to be filled, a name was drawn from the bag. Such a system was meant to guarantee a measure of impartiality in staffing the various public offices.

of her citizens, when the governmental offices are filled by lot, and the honours distributed personally by just persons. Those other citizens for whom it is sufficient to go about their business without fearing the imposition of very high taxes, will also be more satisfied with a personal government than with the Council, for now, knowing that all decisions are made by one man, as long as this person enjoys their confidence, they will be at peace; on the other hand, during the days of the Council there was not a person who could promise them a thing. Therefore, the difficulties associated with the Council could be overcome fairly easily by following the remedies discussed above. If, nevertheless, there still remained some, regardless of their number, who in spite of the above provisions continued to prefer a popular to this government, they should not be feared as long as they are treated well. Because the difference between what they will and what they might have will not be large enough to make them feel that the risk of losing life and property is worth taking. Since they will not be in a position to undertake any innovations their discontent should not give rise to preoccupations. There will still be indigent, desperate and restless men; but these types of people exist in every state. Alone they can accomplish very little, while the rest of the people do not trust them, because no one will want to make company with ruined and inconstant men.

They will also say that Lorenzo's continuous presence in Florence, his use of civilian habits and customs, the fact that he conducted the affairs of state in the public palace, his coming to the square every day granting audiences easily and readily to whomever wished one; and his acquaintance with all the citizens made these latter think of him as a brother and not as someone superior to them. For this reason they loved him more, they were more content with him, and served him faithfully. Now, however, [continuous the argument of Alamanni's opponents] it is not possible to do any of these things, for being in such an exalted position His Excellency the Duke will find it inconvenient to serve the civilians of the state. For this reason, when wishing to see him, they will have to go and find him in his home, and wait for him to open his door to them. Though this is a most convenient arrangement for him, it is most alien to Florentine customs, so that it will be impossible to avoid the ill feeling of the citizens. This difficulty should be taken into account and thought of seriously, but it seems even larger to those who are unimaginative and do not rely on reason but draw their conclusions only from the examples of the past. Yet, as with all other problems, there is a remedy for this one also.

The fact that the Duke can no longer associate with the civilians is not something that will displease the citizens, for it is not injurious but useful to them. The greater the magnificence of his court is, the more easily he will be able to help them in their affairs. Actually, the Florentines are much more committed to some foolish notions than to the concept of liberty: they refuse, in fact, to be reverend to any individual in Florence, even if he merits their respect. They only honour the magistrates ill-willingly, and that they do because they have to. As a result they are by nature more opposed to the ways of a court than any other people. (Nevertheless, when they are outside of Florence, they do not behave in such a manner.) I believe that this is the origin of their view that it is improper to remove their hood[2] when greeting others. This laziness slowly became a habit, and from a habit it was made part of their nature. Probably for this reason, even when outside of Florence, they find it difficult to converse with princes. Old men would never be able to give up this fantastic notion, but the old are wise and the wise are not to be feared for they never undertake novelties. If, however, the prince so wishes, the young could be easily weaned from that habit and accustomed to courtesan manners. In order to do this, the prince should designate all those young men who in our city—either because of their qualities, or those of their father and families—should be kept in high esteem. He should then invite them, one at a time, and tell them that he would be pleased if they were to come and stay with him, and that he would give to all privileges and prerogatives convenient to him. No one would refuse such an invitation, and as soon as they came he should change their civilian clothes for a courtesan habit. Then he could enroll in

[2] A garment commonly worn by artisans and merchants.

his army those who are militarily inclined so that they would be
in the midst of many other Florentines of all conditions. On the
other hand, those who are well-read and intelligent should be
used as secretaries, emissaries and ambassadors—they, too,
should be honoured considerably. Finally, since some will be fit
neither for the army nor for the affairs of state, but rather they
will be inclined toward commercial and business enterprises, the
Prince could accommodate them in many of his other affairs,
one in charge of the Treasury, another at the Customs House,
and still others to keep his accounts and correspondence. By
doing so His Excellency would not have to incur additional
expenses for, in any case, he is obliged to have men in all those
offices, if not Florentines then foreigners. By using his Florentine
subjects he will seem to love his country more, he will be
following ways which will always bring him honour, and he
will be surrounded by men who will augment his own reputation
throughout the world. Beyond that, the benefit of such a system is that he will wean them from that system which now so
alienates them from his customs. For, those who for his Excellency's sake will give up their hood for a cape will be taking
something of a monastic oath, renouncing the republic, and
never again will they be able to depend on the graces and
benevolence of the people. As a result, their full ambition will
be channeled toward earning the favour of His Excellency.
They will be most happy for being chosen, paid and cared for,
they will feel that they are appreciated, and every man is content
where he finds profit and honour. Thus your friends will be all
those who can serve you most and who, if they were your
enemies, could hurt you considerably, because they possess all
the intelligence, spirit and reputation in the city. If ever you
have to wage war outside of Florence, having these men on
your side, you will enjoy the support of the pillars of your
state. Those who will stay in the city to govern it will be
either fathers, uncles or fathers-in-law of these young men,
and either for love or fear they will remain true and faithful.
Gradually, with the passage of years, if the same method of
electing and patronizing the young men is followed, placing
the administration of the city in the hands of those who now
are young but in the future will be old—all of them having

been educated and brought up according to your wishes—it will become impossible for our city to live without a prince who will sustain all. I am certain that in a brief time such a system will acquire such a reputation that he who is not among the elect will consider himself inferior even to the mob. It is also good to remember that it is always wiser to elect ten men who do not deserve such an honour than to omit two who do deserve it.[3]

In Rome, 25th day of November,
M.D.XVI.

30   *Baldassare Castiglione*
The Manners of a Courtier

Born in 1478 in the province of Mantua, Baldassare Castiglione dedicated his life to the pursuit of literary excellence and to serving some of the most powerful and influential signori *of his day. In both realms he acquired a widespread reputation. Charles V, the Hapsburg Emperor, described Castiglione as among the "mejores caballeros" of the world, while his literary name has been firmly secured by his famous essay,* Il Cortegiano. *Written between 1513 and 1518,* The Courtier *obstensibly reproduces a series of conversations held in the Palace of Urbino in 1507, under the aegis of the Duke Guidobaldo of Monte-feltro and his wife, Elisabetta Gonzaga. Surely, if any work of the first half of the* Cinquecento *succeeds in capturing the new aristocratic and courtly spirit that was becoming deeply entrenched in the various signorial courts of Italy,* The Courtier *must be considered to be that work. In the following selection, Castiglione presents an image of the ideal courtier.*

---

[3] That is, it is better to include among your favorites a few who possibly do not deserve that honour, than to exclude two or three very capable men who potentially could become formidable enemies of yours.

"Thus, I would have our Courtier born of a noble and genteel family; because it is far less becoming for one of low birth to fail to do virtuous things than for one of noble birth, who, should he stray from the path of his forebears, stains the family name, and not only fails to achieve anything but loses what has been achieved already. For noble birth is like a bright lamp that makes manifest and visible deeds both good and bad, kindling and spurring on to virtue as much for fear of dishonor as for hope of praise. And since this luster of nobility does not shine forth in the deeds of the lowly born, they lack that spur, as well as that fear of dishonor, nor do they think themselves obliged to go beyond what was done by their forebears; whereas to the wellborn it seems a reproach not to attain at least to the mark set them by their ancestors. Hence, it almost always happens that, in the profession of arms as well as in other worthy pursuits, those who are most distinguished are men of noble birth, because nature has implanted in everything that hidden seed which gives a certain force and quality of its own essence to all that springs from it, making it like itself: as we can see not only in breeds of horses and other animals, but in trees as well, the shoots of which nearly always resemble the trunk; and if they sometimes degenerate, the fault lies with the husbandman. And so it happens with men, who, if they are tended in the right way, are almost always like those from whom they spring, and often are better; but if they lack someone to tend them properly, they grow wild and never attain their full growth.

"It is true that, whether favored by the stars or by nature, some men are born endowed with such graces that they seem not to have been born, but to have been fashioned by the hands of some god, and adorned with every excellence of mind and body; even as there are many others so inept and uncouth that we cannot but think that nature brought them into the world

SOURCE. Baldasar Castiglione, *The Book of the Courtier*, Translated by Charles S. Singleton (New York: Doubleday & Company, 1959). pp. 28–32, 54–59, and 70–72. Copyright by Charles S. Singleton and Edgar de N. Mayhew. Reprinted by permission of Doubleday & Company, Inc. and Charles S. Singleton.

out of spite and mockery. And just as the latter, for the most part, yield little fruit even with constant diligence and good care, so the former with little labor attain to the summit of the highest excellence. And take, as an example, Don Ippolito d'Este, Cardinal of Ferrara, who enjoyed such a happy birth that his person, his appearance, his words, and all his actions are so imbued and ruled by this grace that, although he is young, he evinces among the most aged prelates so grave an authority that he seems more fit to teach than to be taught. Similarly, in conversing with men and women of every station, in play, in laughter, in jest, he shows a special sweetness and such gracious manners that no one who speaks with him or even sees him can do otherwise than feel an enduring affection for him.

"But, to return to our subject, I say that there is a mean to be found between such supreme grace on the one hand and such stupid ineptitude on the other, and that those who are not so perfectly endowed by nature can, with care and effort, polish and in great part correct their natural defects. Therefore, besides his noble birth, I would wish the Courtier favored in this other respect, and endowed by nature not only with talent and with beauty of countenance and person, but with that certain grace which we call an 'air,' which shall make him at first sight pleasing and lovable to all who see him; and let this be an adornment informing and attending all his actions, giving the promise outwardly that such a one is worthy of the company and the favor of every great lord."

At this point, without waiting any longer, signor Gaspar Pallavicino said: "So that our game may have the form prescribed and that we may not appear to esteem little that privilege of opposing which has been allowed us, I say that to me this nobility of birth does not seem so essential. And if I thought I was uttering anything not already known to us all, I would adduce many instances of persons born of the noblest blood who have been ridden by vices; and, on the contrary, many persons of humble birth who, through their virtue, have made their posterity illustrious. And if what you said just now is true, that there is in all things that hidden force of the first seed, then we should all be of the same condition through having the same source, nor would one man be more noble than another.

But I believe that there are many other causes of the differences and the various degrees of elevation and lowliness among us. Among which causes I judge Fortune to be foremost; because we see her hold sway over all the things of this world and, as it seems, amuse herself often in uplifting to the skies whom she pleases and in burying in the depths those most worthy of being exalted.

"I quite agree with what you call the good fortune of those who are endowed at birth with all goodness of mind and body; but this is seen to happen with those of humble as well as with those of noble birth, because nature observes no such subtle distinctions as these. Nay, as I said, the greatest gifts of nature are often to be seen in persons of the humblest origin. Hence, since this nobility of birth is not gained either by talents or by force or skill, and is rather due to the merit of one's ancestors than to one's own, I deem it passing strange to hold that if the parents of our Courtier be of humble birth, all his good qualities are ruined, and that those other qualities which you have named would not suffice to bring him to the height of perfection; that is, talent, beauty of countenance, comeliness of person, and that grace which will make him at first sight lovable to all."

Then Count Ludovico replied: "I do not deny that the same virtues can rule in the lowborn as in the wellborn: but (in order not to repeat what we have said already, along with many further reasons which might be adduced in praise of noble birth, which is always honored by everyone, because it stands to reason that good should beget good), since it is our task to form a Courtier free of any defect whatsoever, and endowed with all that is praiseworthy, I deem it necessary to have him be of noble birth, not only for many other reasons, but also because of that public opinion which immediately sides with nobility. For, in the case of two courtiers who have not yet given any impression of themselves either through good or bad deeds, immediately when the one is known to be of gentle birth and the other not, the one who is lowborn will be held in far less esteem than the one who is of noble birth, and will need much time and effort in order to give to others that good impression of himself which the other will give in an instant and merely by being a gentleman. And everyone knows the importance of these impressions, for, to speak of ourselves, we have seen men come to this house who, though dull-witted and maladroit, had yet the reputation throughout Italy of being very great court-iers; and, even though they were at last discovered and known, still they fooled us for many days and maintained in our minds that opinion of themselves which they found already impressed thereon, even though their conduct was in keeping with their little worth. Others we have seen who at first enjoyed little esteem and who, in the end, achieved a great success.

"And there are various causes of such errors, one being the judgment of princes who, thinking to work miracles, sometimes decide to show favor to one who seems to them to deserve disfavor. And they too are often deceived; but, because they always have countless imitators, their favor engenders a great fame which on the whole our judgments will follow. And if we notice anything which seems contrary to the prevailing opinion, we suspect that we must be mistaken, and we continue to look for something hidden: because we think that such universal opinions must after all be founded on the truth and arise from reasonable causes. And also because our minds are quick to love and hate, as is seen in spectacles of combats and of games and in every sort of contest, where the spectators often side with one of the parties without any evident reason, showing the greatest desire that this one should win and the other should lose. More-over, as for the general opinion concerning a man's qualities, it is good or ill repute that sways our minds at the outset to one of these two passions. Hence, it happens that, for the most part, we judge from love or hate. Consider, then, how important that first impression is, and how anyone who aspires to have the rank and name of good Courtier must strive from the beginning to make a good impression.

"So, as I believe, what is most important and necessary to the Courtier in order to speak and write well is knowledge: because one who is ignorant and has nothing in his mind worth listening to can neither speak nor write well.

"Next, what one has to say or write must be given a good order. It must then be well expressed in words, which words (if I am not mistaken) must be proper, select, lustrous, and well formed, but above all be words which are still used by the people. Now it is the words themselves that make the greatness and magnificence of an oration; for if a speaker uses good judgment and care, and understands how to choose those words which best express what he wishes to say; and if he elevates them, and shapes them to his purpose like so much wax, he can give them such a disposition and an order such as to cause them to reveal at a glance their dignity and splendor, like paintings when placed in a good and natural light. And I say this as well of writing as of speaking; except that in speaking some things are required that are not needed in writing: such as a good voice, not too thin or soft as a woman's, nor yet so stern and rough as to have a boorish quality, but sonorous, clear, gentle, and well constituted, with distinct enunciation and with fitting manner and gestures. The latter, in my opinion, consist in certain movements of the entire body, not affected or violent, but tempered by a seemly expression of the face and a movement of the eyes such as to give grace and be consonant with the words, together with such gestures as shall signify as well as possible the intention and the feeling of the orator. But all this would be empty and of little moment if the thoughts expressed by the words were not fine, witty, acute, elegant, and solemn, according to the need."

Then signor Morello said: "If this Courtier of ours speaks with so much elegance and gravity, I fear there may be those among us who will not understand him."

"Nay," replied the Count, "all will understand him, because words that are easy to understand can still be elegant. Nor would I have him always speak of grave matters, but of amusing things, of games, jests, and jokes, according to the occasion; but sensibly in everything, with readiness and a lucid fullness; nor must he show vanity or a childish folly in any way. Then, whenever he speaks of anything that is obscure or difficult, I would have him explain his meaning down to a fine point, with precision in both words and thoughts, making every ambiguity clear and plain in a manner that is careful but not tiresome. Likewise, when occasion demands, let him know how to speak with dignity and force, and how to stir up those sentiments which are latent within us, kindling and moving them as the need may be; and speak at other times with such simple candor as to make it seem that nature herself is speaking, to soften such sentiments and inebriate them with sweetness, and all this with such ease as to cause the one who listens to believe that with little effort he too could attain to such excellence—but who, when he tries, discovers that he is very far from it.

"Such is the manner in which I would have our Courtier speak and write; and let him not only choose fine and elegant words from every part of Italy, but I should praise him as well if sometimes he used some of those French or Spanish terms that are already current with us. Thus, should the need arise, I should not be displeased if he used *primor* (excellence); or used *accertare* (to succeed); *avventurare* (to hazard); or *ripassare una persona con ragionamento*, meaning to observe someone and associate with him in order to get to know him well; or *un cavaliere senza rimproccio* (a knight without reproach), *attilato* (elegant), *creato d'un principe* (the dependent of a prince) and other like terms, provided he has reason to think he will be understood. I would have him use certain words sometimes in a sense they do not usually have, transferring them aptly, and, so to say, grafting them like the scion of a tree on some better trunk, in order to make them more attractive and beautiful and, as it were, put things before our very eyes; and, as we say, make us feel them with our hands, to the delight of the listener or the reader. Nor would I have him be afraid even to coin some new words; and he should use new figures of speech, taking these elegantly from the Latins, even as the Latins themselves once took them from the Greeks.

"Therefore if today, among men of letters of good talent and judgment, some took pains to write in this language (in the manner I have described) things worthy of being read, we should soon see it polished and replete with terms and fine figures, and capable of being used in writing as well as any other; and if this were then not pure old Tuscan, it would be Italian, universal, copious, and varied, and like a delightful garden full of a variety of flowers and fruits. Nor would this be anything new, for out of the four languages of which they were able to avail themselves, Greek writers chose words, expressions, and figures from each as they saw fit, and brought forth another that was called the common language; then later all five were called simply Greek. And although Athenian was more elegant, pure, and copious than the others, good writers who were not Athenian by birth did not affect it so much as to be unrecognizable by their style and, as it were, by the savor and essence of their native speech. Yet they were not scorned for this; on the contrary, those who tried to seem too Athenian were blamed for it. Among Latin writers also there were many non-Romans who were much esteemed in their day, even though they were not seen to possess that purity of the Roman tongue which is rarely acquired by men born elsewhere. Certainly Titus Livius was not rejected, although there was one who claimed to find a Paduan flavor in him; nor was Virgil rejected on any charge that he did not speak Roman. Moreover, as you know, many writers of barbarian extraction were read and esteemed at Rome.

"But we, being far more strict than the ancients, impose upon ourselves certain new laws that are inept; and although we have well-traveled roads before our eyes, we try to proceed along byways, for in our own language—the function of which, as of all other languages, is to express well and clearly what the mind conceives—we take pleasure in what is obscure; and, calling it the 'vulgar tongue,' we choose to use words in it which are not only not understood by the vulgar, but not even by noble men of letters, and are no longer in use anywhere, careless of the fact that all good writers among the ancients condemn words that have been rejected by usage. Which usage you do not well understand, in my opinion, because you say that if some fault of speech has become prevalent among the ignorant, it ought not to be called usage for that reason, nor accepted as a rule of speech; and, from what I have heard you state on other occasions, you would have us say *Campidoglio* instead of *Capitolio;* *Girolamo* instead of *Jeronimo; aldace* instead of *audace; padrone* instead of *patrone*—and other like words which are corrupt and spoiled—because they are so written by some ignorant old Tuscan, and because they are so used by Tuscan peasants today.

"Thus, good usage in speech, as I believe, springs from men who have talent, and who through learning and experience have attained good judgment, and who thereby agree among themselves and consent to adopt those words which to them seem good; which words are recognized by virtue of a certain natural judgment and not by any art or rule. Do you know that figures of speech, which give so much grace and luster to discourse, are all abuses of grammatical rules, yet are accepted and confirmed by usage, because (it being impossible to give any other reason for this) they please, and seem to offer suavity and sweetness to the ear itself? And this, I believe, is what good usage is, whereof Romans, Neapolitans, Lombards, and the rest can be quite as capable as Tuscans.

"It is indeed true that in all languages some things are always good, such as facility, good order, fullness, fine periods of harmonious clauses; and that, on the contrary, affectation and the other things that are opposed to these are bad. But among words there are some that remain good for a time, then grow old and lose their grace completely, whereas others gain in strength and come into favor; because, just as the seasons of the year divest the earth of her flowers and fruits, and then clothe her again with others, so time causes those first words to fall, and usage brings others to life, giving them grace and dignity, until they are gradually consumed by the envious jaws of time, when they too go to their death; because, in the end, we and all our things are mortal. Consider that we no longer have any knowledge of the Oscan tongue. Provençal, which we might say was but recently celebrated by noble writers, is not now understood by the inhabitants of that region. Hence, I think, even as the Magnifico has well said, that if Petrarch and Boccaccio were living today, they would not use many of the words we find in their writings: hence, it does not seem good to me that we should imitate them in those words. I do indeed praise highly those who can imitate what is to be imitated; nonetheless, I do not think it at all impossible to write well without imitation; and particularly in this language of ours in which we can be helped by usage—which is something I would not venture to say of Latin."

"I would have him more than passably learned in letters, at least in those studies which we call the humanities. Let him be conversant not only with the Latin language, but with Greek as well, because of the abundance and variety of things that are so divinely written therein. Let him be versed in the poets, as well as in the orators and historians, and let him be practiced also in writing verse and prose, especially in our own vernacular; for, besides the personal satisfaction he will take in this, in this way he will never want for pleasant entertainment with the ladies, who are usually fond of such things. And if, because of other occupations or lack of study, he does not attain to such a perfection that his writings should merit great praise, let him take care to keep them under cover so that others will not laugh at him, and let him show them only to a friend who can be trusted; because at least they will be of profit to him in that, through such exercise, he will be capable of judging the writing of others. For it very rarely happens that a man who is unpracticed in writing, however learned he may be, can ever wholly understand the toils and industry of writers, or taste the sweetness and excellence of styles, and those intrinsic niceties that are often found in the ancients.

"These studies, moreover, will make him fluent, and (as Aristippus said to the tyrant) bold and self-confident in speaking with everyone. However, I would have our Courtier keep one precept firmly in mind, namely, in this as in everything else, to be cautious and reserved rather than forward, and take care not to get the mistaken notion that he knows something he does not know. For we are all by nature more avid of praise than we ought to be and, more than any other sweet song or sound, our ears love the melody of words that praise us; and thus, like Sirens' voices, they are the cause of shipwreck to him who does not stop his ears to such beguiling harmony. This danger was recognized by the ancients, and books were written to show how the true friend is to be distinguished from the flatterer. But to what avail is this, if many, indeed countless persons know full well when they are being flattered, yet love the one who flatters them and hate the one who tells them the truth? And finding him who praises them to be too sparing in his words, they even help him and proceed to say such things of themselves that they make the impudent flatterer himself feel ashamed.

"Let us leave these blind ones to their error, and let us have our Courtier be of such good judgment that he will not let himself be persuaded that black is white, or presume of himself more than he clearly knows to be true; and especially in those points which (if your memory serves you) messer Cesare said we had often used as the means of bringing to light the folly of many persons. Indeed, even if he knows that the praises bestowed upon him are true, let him avoid error by not assenting too openly to them, nor concede them without some protest; but let him rather disclaim them modestly, always showing and really esteeming arms as his chief profession, and the other good accomplishments as ornaments thereto; and do this especially when among soldiers, in order not to act like those who in studies wish to appear as soldiers, and, when in the company of warriors, wish to appear as men of letters. In this way, for the reasons we have stated, he will avoid affectation and even the ordinary things he does will appear to be very great things."

31   *Anton Francesco Donni*
The Justice of the New Court

Anton Francesco Donni (1513-1574), born in Florence and a resident of Venice for the better part of his mature life, was an acerbic and sharp-tongued story teller, much in the tradition of Boccaccio and Sacchetti. In the following tale, written well after the establishment of the Medicean Duchy in Florence (1531), the reader has a chance to assess the expectations and mythology developing around the figure of the 16th century princes. Gallant, courageous, judicious, and witty, the prince dispenses justice and rules his state magnanimously, exhibiting in the process not only a significant measure of statecraft but also those qualities expected of a courtier by Castiglione.

Two young courtiers once laid a plot together to carry off a beautiful young girl from her mother's protection; one of

SOURCE: Anton Francesco Donni, "The Justice of the New Court" from Thomas Roscoe, editor and translator, *The Italian Novelists* (London: 1825), Vol. III, pp. 198-203.

whom, having already engaged her affections, succeeded, under the most solemn promises of marriage, in seducing her from the path of duty. Though of humble origin, she was as intelligent and accomplished as she was beautiful, yet her youth and inexperience, united to the pleadings of affection, at length betrayed her to her ruin. She nevertheless placed such unbounded confidence in her lover's honour, and such was the ascendancy he acquired over her, that she was prevailed upon, when the ardour of his love had passed away, to resume her former dress, and consent to return to her mother's home, in the belief that on the appointed day he would come and claim her hand in marriage. In this way she was, late one evening, borne by these bad friends to her former dwelling, one of them pretending to bind himself for the fulfillment of the other's engagements. They left her a little money, and took their leave of their weeping victim, repeating their false promises of a speedy return.

Here her unhappy situation could not long be concealed from her mother, whose mingled grief and passion on learning the fatal truth, were such as only a mother can fully appreciate, but which it is impossible to convey in words. Drowned in tears of anguish, her daughter in vain attempted to inspire her with the hopes she herself felt, to excuse the conduct and assert the honourable intentions of her lover. The mother soon saw the full extent of her poor girl's misfortune, the long tissue of premeditated cruelty and deceit to which she had fallen a prey; and the hand which had been suddenly raised, as if to strike her to the earth, only clasped her neck in the fulness of maternal sorrow and affection. But their unhappiness did not rest here; the tongue of scandal soon became busy with their good name, which had lately ranked among the best and purest, and the mother, goaded with redoubled anguish, now insisted upon their appealing to the Duke Alexander for redress, not the least distinguished among the Medici for his love of justice throughout Florence. With patient attention the duke listened to her unhappy story, and told her to wipe away her tears, for that, as far as depended upon him, she should no longer have occasion to weep. Then taking her mother aside, he said, "I wish you to be civil to these gentlemen: invite them to your house; let your daughter entertain

them like other company, and contrive that they shall sup
together. Moreover, observe my commands in every thing I
shall direct, and despair not, for we will secure the future
happiness of your daughter. But breathe not a word of what I
say to you; if you have the weakness, like most women; to talk
of your own affairs, and let my name appear in this, ill betide the
fortunes of your family, for you will forfeit my favour, and the
dowry which it is my intention to bestow upon your daughter,
and remain in greater disgrace than before. Be secret, therefore,
and let me hear from you on the occasion I have mentioned."

In obedience to the duke's wishes, the lady put the whole
affair into train; and one day as the fair girl sat binding her
hair upon the sunny side of a gentle hill, lying beyond her
flower garden, she perceived the two cavaliers approaching her.
They saw, and accosted her, while her mother received them
with cheerful looks at the door, and inviting them in, proceeded
to regale them in the best style she could. In the mean time she
informed the duke of their arrival, who, accompanied by a few
select officers, directly set off, and joined the lady at her house.
Soon after alighting, he took occasion to entreat the lady to
show him through her mansion. This she was apparently compelled to do; and when they approached the apartment where
the party were supping together, she affected to turn his excellency aside, observing aloud, "There is nothing further worthy
of your excellency's notice; a mere lumber room." "But I will
see it, nevertheless," interrupted his grace, "I will see it;" and
suddenly opening the door, he beheld his two courtiers, with
the lovely girl seated between them, enjoying themselves in the
best style, and imagining, in their conceit, that they were now
equally acceptable to both the ladies of the house. "Good night,
my lords," cried the duke, "I wish you joy; you seem extremely
comfortable here." They both directly rose in the utmost confusion at the sight of the duke, while the timid girl, unable to
contend with her feelings, burst into a flood of tears. "Weep
not," said the duke to her, in a gentle voice, "good girls are always to be found at home; they do not run after courtiers to
other people's houses; you confer honour upon your household
by staying where you are." Though there was a tone of irony
in this, followed by some severe yet well meant reflections and

advice, he mingled with them so much gentleness and pity, that she thanked him even in her tears. He then declared that he had come for the sole purpose of bestowing her hand in marriage, and of conferring on her a dowry of five hundred crowns. Turning next towards one of his first officers, he continued, "Would you deign to accept this gentleman as your husband? Does he please you?" Drooping her fair head, unable for some minutes to reply, she could only at length sob out: "No, no husband, but he who promised to take me as his wedded wife." "What," said the duke, "are you then already married?" "This, my lord, is the gentleman who gave me his vows and swore to make me his wife." The duke then turning round upon the courtier, with a noble and determined air, "If this be the truth," he continued, "how happens it that I find the lady in this house, and in company with this other gentleman at table? Wherefore does she not sit at your table? What am I to think of this?" "He is my friend," said the guilty courtier, "he will witness for me" —but he stammered out only some unmeaning words, and stood covered with confusion as the duke proceeded; "And had you both forgotten that there was yet such a governor as Alexander de' Medici alive? that there was yet justice in the land? Speak, fair lady; which of these gentlemen do you fix upon as your lawful husband?" "No other, so please your excellency," she replied, "but he who has often promised to make me his." "It is enough," continued the duke, "what you ask is only just; and to show you that justice is one of the virtues that I love, receive this ring, signor, and espouse the young woman before my eyes. And you," he observed, addressing the courtier's companion, "will be kind enough to add to the lady's dowry, the sum of five hundred crowns, the same amount that I have myself given her." Then, having been witness to the marriage, he departed with the whole of his train, including the bridegroom's false friend, leaving the happy young bride and her husband in their mother's house.

SUGGESTIONS FOR FURTHER READING

I have made no attempt to provide a complete bibliography on the Italian Renaissance. Instead, I have listed a small number of works each covering, in ways which seemed interesting and suggestive to me, some particular historical problem of that period.

General Works

Numerous manuals and textbooks on the Renaissance have been published in the last quarter of a century. Most of them are not very satisfactory, although each author, in his own way, has illustrated some aspect of the period that he considers particularly interesting or important. A notable exception to this generalization is R. Romano and A. Tenenti, *Alle Origini del Mondo Moderno (1350–1550)* (Milan, 1967), a work which, in my estimation, offers any number of brilliant insights and summarizes in an incisive manner much recent research. It is particularly strong in the chapters dealing with economic and social history. Other such manuals are W. K. Ferguson, *Europe in Transition 1300–1520* (Boston, 1962); Myron P. Gilmore, *The World of Humanism—1453–1517* (New York, 1952); E. P. Cheyney, *The Dawn of a New Era* (New York, 1936); Denys Hay, *The Italian Renaissance in its Historical Background* (Cambridge, 1961); H. Hauser and A. Renaudet, *Les Debuts de l'Age Moderne* (Paris, 1956); P. Pieri, *Il Rinascimento e la Crisi Militare Italiana* (Turin, 1952): this work includes much useful information not only on military history but on social, economic, and diplomatic developments of the 15th century; F. Braudel, *La Méditerranee et le Monde Mediterraneen* à l'Epoque de Philippe II, 2nd revised, edition, 2 vols. (Paris, 1966): this is an historical masterpiece that deals with the second half of the 16th century, but offers much useful information on the entire

Cinquecento. On economic developments in general are Gino Luzzatto, *Storia Economica d'Italia: Il Medioevo* (Florence, 1963), and Armando Sapori, *Studi di Storia Economica,* 3 vols. (Florence, 1967): this is a collection of many of Sapori's fundamental articles and specialized studies published in the last three decades. A very useful book is F. Edler, *Glossary of Medieval Terms of Business* (Cambridge, Mass., 1934). Finally, indispensable for the study of the historiography of the concept of the "Renaissance" from the 15th century to the present is W. K. Ferguson, *The Renaissance in Historical Thought: Five Centuries of Interpretation* (Boston, 1948).

Agriculture

C. M. Cipolla, "Une crise ignorée. Comment s'est perdue la propriété ecclésiastique dans l' Italie du Nord entre le XIᵉ et le XVIᵉ siècle," *Annales,* II (1947); Elio Conti, *La Formazione Agraria Moderna nel Contado Fiorentino,* 3 vols, in 4 (Rome, 1965–1967); Georges Duby, "Sur l'histoire agraire de l' Italie," *Annales,* XVIII (1963); P. J. Jones, "Medieval Agrarian Society in its Prime–Italy," *Cambridge Economic History,* I, rev. ed. (Cambridge, 1966): this may well be the most useful survey of the agricultural problem in Italy available in English; P. S. Leicht, *Operai, Artigiani, Agricoltori in Italia dal Secolo VI al XVI* (Milan, 1959); G. Luzzatto, *Dai Servi della Gleba Agli Albori del Capitalismo* (Bari, 1966), a collection of brilliant articles published over a period of nearly six decades by one of the great economic historians of the 20th century; G. Luzzatto, "Per la storia dell'economia rurale in Italia nel secolo XIV," *Homage à Lucien Febvre,* II (Paris, 1953); Aldo de Maddalena, "Il mondo rurale italiano nel cinque e nel seicento (Rassegna di studi recenti)," *Rivista Storica Italiana,* LXXVI (1964); Gemma Miani, "L' Economie lombarde aux XIVe et XVe siècles: une exception à la règle?" *Annales,* XIX (1964); E. Sereni, *Storia del Paesaggio Agrario Italiano* (Bari, 1961); Aldo Stella, "La proprietà ecclesiastica nella repubblica di Venezia dal secolo XV al XVII," Nuova *Rivista Storica,* XLII (1958).

Demography

J. M. W. Bean, "Plague, Population and Economic Decline in

the Later Middle Ages," Economic History Review, XV (1963); K. J. Beloch, *Bevölkerungsgeschichte Italiens, 3* vols. (Berlin, 1937–1961); Paolo Montanari, *Documenti su la Popolazione di Bologna alla Fine del Trecento* (Bologna, 1967); Carlo Pasero, "Dati statistici e notizie intorno al movimento della popolazione bresciana durante il dominio veneto (1426–1797)," *Archivio Storico Lombardo*, LXXXVIII (1963); J. C. Russell, *Late Ancient and Medieval Population* (Philadelphia, 1958).

Some Cities and Regions

C. C. Bayley, *War and Society in Renaissance Florence* (Toronto, 1961); Marvin B. Becker, *Florence in Transition* (Baltimore, 1967); Federico Chabod, Lo Stato Di *Milano nella Prima Meta del Secolo XVI* (Rome, 1955); G. Coniglio, *Il Regno di Napoli al Tempo de Carlo V* (Naples, 1951); R. Davidsohn, *Geschichte von Florenz*, 4 vols. (Berlin, 1896–1927); J. Delumeau, *Vie Economique et Sociale de Rome dans la Seconde Moitie du XVIe Siècle*, 2 vols. (Paris, 1957–1959); J. Heers, *Genes au XVe Siècle* (Paris, 1961); David Herlihy, *Pisa in the Early Renaissance* (New Haven, 1958); H. Kretschmayr, *Geschichte von Venedig*, 3 vols. (Gotha-Stuttgart, 1905-1934); John Larner, *The Lords of the Romagna* (Ithaca, 1966); *Mantova—la Storia*, 3 vols. (Mantua, 1958–1963); F. T. Perrens, *Histoire de Florence*, 9 vols. (Paris, 1877–1883); Storia di Milano, 18 vols. (Milano, 1955–1967).

Commerce, Industry, and Banking

Philip P. Argenti, *The Occupation of Chios by the Genoese and Their Administration of the Island*, 1346–1566, 3 vols. (Cambridge, 1958); B. Barbadoro, *Le Finanze della Republica Fiorentina—Imposta Diretta e Debito Publico Fino all' Istituzione del Monte* (Florence, 1929); C. Cipolla, *Money, Prices and Civilization* (Princeton, 1955); Jean Delumeau, *L'Alun de Rome, XVe-XIXe Siècle* (Paris, 1962); R. de Roover, *The Rise and Decline of the Medici Bank—1397–1494* (Cambridge, Mass., 1964); R. de Roover, *L' Evolution de la Lettre de Change* (Paris, 1953); A. Doren, *Die Florentiner Wollentuch-Industrie* (Stuttgart, 1901); A. Doren, *Le Arti Fiorentine*, 2 vols. (Florence, 1940); Domenico Gioffrè, *Genes et les Foires de Change—de Lyons a Besançon* (Paris, 1960); F. Lane, *Andrea Barbarigo, Merchant of Venice*,

1418–1449 (Baltimore, 1944); F. Lane, *Venetian Ships and Ship-builders of the Renaissance* (Baltimore, 1934); R. S. Lopez, *Genova Marinara nel Duecento: Benedetto Zaccaria* (Messina, 1933); R. S. Lopez, *Studi sull' Economia Genovese nel Medioevo* (Turin, 1936); Gino Luzzatto, *Il Debito Publico della Repubblica di Venezia Dagli Ultimi Decenni del XII Secolo alla Fine del XV* (Milan, 1963); G. Luzzatto, *Storia Economica di Venezia dall' XI al XVI Secolo* (Venice, 1961); Michael Mallett, The Florentine Galleys in the Fifteenth Century (Oxford, 1967); B. N. Nelson, The Idea of Usury (Princeton, 1949); G. Pagnini, *Della Decima e di Varie Altre Gravezze Imposte dal Comune di Firenze* (Lisbon, 1765); M. M. Postan, "The Rise of a Money Economy," *Economic History Review*, XIV (1944); Yves Renouard, "Affaires et hommes d'affaires italiens du moyen âge," *Annales*, VII (1952); G. R. B. Richards, *Florentine Merchants in the Age of the Medici* (Cambridge, Mass., 1932); A. A. Ruddock, *Italian Merchants and Shipping in Southampton, 1270–1600* (Southampton, 1951); A. Sapori, *Le Marchand Italien au Moyen Age* (Paris, 1952); A. Sapori (ed.), *I Libri degli Alberti del Giudice* (Milan, 1952); A. Sapori, *La Crisi delle Compagnie Mercantili dei Bardi e dei Peruzzi* (Florence, 1925); Alberto Tenenti and Corrado Vivanti, "Le film d'un grand systeme de navigation: Les galères venitiennes, XIVe–XVIe siècles," *Annales*, XVI (1961); U. Tucci, "Alle origini dello spirito capitalistico a Venezia: La previsione economica," *Studi in Onore di Amintore Fanfani* (Milan, 1962); A. P. Usher, *The Early History of Deposit Banking in Mediterranean Europe* (Cambridge, Mass., 1943).

Economic Trends: 1348–1500

Gino Barbieri, *Origini del Capitalismo Lombardo* (Milan, 1961); Bruno Caizzi, "I tempi della decadenza di Cremona," *Studi in Onore di Armando Sapori* (Milan, 1957); Carlo Cipolla, "The Economic Depression of the Renaissance," *The Economic History Review*, XVI (1964); Carlo Cipolla, "Revisions in Economic History: The Trends in Italian Economic History in the Later Middle Ages." *The Economic History Review*, 1949; Enrico Fiumi, "Sui rapporti fra città e contado," *Archivio Storico Italiano*, CXIV (1956); Enrico Fiumi, "Fioritura e decadenza dell' economia fiorentina," *Archivio Storico Italiano*, CXV (1957); CXVI (1958);

CXVII (1959); David Herlihy, "Direct and Indirect Taxation in Tuscan Urban Finance, ca. 1200–1400," *Collection Histoire*, VII (1964); R. S. Lopez and H. A. Miskimin, "The Economic Depression of the Renaissance," *The Economic History Review*, XIV (1962); M. Mollat, P. Joansen, M. Postan, A. Sapori, C. Verlinden, "L'economie européenne aux deux derniers siècles du Moyen Age," *Xᵉ Congresso Internazionale di Scienze Storiche*, VI (Florence, 1955); Peter Partner, "The 'Budget' of the Roman Church in the Renaissance Period," *Italian Renaissance Studies* (London, 1960); M. M. Postan, "Some Economic Evidence of Declining Population in the Later Middle Ages," *The Economic History Review*, n.s., II (1950); E. Perroy, "A L'origine d'une économie contractée. Les crises du XIV siècle," *Annales*, II (1949).

Social Classes

H. Baron, "The Social Background of Political Liberty in the Early Italian Renaissance," *Comparative Studies in Society and History*, II (1960); Giorgio Cracco, *Societa e Stato nel Medioevo Veneziano* (Florence, 1967); E. Cristiani, *Societa e Popolo nel Comune di Pisa* (Naples, 1962); L. F. Marks, "The Financial Oligarchy in Florence Under Lorenzo," *Italian Renaissance Studies* (London, 1960); A. von Martin, *Sociology of the Renaissance* (New York, 1963); J. Plesner, *L'Emigration de la Campagne à la Ville de Florence au XIV Siècle* (Kopenhagen, 1934); R. L. Reynolds, "In Search of a Business Class in 13th Century Genoa," *The Journal of Economic History*, Supplement V (1945); N. Rodolico, *I Ciompi* (Florence, 1945); N. Rodolico, "The Struggle for the Right of Association in Fourteenth Century Florence," *History*, VIII (1924); G. Volpe, *Medioevo Italiano* (Florence, 1961).

The Merchant and His Culture

C. Ady, *Morals and Manners of the Quattrocento* (London, 1942); F. Antal, *Florentine Painting and Its Social Background* (London, 1947); H. Baron, *The Crisis of the Early Italian Renaissance* (Princeton, 1966); G. Brucker (ed.), *Two Memoirs of Renaissance Florence* (New York, 1967); E. Bensa, *Francesco di Marco da Prato: Notizie e Documenti Sulla Mercatura Italiana del Secolo XIV* (Milano, 1928); R. Kelso, *Doctrine for the Lady of the Renaissance* (Urbana, 1956); I. Origo, *The Merchant of Prato: The Life and Papers of Francesco Di Marco Datini* (London, 1957); M. Meiss, *Painting in Florence and Siena after the Black Death* (Princeton, 1951); A. Tenenti, *Il Senso Della Morte e l'Amore Della Vita Nel Rinascimento* (Turin, 1957).

The Articulation of a New Elite

A. Ady, *The Bentivoglio of Bologna: a Study in Despotism* (London, 1937); R. von Albertini, *Das Florentinische Staatsbewustsein im Ubergang von der Republik zum Prinzipat* (Bern, 1955); M. Berengo, *Nobili e Mercanti nella Lucca del Cinquecento* (Turin, 1965); Paul Coles, "The Crisis of Renaissance Society: Genoa, 1488–1507," *Past and Present*, XI (1957); G. Peyronnet, "Il ducato di Milano sotto Francesco Sforza (1450–1466); politica interna, vita economica e sociale," *Archivio Storico Italiano*, CXVI (1958).